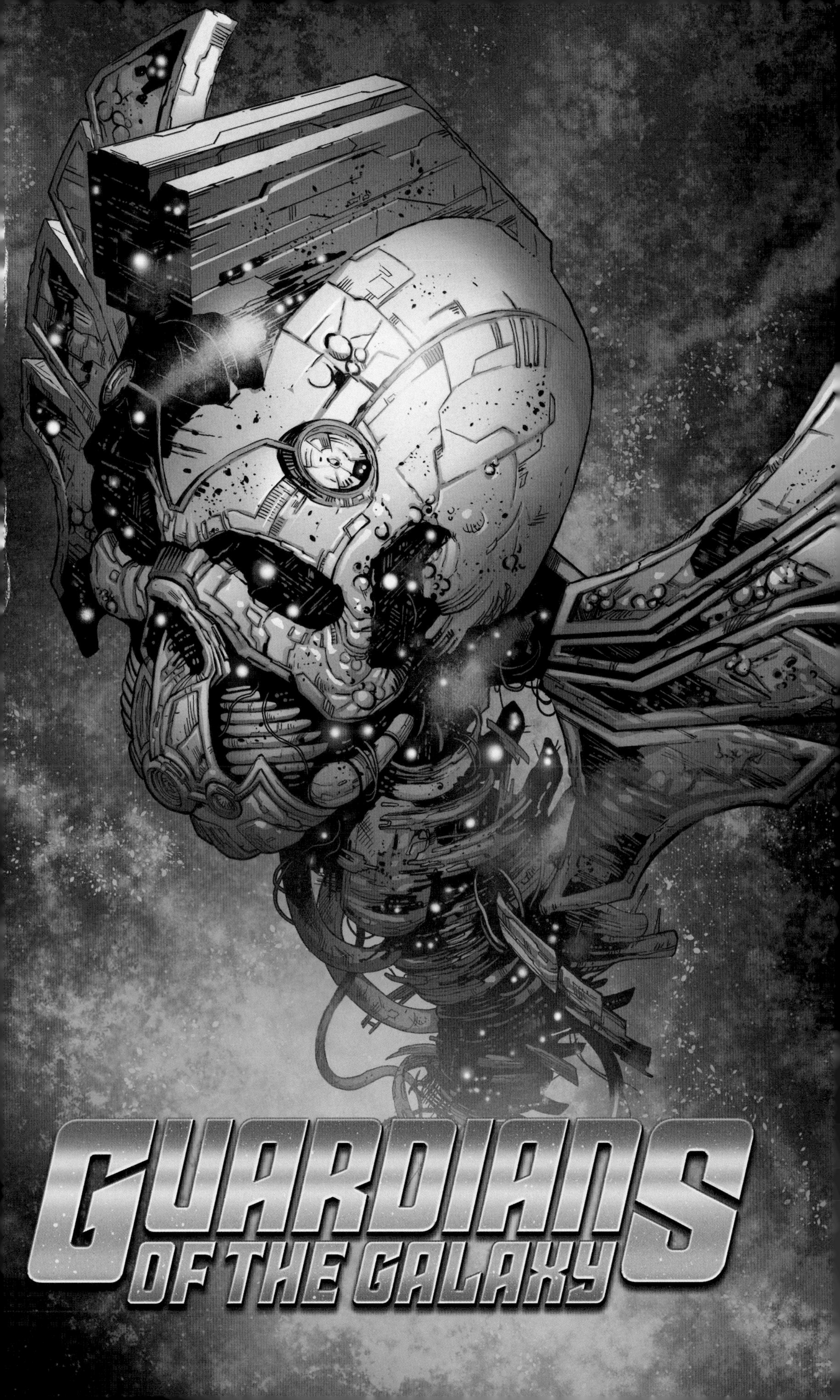
GUARDIANS
OF THE GALAXY

GUARDIANS OF THE GALAXY: NEW GUARD VOL. 2 — WANTED. Contains material originally published in magazine form as GUARDIANS OF THE GALAXY #6-10. First printing 2016. ISBN# 978-0-7851-9519-1. Published by MARVEL WORLDWIDE, INC., a subsidiary of MARVEL ENTERTAINMENT, LLC. OFFICE OF PUBLICATION: 135 West 50th Street, New York, NY 10020. Copyright © 2016 MARVEL No similarity between any of the names, characters, persons, and institutions in this magazine with those of any living or dead person or institution is intended, and any such similarity which may exist is purely coincidental. **Printed in the U.S.A.** ALAN FINE, President, Marvel Entertainment; DAN BUCKLEY, President, TV, Publishing & Brand Management; JOE QUESADA, Chief Creative Officer; TOM BREVOORT, SVP of Publishing; DAVID BOGART, SVP of Business Affairs & Operations, Publishing & Partnership; C.B. CEBULSKI, VP of Brand Management & Development, Asia; DAVID GABRIEL, SVP of Sales & Marketing, Publishing; JEFF YOUNGQUIST, VP of Production & Special Projects; DAN CARR, Executive Director of Publishing Technology; ALEX MORALES, Director of Publishing Operations; SUSAN CRESPI, Production Manager; STAN LEE, Chairman Emeritus. For information regarding advertising in Marvel Comics or on Marvel.com, please contact Vit DeBellis, Integrated Sales Manager, at vdebellis@marvel.com. For Marvel subscription inquiries, please call 888-511-5480. **Manufactured between 9/23/2016 and 11/7/2016 by LSC COMMUNICATIONS INC., SALEM, VA, USA.**

10 9 8 7 6 5 4 3 2 1

GUARDIANS OF THE GALAXY

WANTED

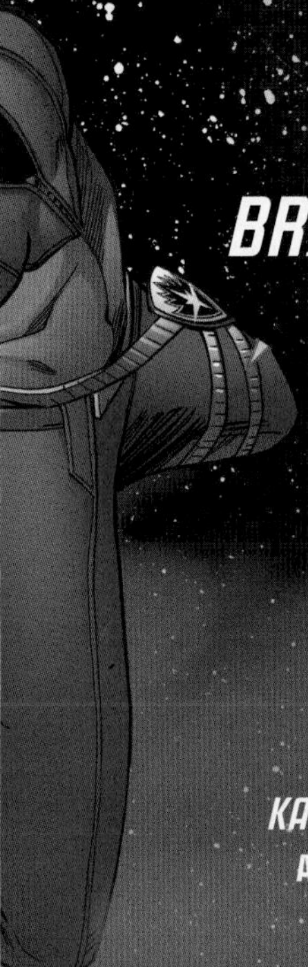

BRIAN MICHAEL BENDIS
WRITER

VALERIO SCHITI
ARTIST

RICHARD ISANOVE
COLOR ARTIST

VC'S CORY PETIT
LETTERER

ART ADAMS & JASON KEITH
COVER ART

KATHLEEN WISNESKI
ASSISTANT EDITOR

JAKE THOMAS
ASSOCIATE EDITOR

NICK LOWE
EXECUTIVE EDITOR

COLLECTION EDITOR: JENNIFER GRÜNWALD
ASSOCIATE MANAGING EDITOR: KATERI WOODY
ASSOCIATE EDITOR: SARAH BRUNSTAD
EDITOR, SPECIAL PROJECTS: MARK D. BEAZLEY
VP PRODUCTION & SPECIAL PROJECTS: JEFF YOUNGQUIST
SVP PRINT, SALES & MARKETING: DAVID GABRIEL

EDITOR IN CHIEF: AXEL ALONSO
CHIEF CREATIVE OFFICER: JOE QUESADA
PUBLISHER: DAN BUCKLEY
EXECUTIVE PRODUCER: ALAN FINE

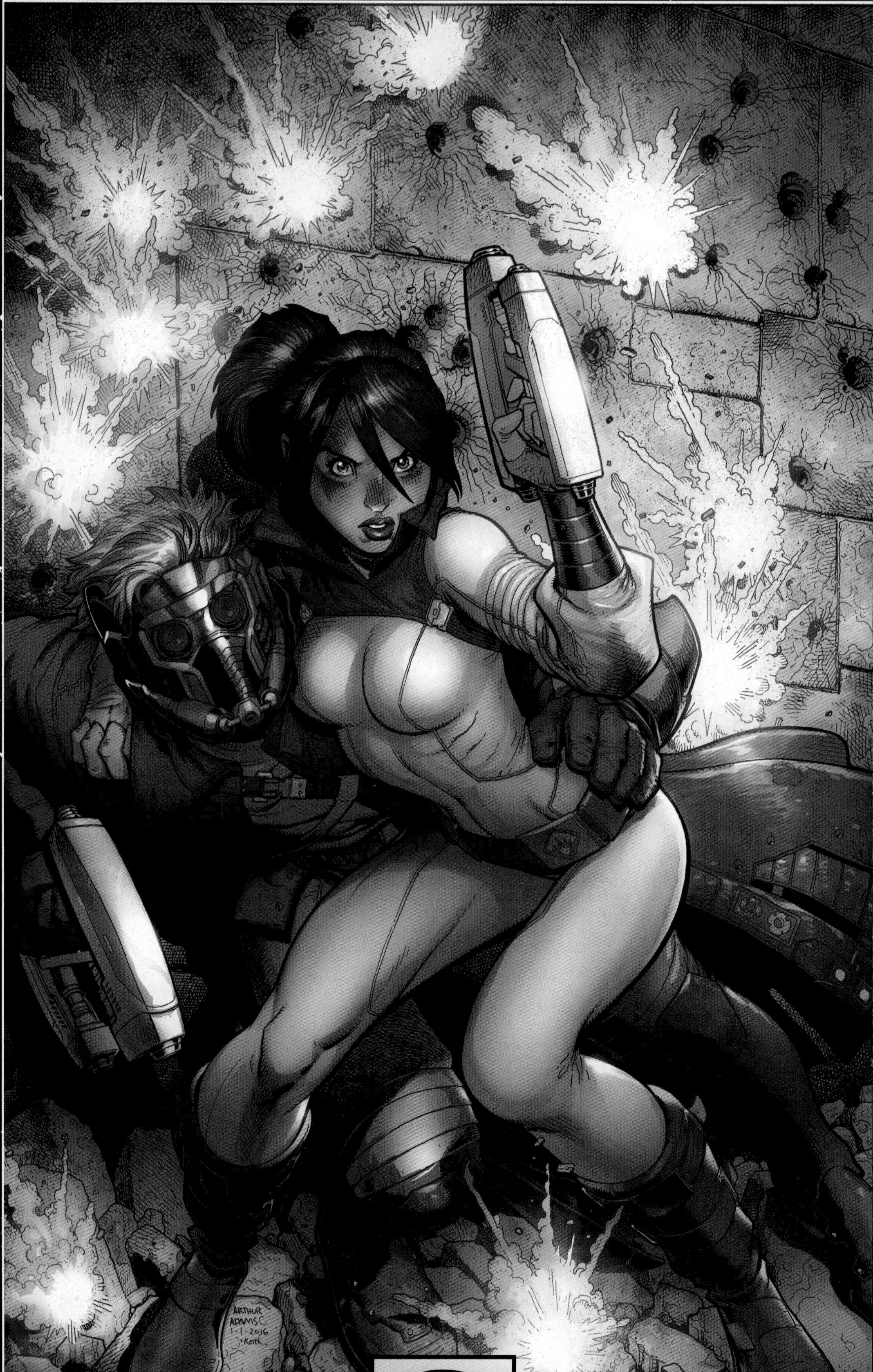
ARTHUR
ADAMS C.
1-1-2016
+Keith

6

he entire galaxy is a mess. Warring empires and cosmic terrorists plague every corner. omeone has to rise above it all and fight for those who have no one to fight for them. A group f misfits--***Drax the Destroyer***, ***Gamora***, ***Rocket Raccoon***, ***Groot***, and ***Flash Thompson***, k.a. ***Venom***--joined together under the leadership of ***Peter Quill, Star-Lord.*** With new embers ***Kitty Pryde*** and ***Ben Grimm***, a.k.a. ***The Thing***, they serve a higher cause as the…

GUARDIANS OF THE GALAXY

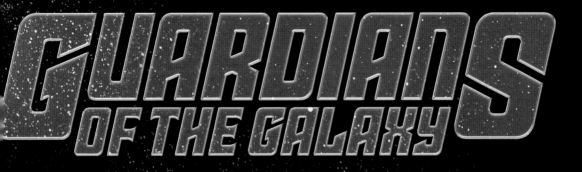

ala, the last Kree Accuser, held Peter Quill responsible for the destruction of er home planet, and ransacked Spartax as revenge. Working together, all nine uardians of the Galaxy managed to bring her down, but not before she demolished e capital. In their crumbling offices, Spartax government administrators were ll too eager to blame Star-Lord for the disaster.

e's now *former* president, and current fugitive, of Spartax. So the Guardians are n the run, and all together again…mostly.

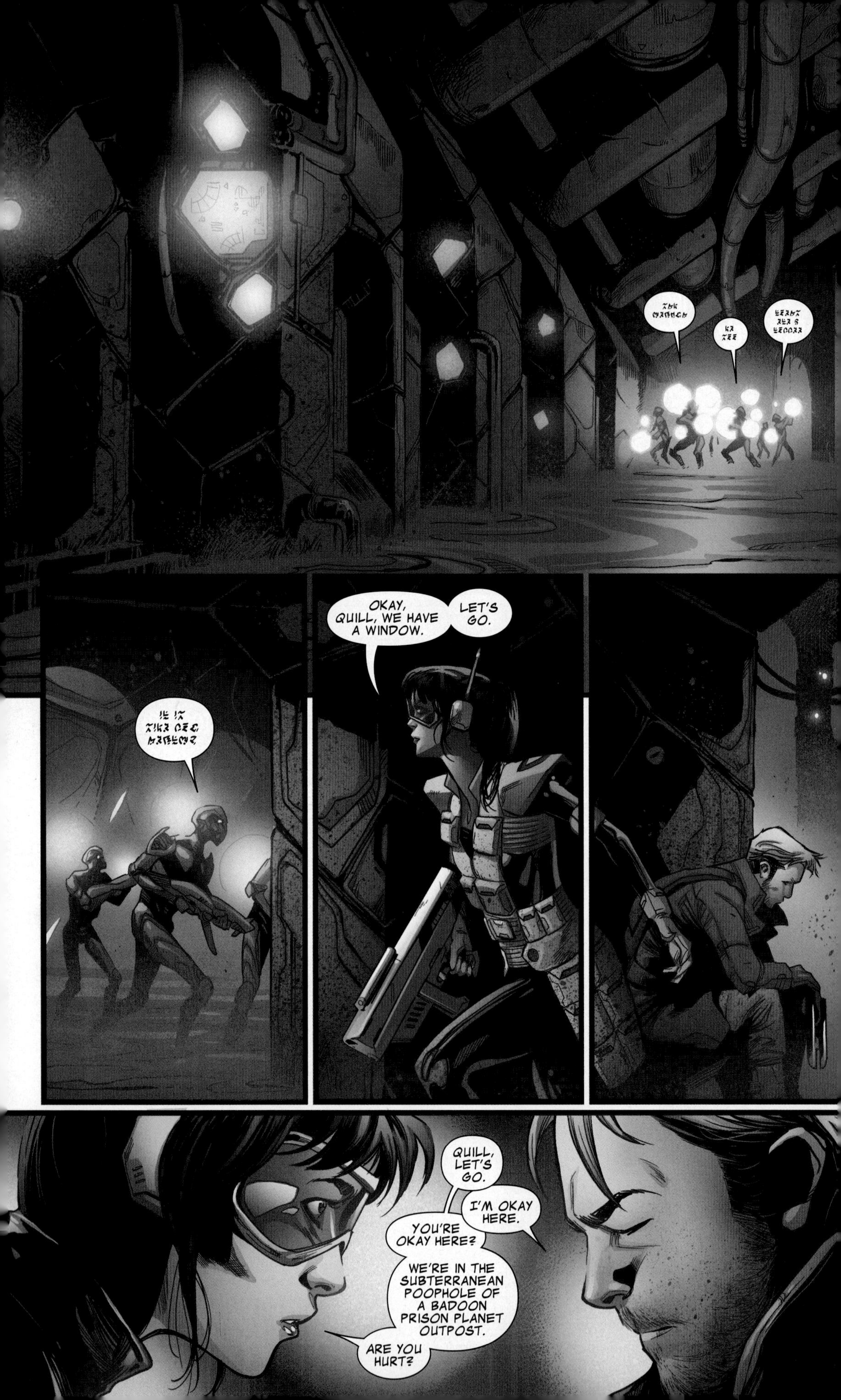

OKAY, QUILL, WE HAVE A WINDOW.
LET'S GO.
QUILL, LET'S GO.
I'M OKAY HERE.
YOU'RE OKAY HERE?
WE'RE IN THE SUBTERRANEAN POOPHOLE OF A BADOON PRISON PLANET OUTPOST.
ARE YOU HURT?

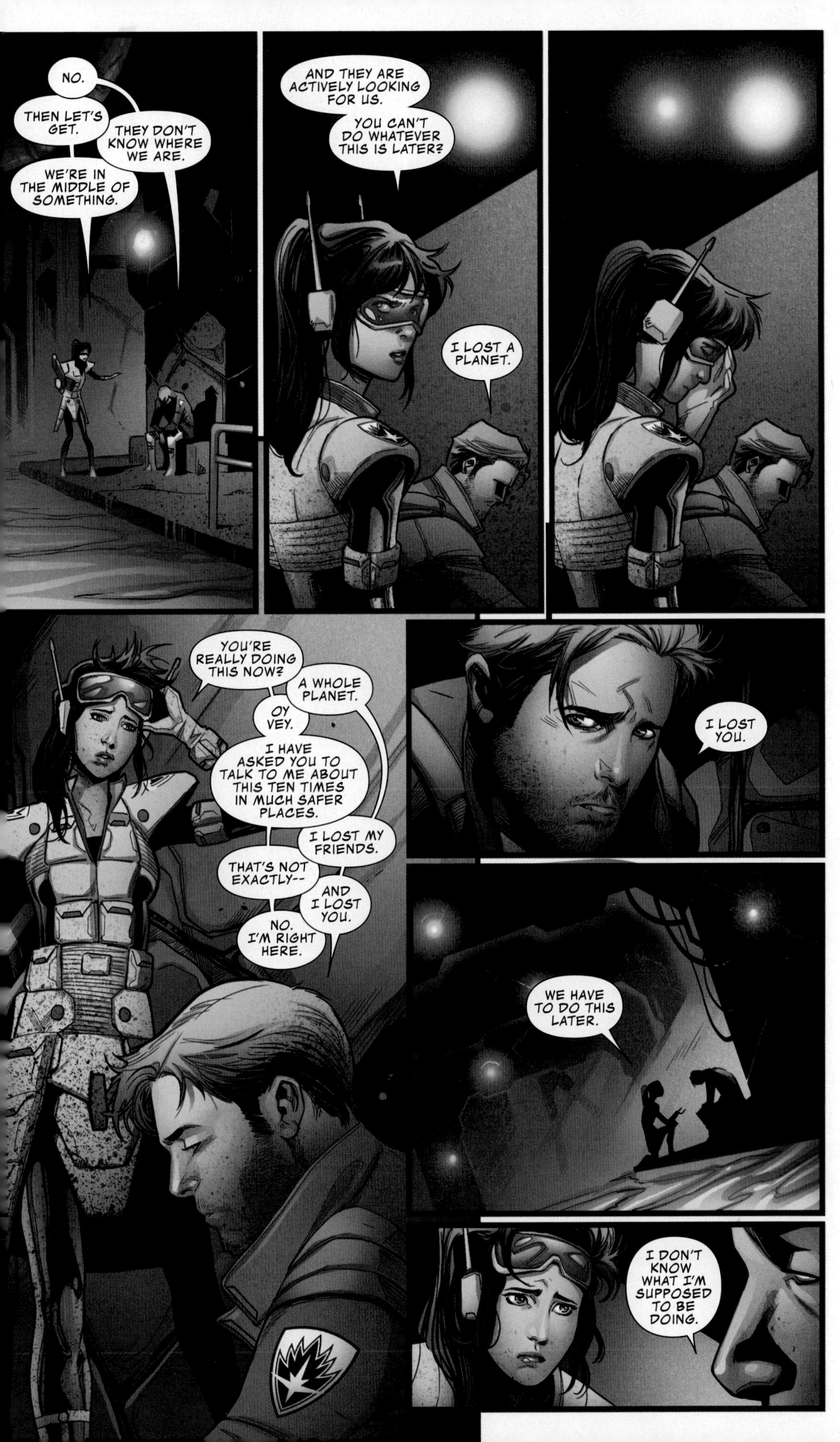
NO.
THEN LET'S GET.
THEY DON'T KNOW WHERE WE ARE.
WE'RE IN THE MIDDLE OF SOMETHING.
AND THEY ARE ACTIVELY LOOKING FOR US.
YOU CAN'T DO WHATEVER THIS IS LATER?
I LOST A PLANET.
YOU'RE REALLY DOING THIS NOW?
A WHOLE PLANET.
OY VEY.
I HAVE ASKED YOU TO TALK TO ME ABOUT THIS TEN TIMES IN MUCH SAFER PLACES.
I LOST MY FRIENDS.
THAT'S NOT EXACTLY--
AND I LOST YOU.
NO. I'M RIGHT HERE.
I LOST YOU.
WE HAVE TO DO THIS LATER.
I DON'T KNOW WHAT I'M SUPPOSED TO BE DOING.

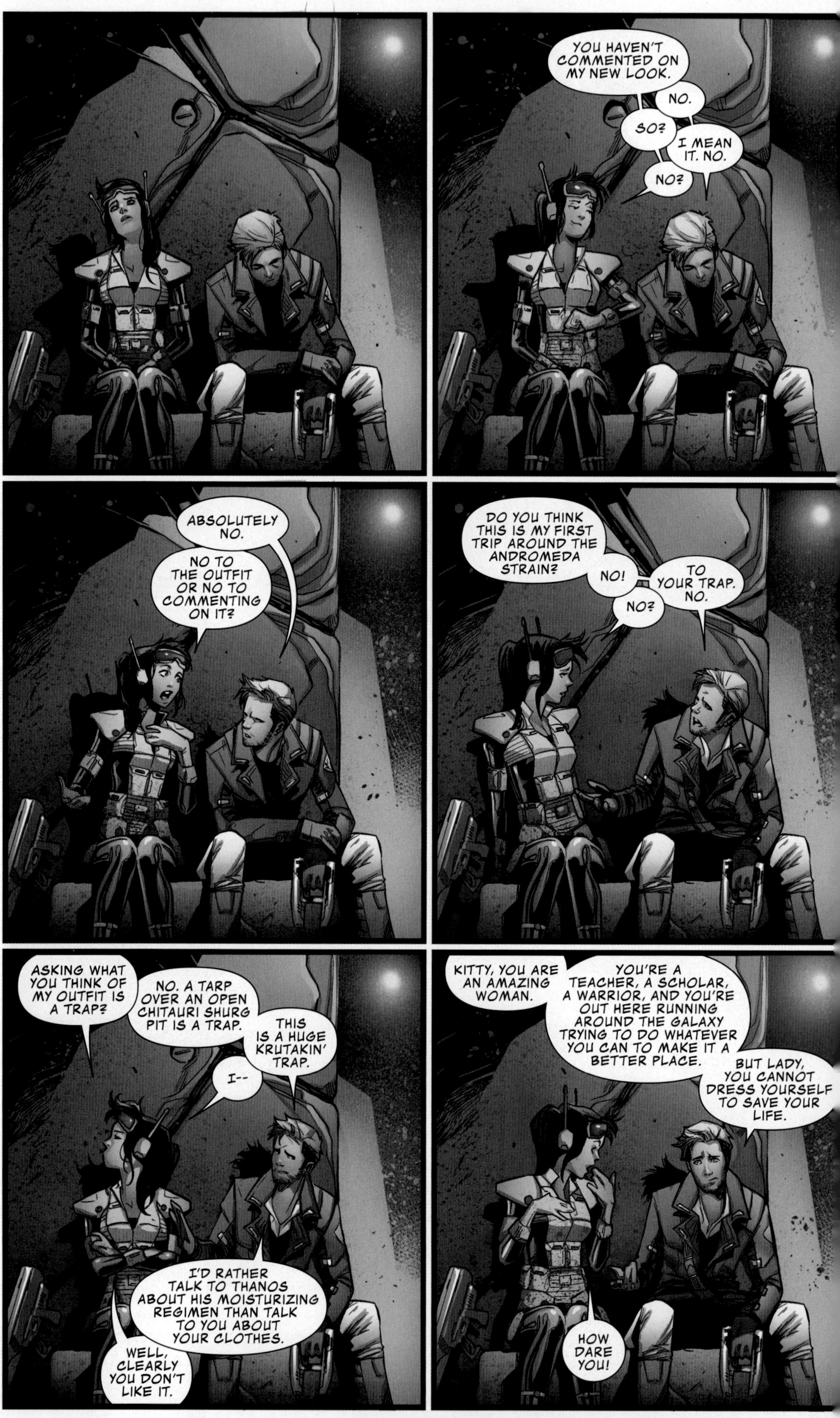

YOU HAVEN'T COMMENTED ON MY NEW LOOK.
NO.
SO?
I MEAN IT. NO.
NO?
ABSOLUTELY NO.
NO TO THE OUTFIT OR NO TO COMMENTING ON IT?
DO YOU THINK THIS IS MY FIRST TRIP AROUND THE ANDROMEDA STRAIN?
NO!
NO?
TO YOUR TRAP. NO.
ASKING WHAT YOU THINK OF MY OUTFIT IS A TRAP?
NO. A TARP OVER AN OPEN CHITAURI SHURG PIT IS A TRAP.
I--
THIS IS A HUGE KRUTAKIN' TRAP.
I'D RATHER TALK TO THANOS ABOUT HIS MOISTURIZING REGIMEN THAN TALK TO YOU ABOUT YOUR CLOTHES.
WELL, CLEARLY YOU DON'T LIKE IT.
KITTY, YOU ARE AN AMAZING WOMAN.
YOU'RE A TEACHER, A SCHOLAR, A WARRIOR, AND YOU'RE OUT HERE RUNNING AROUND THE GALAXY TRYING TO DO WHATEVER YOU CAN TO MAKE IT A BETTER PLACE.
BUT LADY, YOU CANNOT DRESS YOURSELF TO SAVE YOUR LIFE.
HOW DARE YOU!

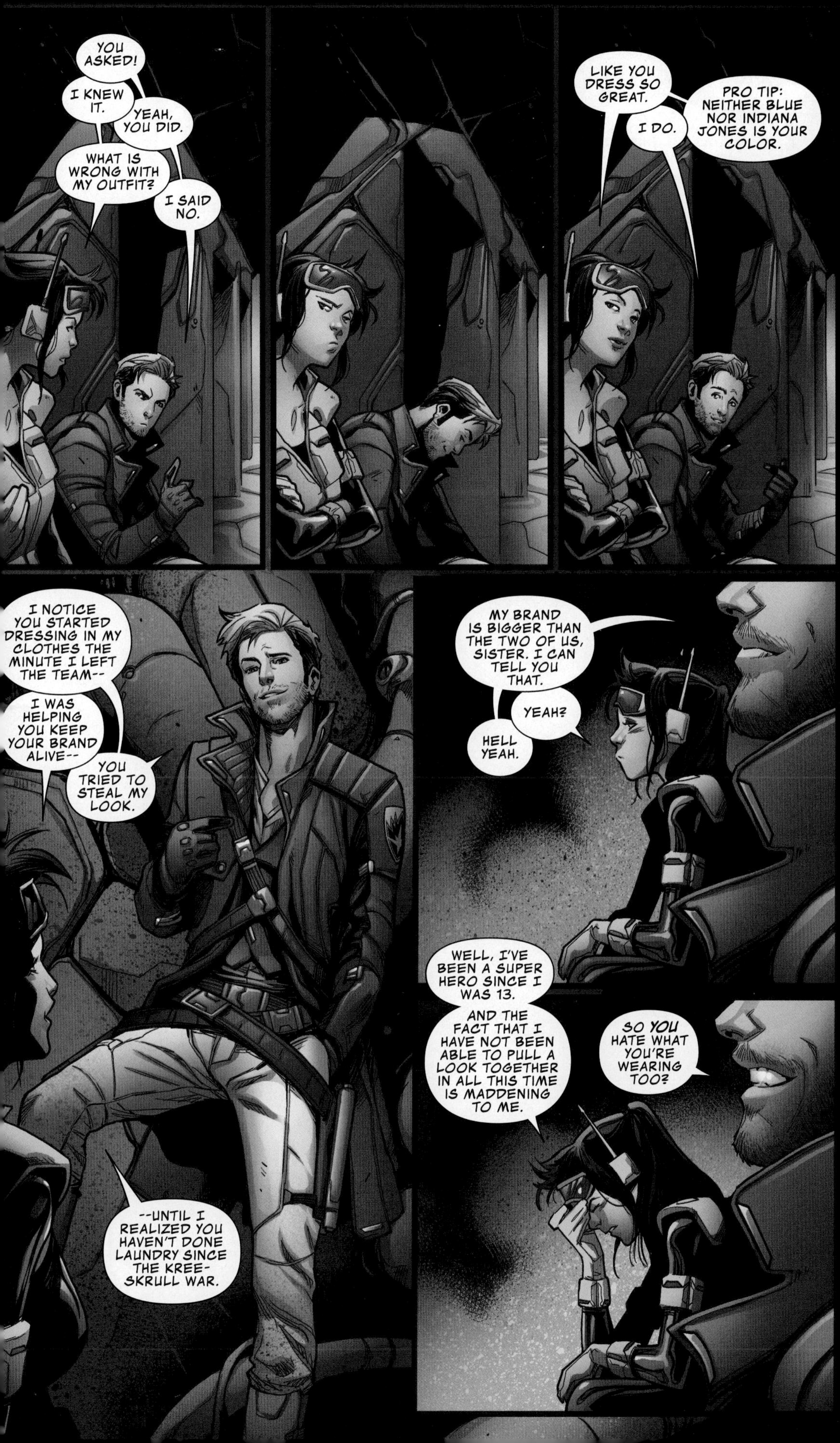
YOU ASKED!
I KNEW IT.
YEAH, YOU DID.
WHAT IS WRONG WITH MY OUTFIT?
I SAID NO.
LIKE YOU DRESS SO GREAT.
I DO.
PRO TIP: NEITHER BLUE NOR INDIANA JONES IS YOUR COLOR.
I NOTICE YOU STARTED DRESSING IN MY CLOTHES THE MINUTE I LEFT THE TEAM--
I WAS HELPING YOU KEEP YOUR BRAND ALIVE--
YOU TRIED TO STEAL MY LOOK.
--UNTIL I REALIZED YOU HAVEN'T DONE LAUNDRY SINCE THE KREE-SKRULL WAR.
MY BRAND IS BIGGER THAN THE TWO OF US, SISTER. I CAN TELL YOU THAT.
YEAH?
HELL YEAH.
WELL, I'VE BEEN A SUPER HERO SINCE I WAS 13.
AND THE FACT THAT I HAVE NOT BEEN ABLE TO PULL A LOOK TOGETHER IN ALL THIS TIME IS MADDENING TO ME.
SO YOU HATE WHAT YOU'RE WEARING TOO?

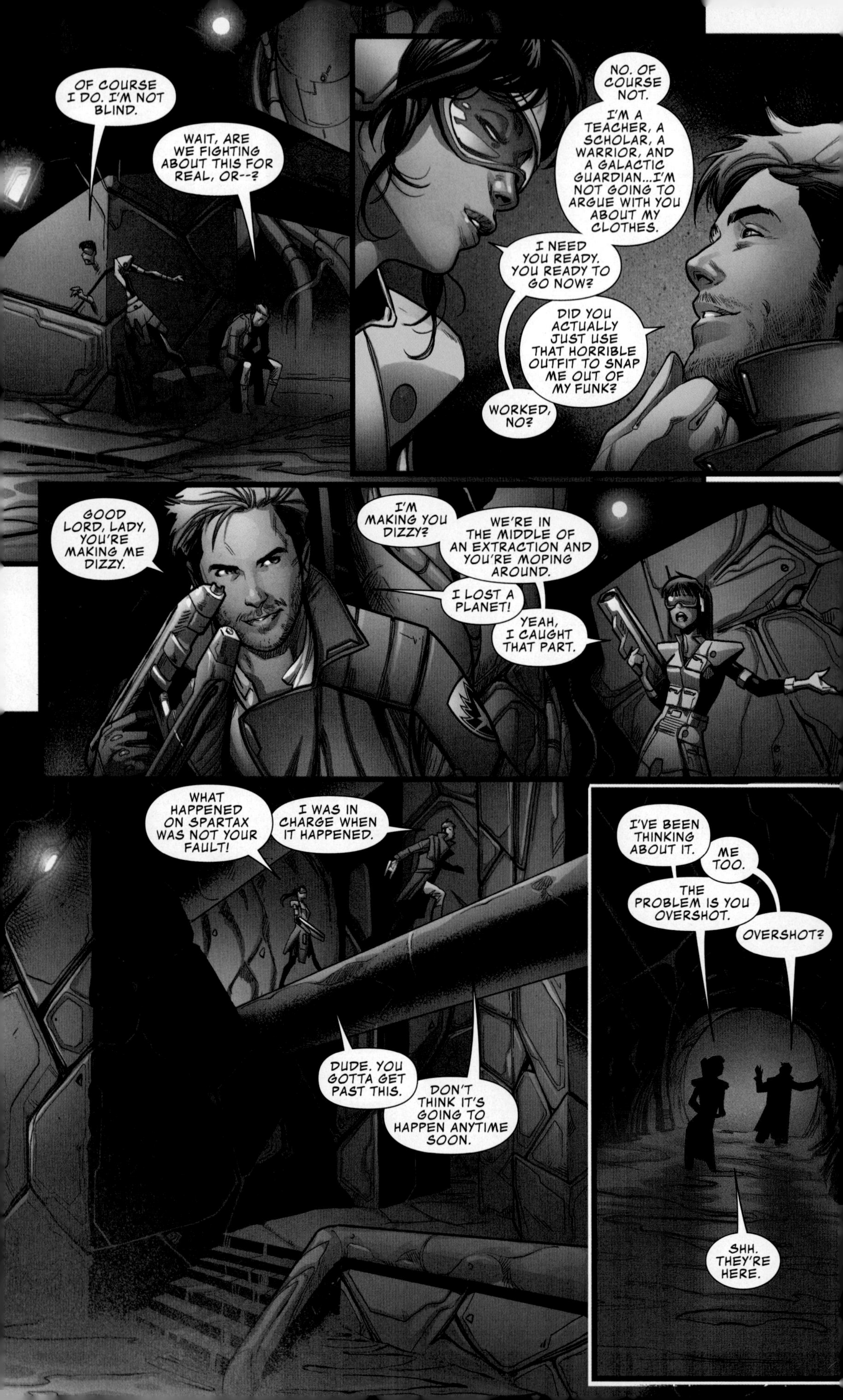

OF COURSE I DO. I'M NOT BLIND.
WAIT, ARE WE FIGHTING ABOUT THIS FOR REAL, OR--?
NO. OF COURSE NOT.
I'M A TEACHER, A SCHOLAR, A WARRIOR, AND A GALACTIC GUARDIAN...I'M NOT GOING TO ARGUE WITH YOU ABOUT MY CLOTHES.
I NEED YOU READY. YOU READY TO GO NOW?
DID YOU ACTUALLY JUST USE THAT HORRIBLE OUTFIT TO SNAP ME OUT OF MY FUNK?
WORKED, NO?
GOOD LORD, LADY, YOU'RE MAKING ME DIZZY.
I'M MAKING YOU DIZZY?
WE'RE IN THE MIDDLE OF AN EXTRACTION AND YOU'RE MOPING AROUND.
I LOST A PLANET!
YEAH, I CAUGHT THAT PART.
WHAT HAPPENED ON SPARTAX WAS NOT YOUR FAULT!
I WAS IN CHARGE WHEN IT HAPPENED.
DUDE. YOU GOTTA GET PAST THIS.
DON'T THINK IT'S GOING TO HAPPEN ANYTIME SOON.
I'VE BEEN THINKING ABOUT IT.
ME TOO.
THE PROBLEM IS YOU OVERSHOT.
OVERSHOT?
SHH. THEY'RE HERE.

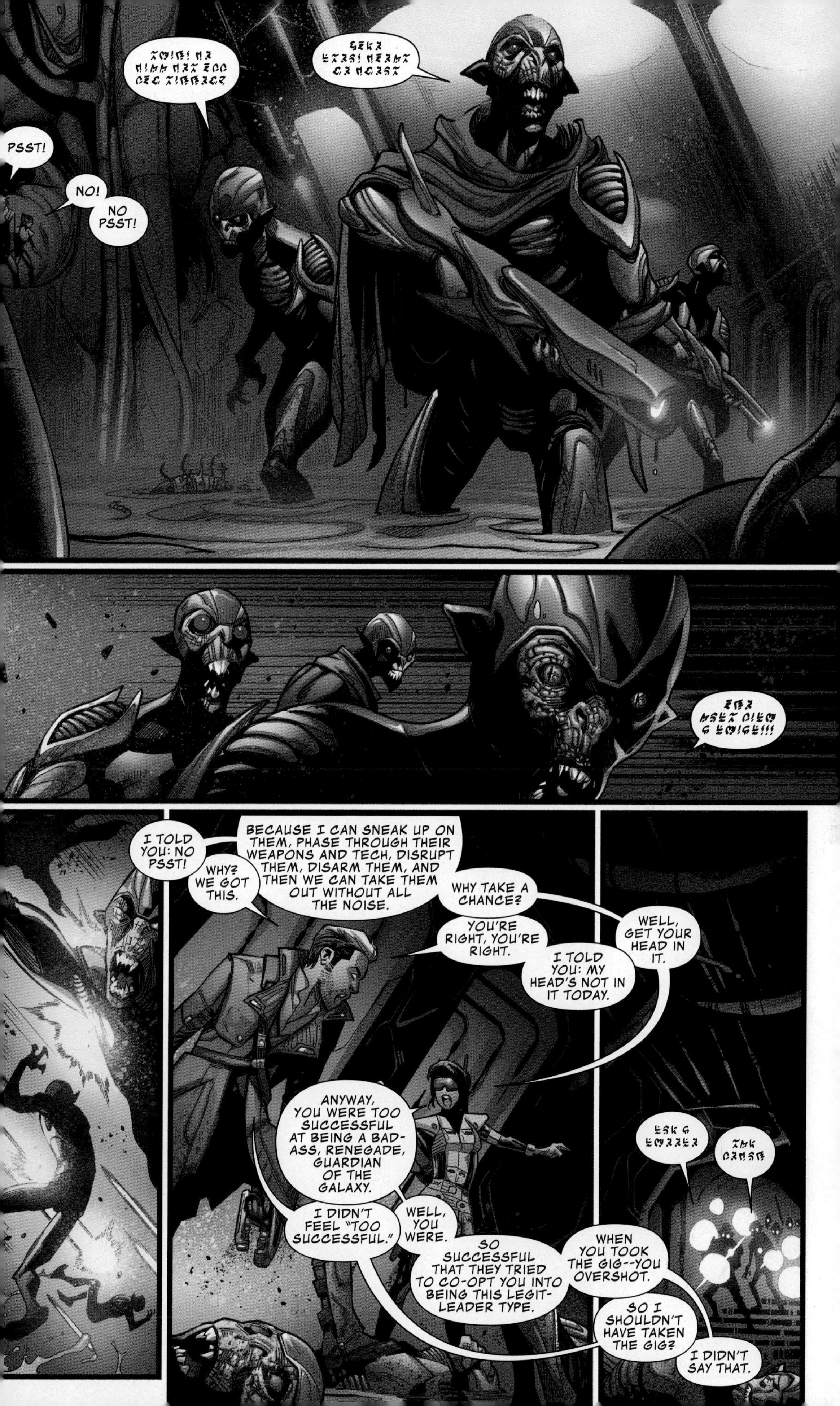

PSST!
NO! NO PSST!
I TOLD YOU: NO PSST!
WHY? WE GOT THIS.
BECAUSE I CAN SNEAK UP ON THEM, PHASE THROUGH THEIR WEAPONS AND TECH, DISRUPT THEM, DISARM THEM, AND THEN WE CAN TAKE THEM OUT WITHOUT ALL THE NOISE.
WHY TAKE A CHANCE?
YOU'RE RIGHT, YOU'RE RIGHT.
WELL, GET YOUR HEAD IN IT.
I TOLD YOU: MY HEAD'S NOT IN IT TODAY.
ANYWAY, YOU WERE TOO SUCCESSFUL AT BEING A BAD-ASS, RENEGADE, GUARDIAN OF THE GALAXY.
I DIDN'T FEEL "TOO SUCCESSFUL."
WELL, YOU WERE.
SO SUCCESSFUL THAT THEY TRIED TO CO-OPT YOU INTO BEING THIS LEGIT-LEADER TYPE.
WHEN YOU TOOK THE GIG--YOU OVERSHOT.
SO I SHOULDN'T HAVE TAKEN THE GIG?
I DIDN'T SAY THAT.

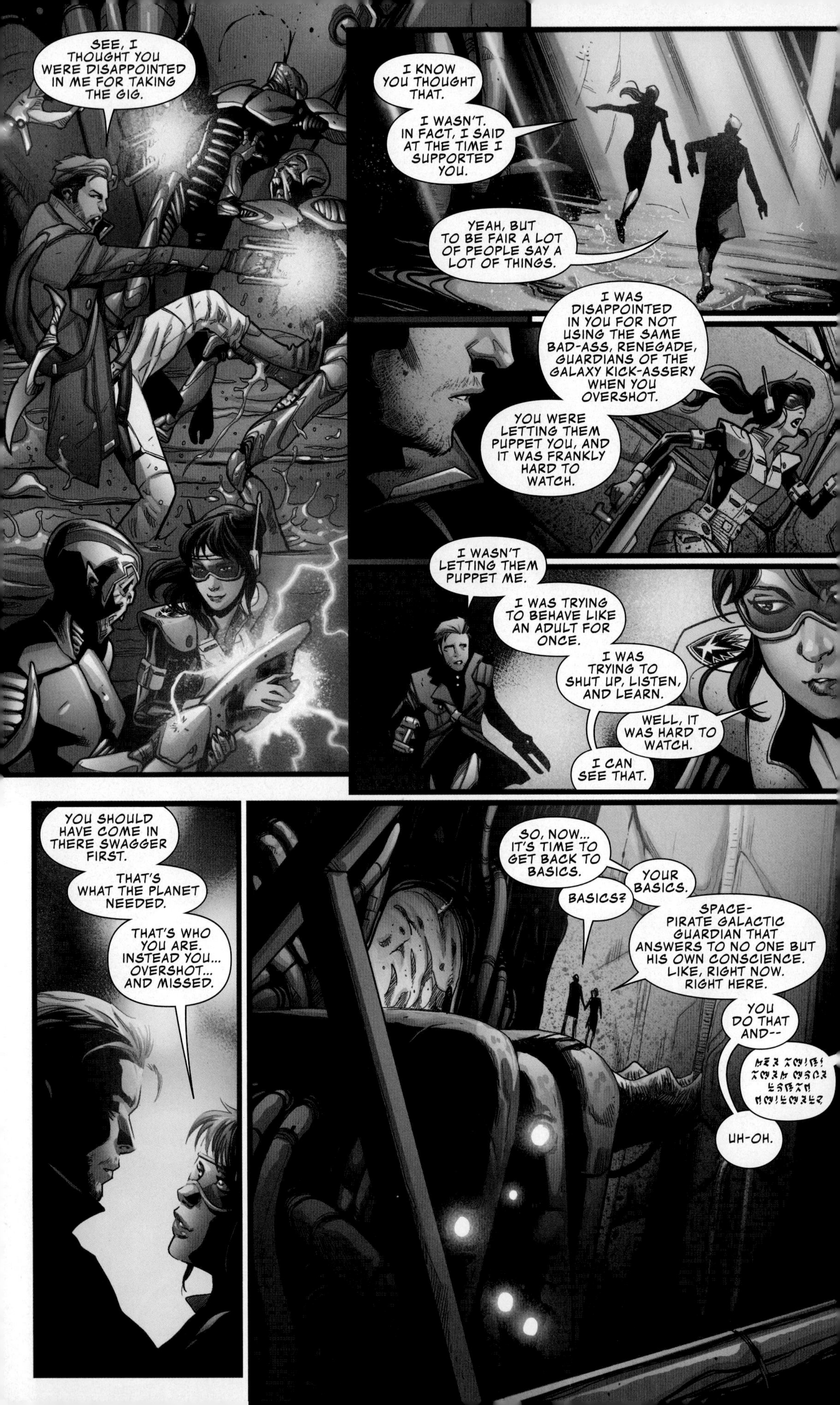
SEE, I THOUGHT YOU WERE DISAPPOINTED IN ME FOR TAKING THE GIG.
I KNOW YOU THOUGHT THAT.
I WASN'T. IN FACT, I SAID AT THE TIME I SUPPORTED YOU.
YEAH, BUT TO BE FAIR A LOT OF PEOPLE SAY A LOT OF THINGS.
I WAS DISAPPOINTED IN YOU FOR NOT USING THE SAME BAD-ASS, RENEGADE, GUARDIANS OF THE GALAXY KICK-ASSERY WHEN YOU OVERSHOT.
YOU WERE LETTING THEM PUPPET YOU, AND IT WAS FRANKLY HARD TO WATCH.
I WASN'T LETTING THEM PUPPET ME.
I WAS TRYING TO BEHAVE LIKE AN ADULT FOR ONCE.
I WAS TRYING TO SHUT UP, LISTEN, AND LEARN.
WELL, IT WAS HARD TO WATCH.
I CAN SEE THAT.
YOU SHOULD HAVE COME IN THERE SWAGGER FIRST.
THAT'S WHAT THE PLANET NEEDED.
THAT'S WHO YOU ARE. INSTEAD YOU... OVERSHOT... AND MISSED.
SO, NOW... IT'S TIME TO GET BACK TO BASICS.
BASICS?
YOUR BASICS.
SPACE-PIRATE GALACTIC GUARDIAN THAT ANSWERS TO NO ONE BUT HIS OWN CONSCIENCE. LIKE, RIGHT NOW. RIGHT HERE.
YOU DO THAT AND--
UH-OH.

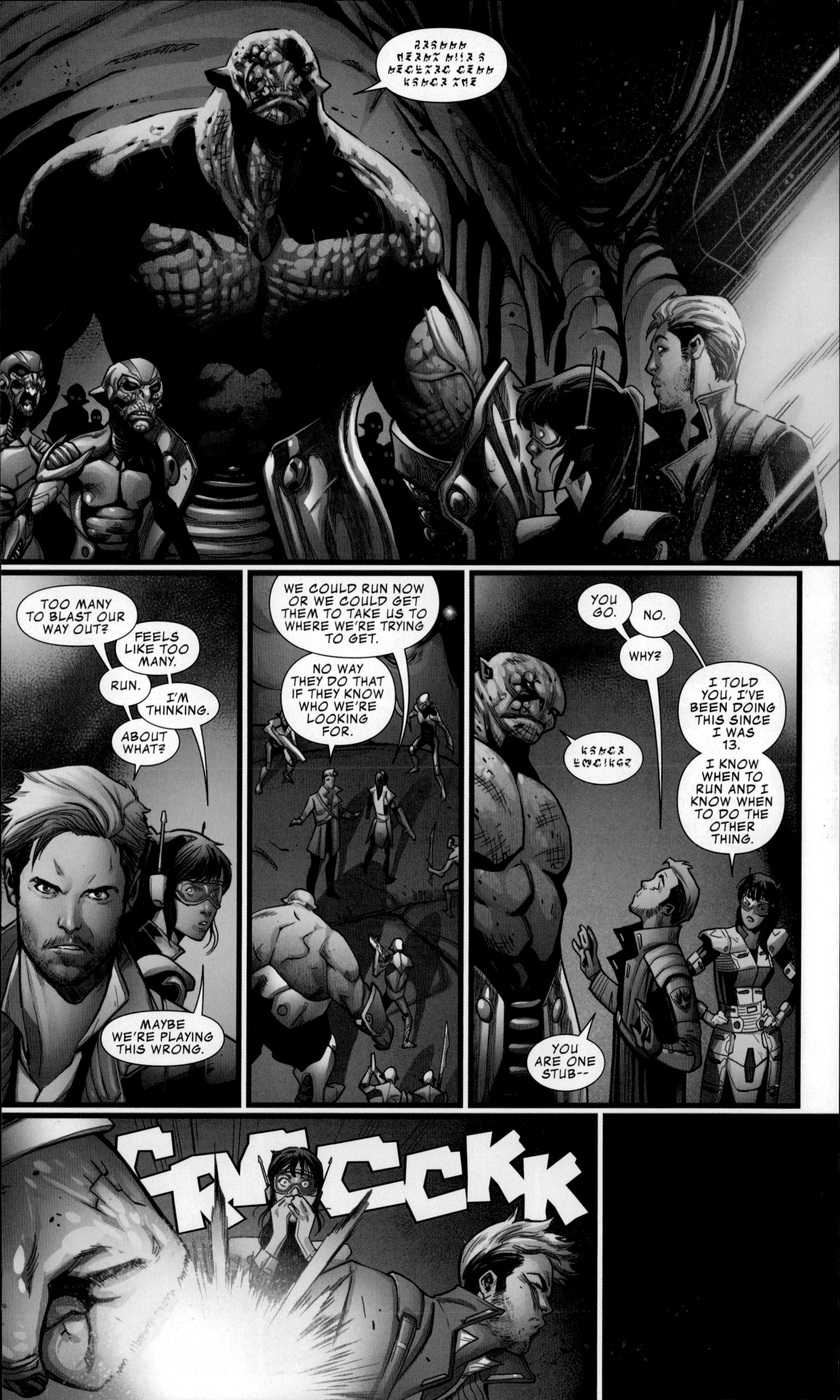

TOO MANY TO BLAST OUR WAY OUT?
FEELS LIKE TOO MANY.
RUN.
I'M THINKING.
ABOUT WHAT?
MAYBE WE'RE PLAYING THIS WRONG.
WE COULD RUN NOW OR WE COULD GET THEM TO TAKE US TO WHERE WE'RE TRYING TO GET.
NO WAY THEY DO THAT IF THEY KNOW WHO WE'RE LOOKING FOR.
YOU GO.
NO.
WHY?
I TOLD YOU, I'VE BEEN DOING THIS SINCE I WAS 13.
I KNOW WHEN TO RUN AND I KNOW WHEN TO DO THE OTHER THING.
YOU ARE ONE STUB--

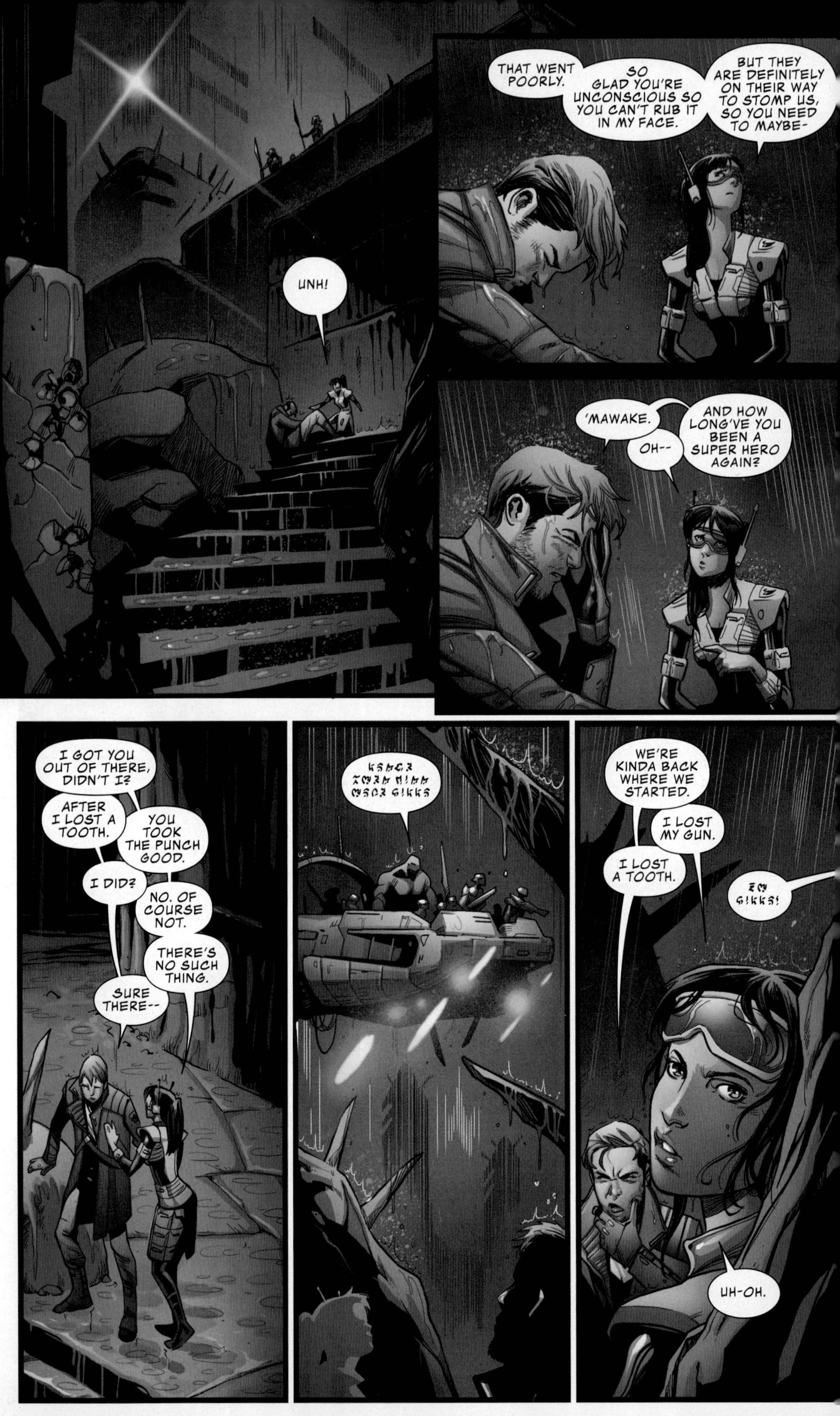
UNH!
THAT WENT POORLY.
SO GLAD YOU'RE UNCONSCIOUS SO YOU CAN'T RUB IT IN MY FACE.
BUT THEY ARE DEFINITELY ON THEIR WAY TO STOMP US, SO YOU NEED TO MAYBE-
'MAWAKE.
OH--
AND HOW LONG'VE YOU BEEN A SUPER HERO AGAIN?
I GOT YOU OUT OF THERE, DIDN'T I?
AFTER I LOST A TOOTH.
YOU TOOK THE PUNCH GOOD.
I DID?
NO. OF COURSE NOT.
THERE'S NO SUCH THING.
SURE THERE--
WE'RE KINDA BACK WHERE WE STARTED.
I LOST MY GUN.
I LOST A TOOTH.
UH-OH.

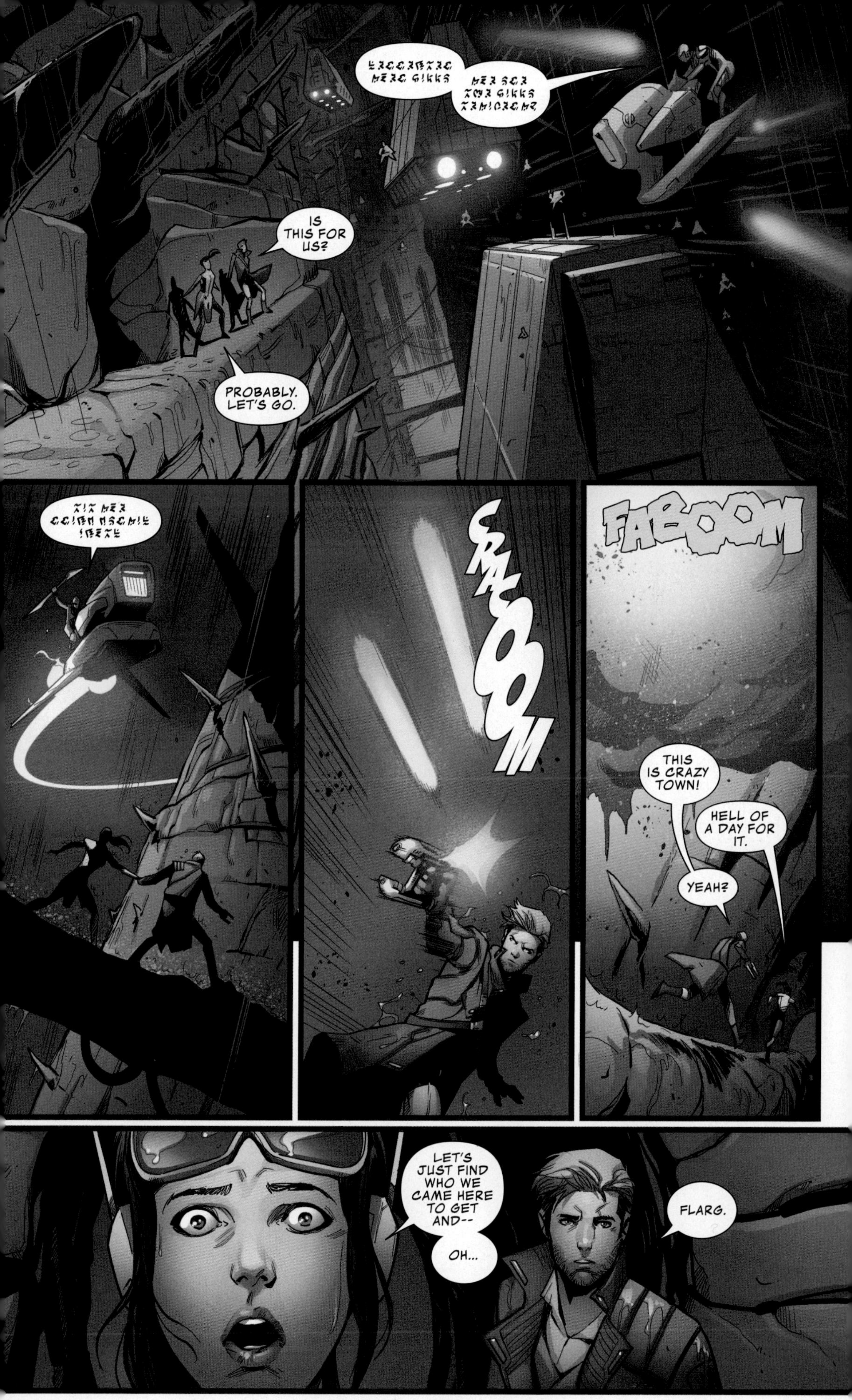
IS THIS FOR US?
PROBABLY. LET'S GO.
CRACOOOM
FABOOM
THIS IS CRAZY TOWN!
HELL OF A DAY FOR IT.
YEAH?
LET'S JUST FIND WHO WE CAME HERE TO GET AND--
OH...
FLARG.

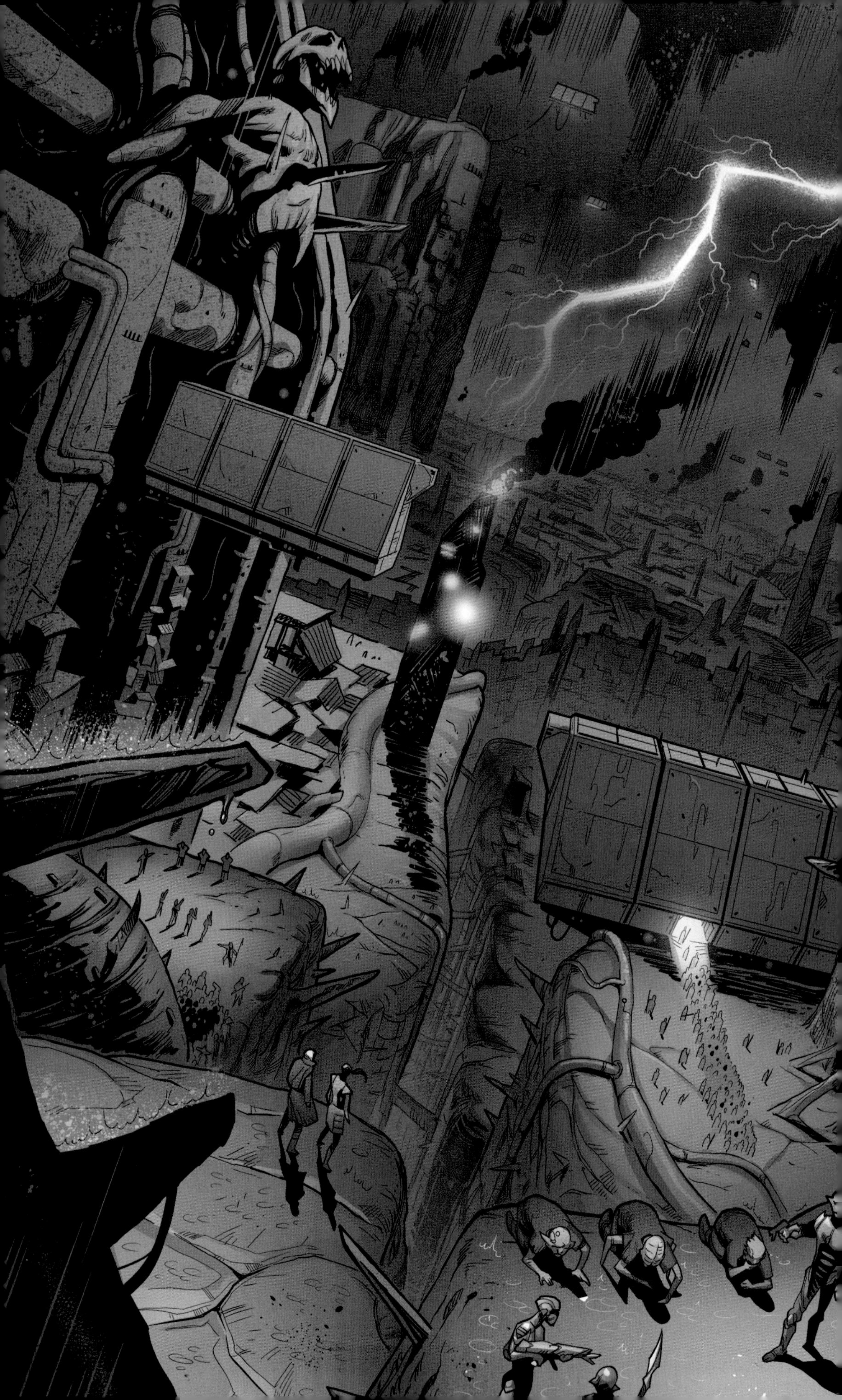

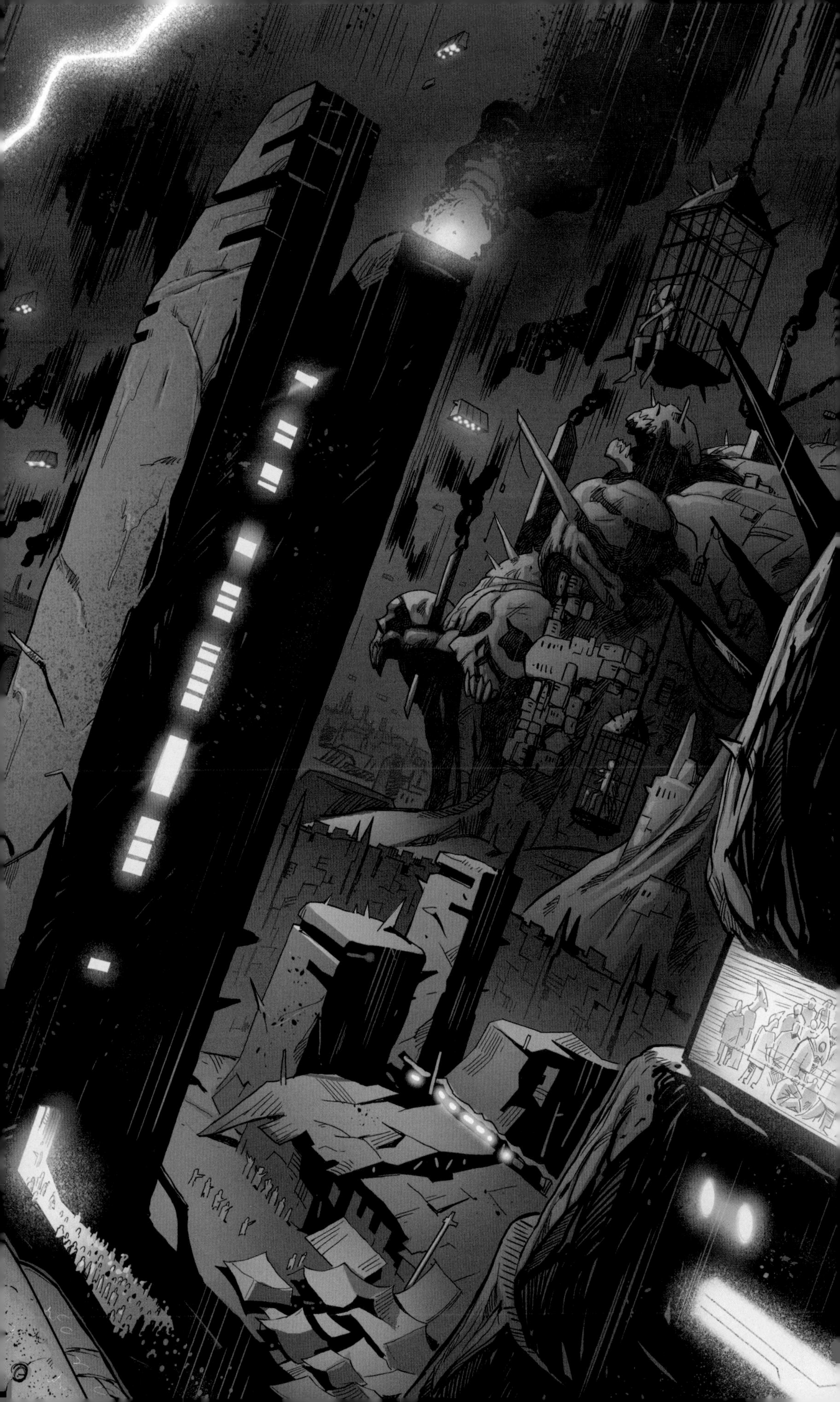

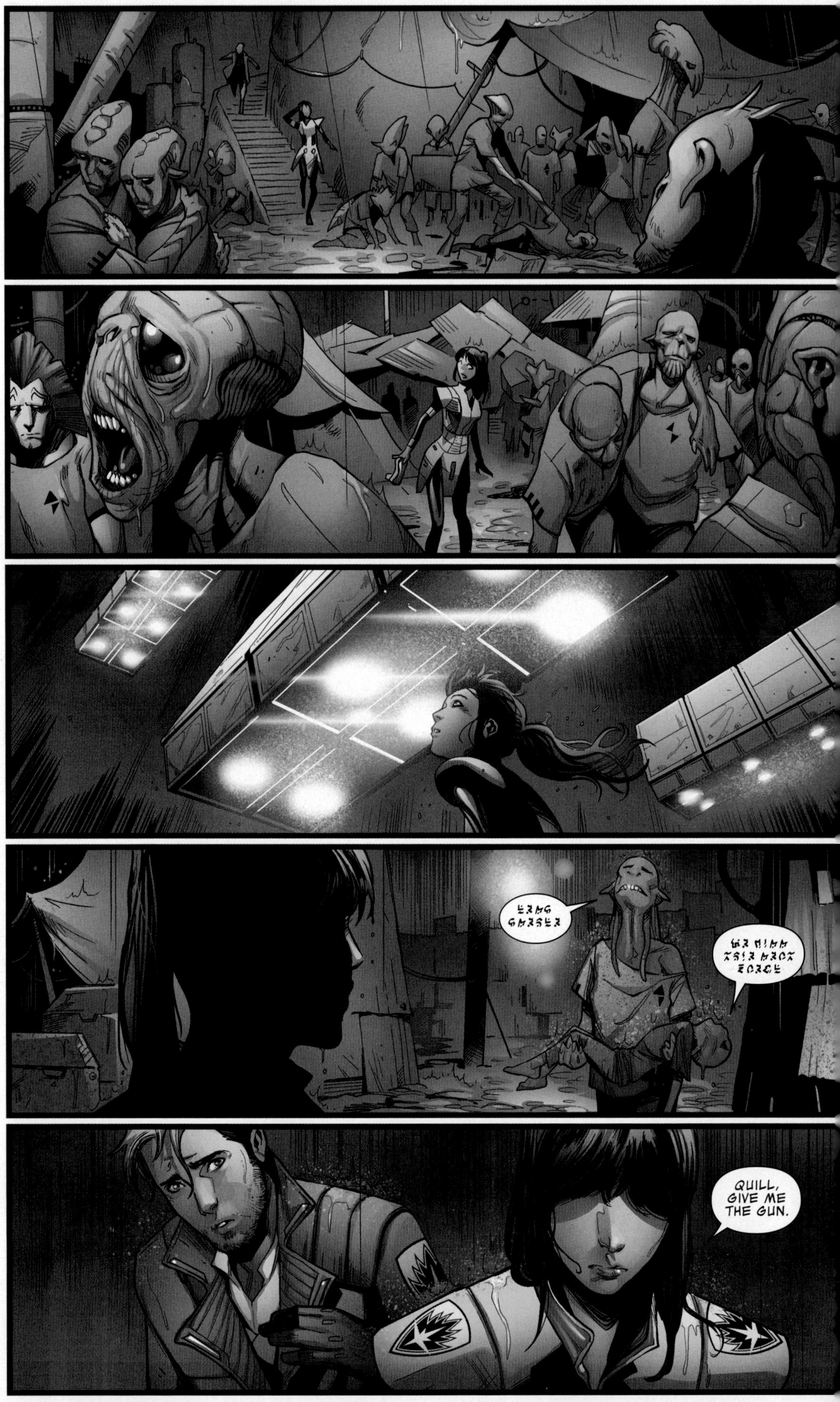
QUILL, GIVE ME THE GUN.

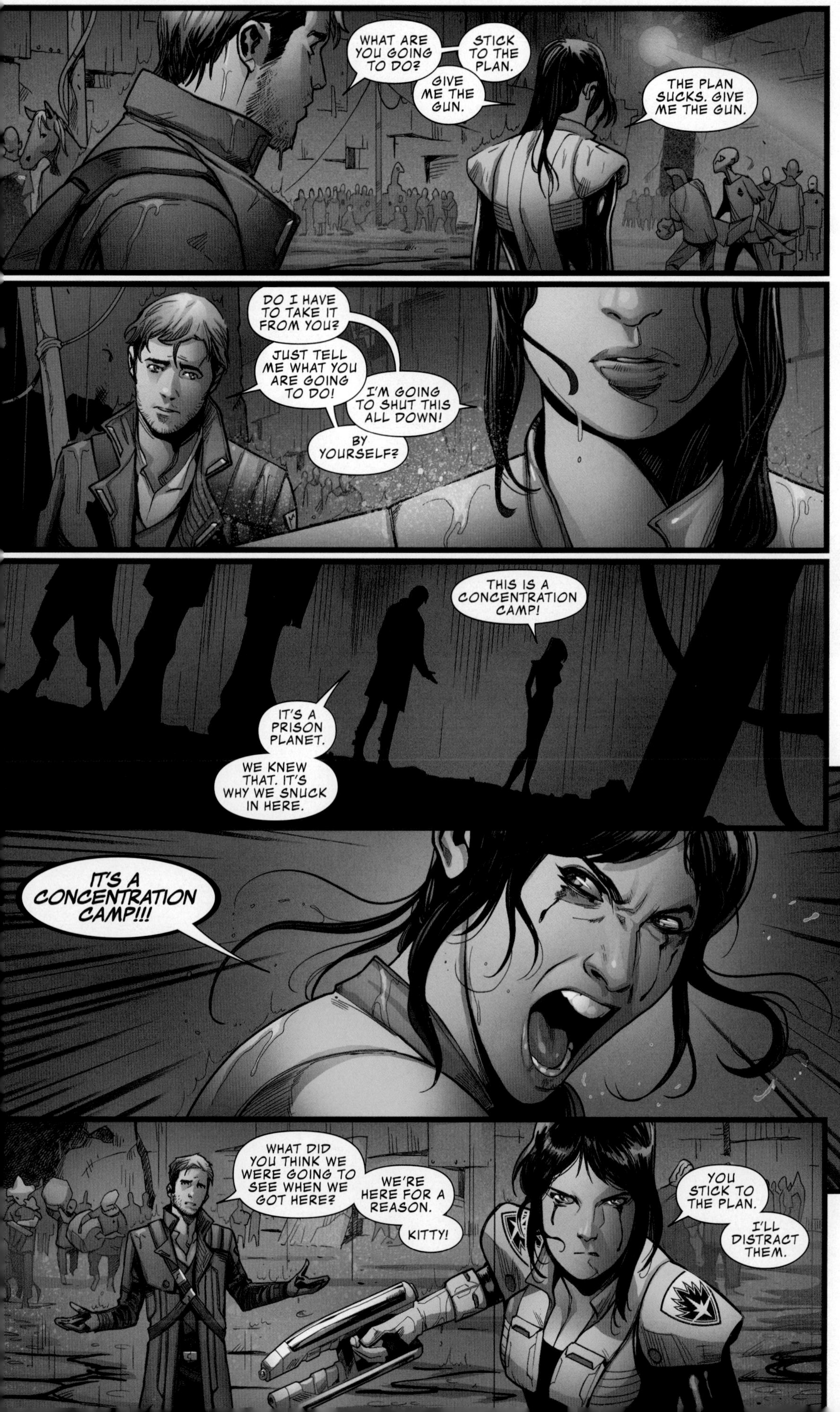
WHAT ARE YOU GOING TO DO?
STICK TO THE PLAN.
GIVE ME THE GUN.
THE PLAN SUCKS. GIVE ME THE GUN.
DO I HAVE TO TAKE IT FROM YOU?
JUST TELL ME WHAT YOU ARE GOING TO DO!
I'M GOING TO SHUT THIS ALL DOWN!
BY YOURSELF?
THIS IS A CONCENTRATION CAMP!
IT'S A PRISON PLANET.
WE KNEW THAT. IT'S WHY WE SNUCK IN HERE.
IT'S A CONCENTRATION CAMP!!!
WHAT DID YOU THINK WE WERE GOING TO SEE WHEN WE GOT HERE?
WE'RE HERE FOR A REASON.
KITTY!
YOU STICK TO THE PLAN.
I'LL DISTRACT THEM.

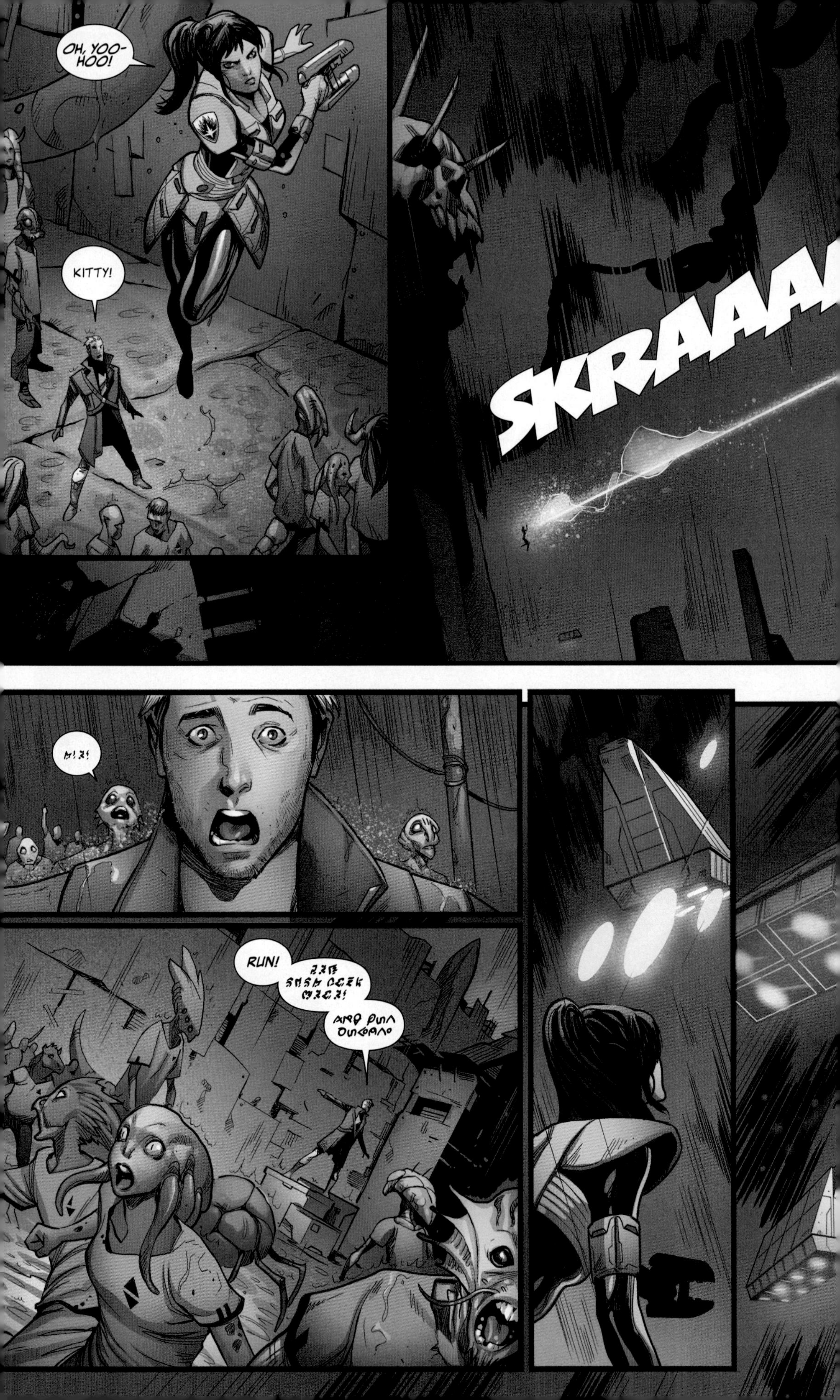
OH, YOO-HOO!
KITTY!
SKRAAA
RUN!

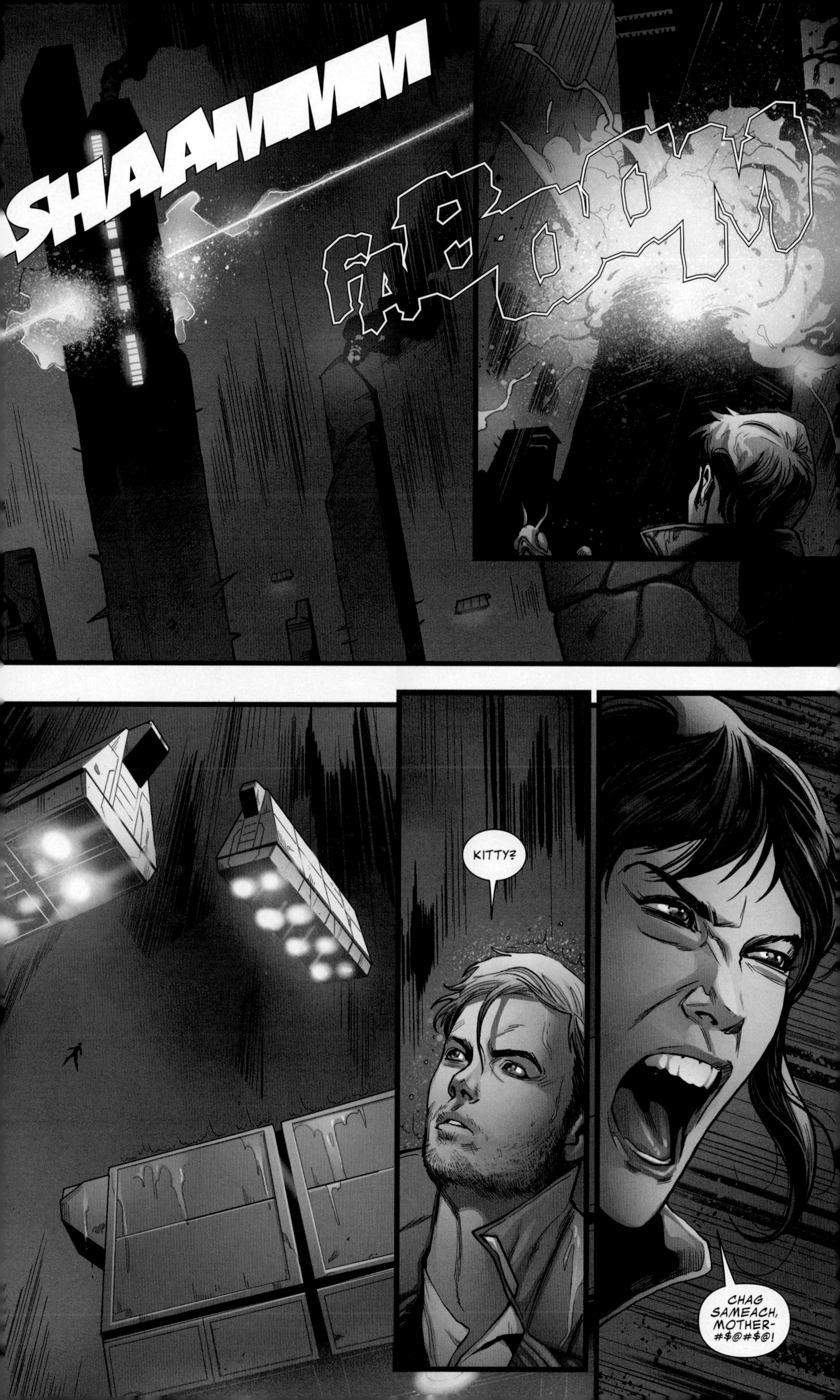
SHAAMMMM
FaBOOOOM
KITTY?
CHAG SAMEACH, MOTHER-#$@#$@!

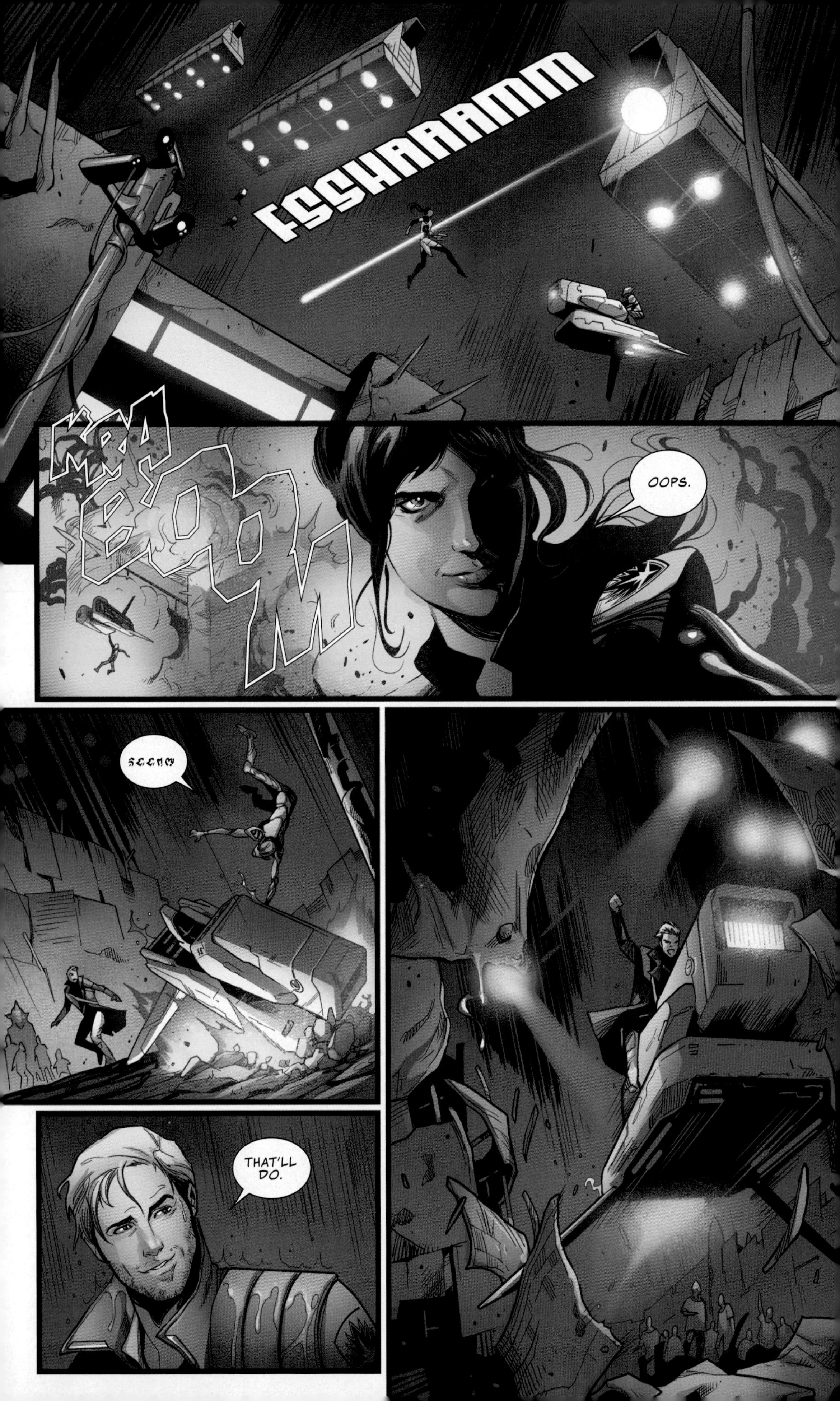
FSSHRAAMM
KRA-BOOM
OOPS.
THAT'LL DO.

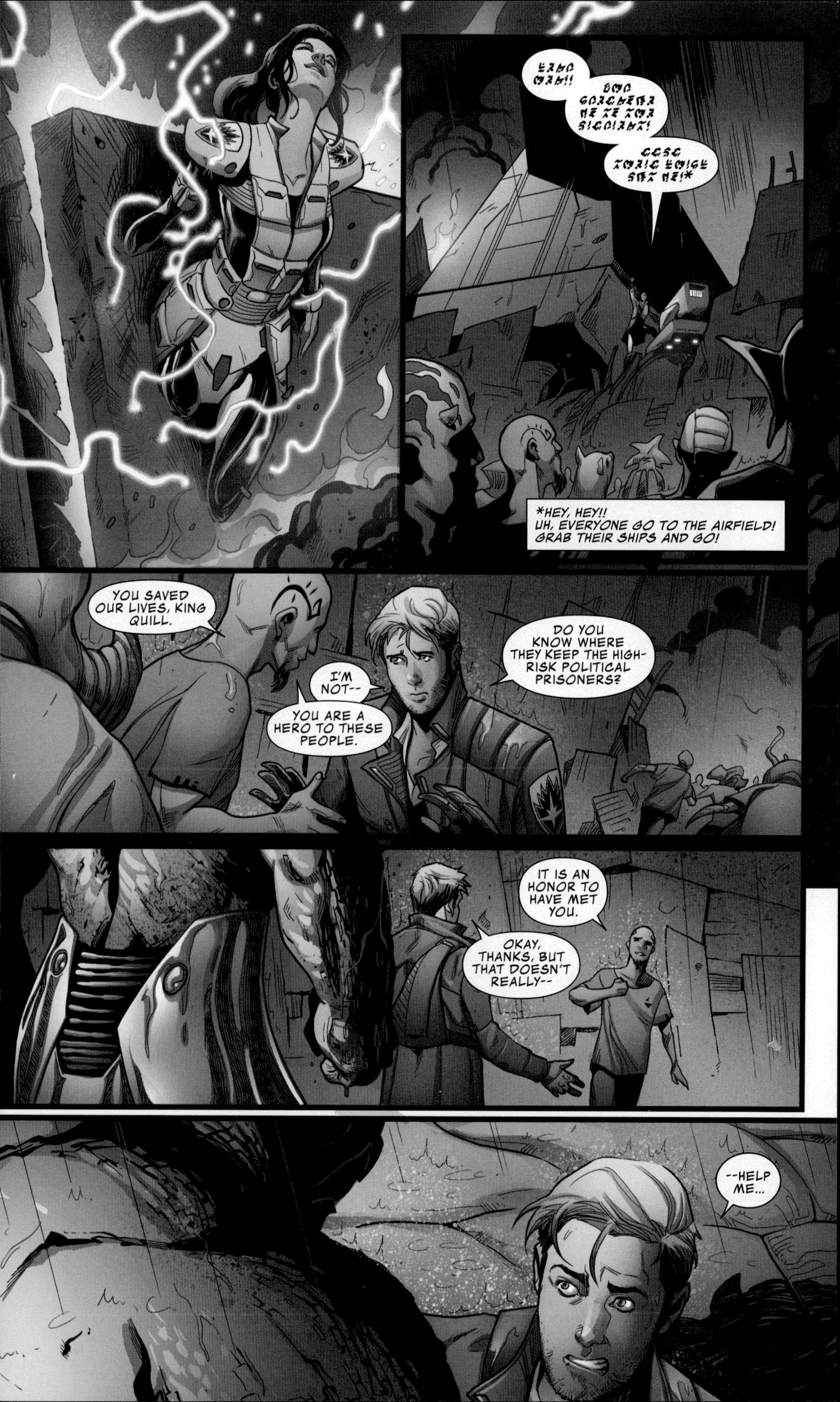
*HEY, HEY!!
UH, EVERYONE GO TO THE AIRFIELD!
GRAB THEIR SHIPS AND GO!
YOU SAVED OUR LIVES, KING QUILL.
I'M NOT--
YOU ARE A HERO TO THESE PEOPLE.
DO YOU KNOW WHERE THEY KEEP THE HIGH-RISK POLITICAL PRISONERS?
IT IS AN HONOR TO HAVE MET YOU.
OKAY, THANKS, BUT THAT DOESN'T REALLY--
--HELP ME...

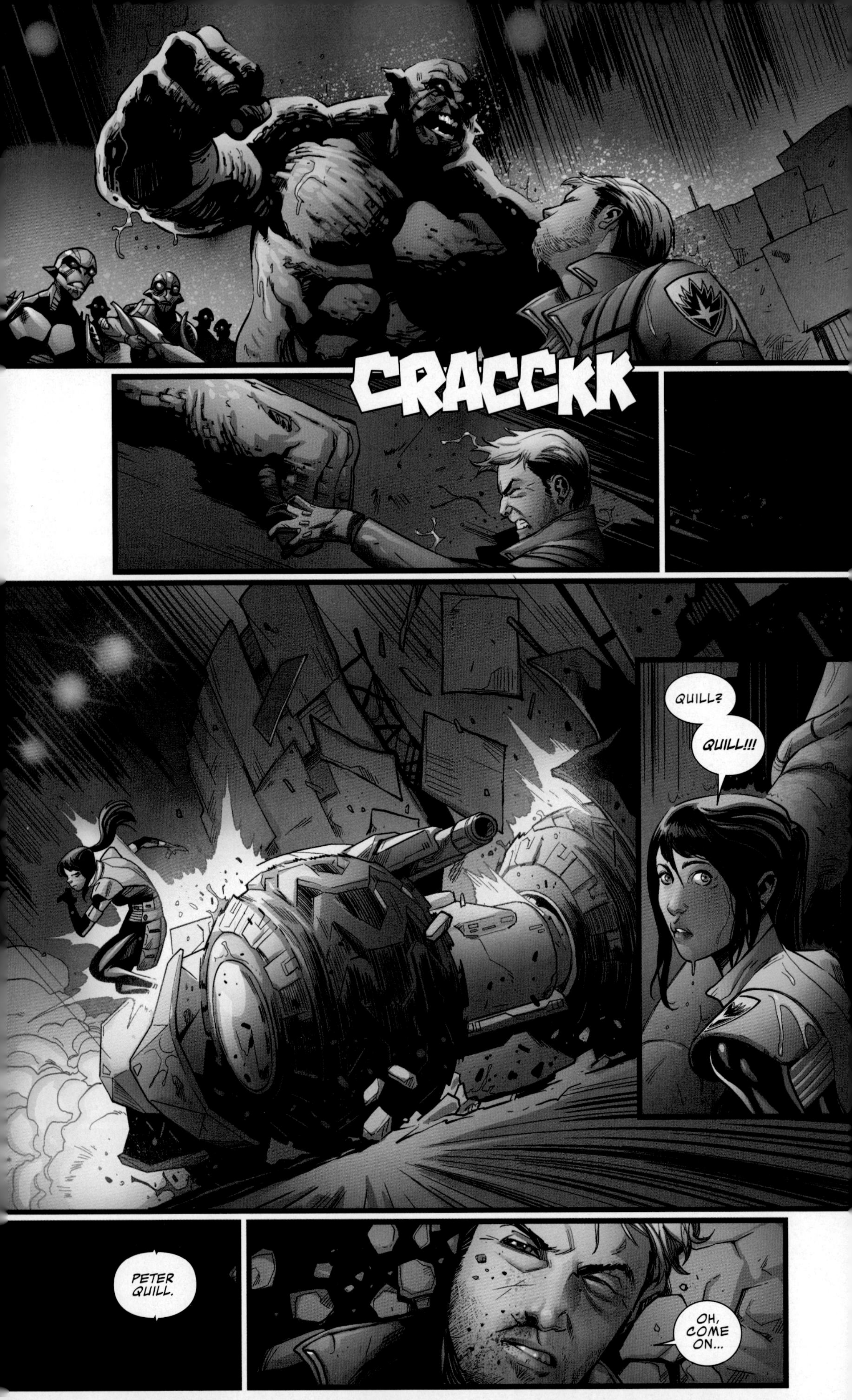
CRACCKK
QUILL?
QUILL!!!
PETER QUILL.
OH, COME ON...

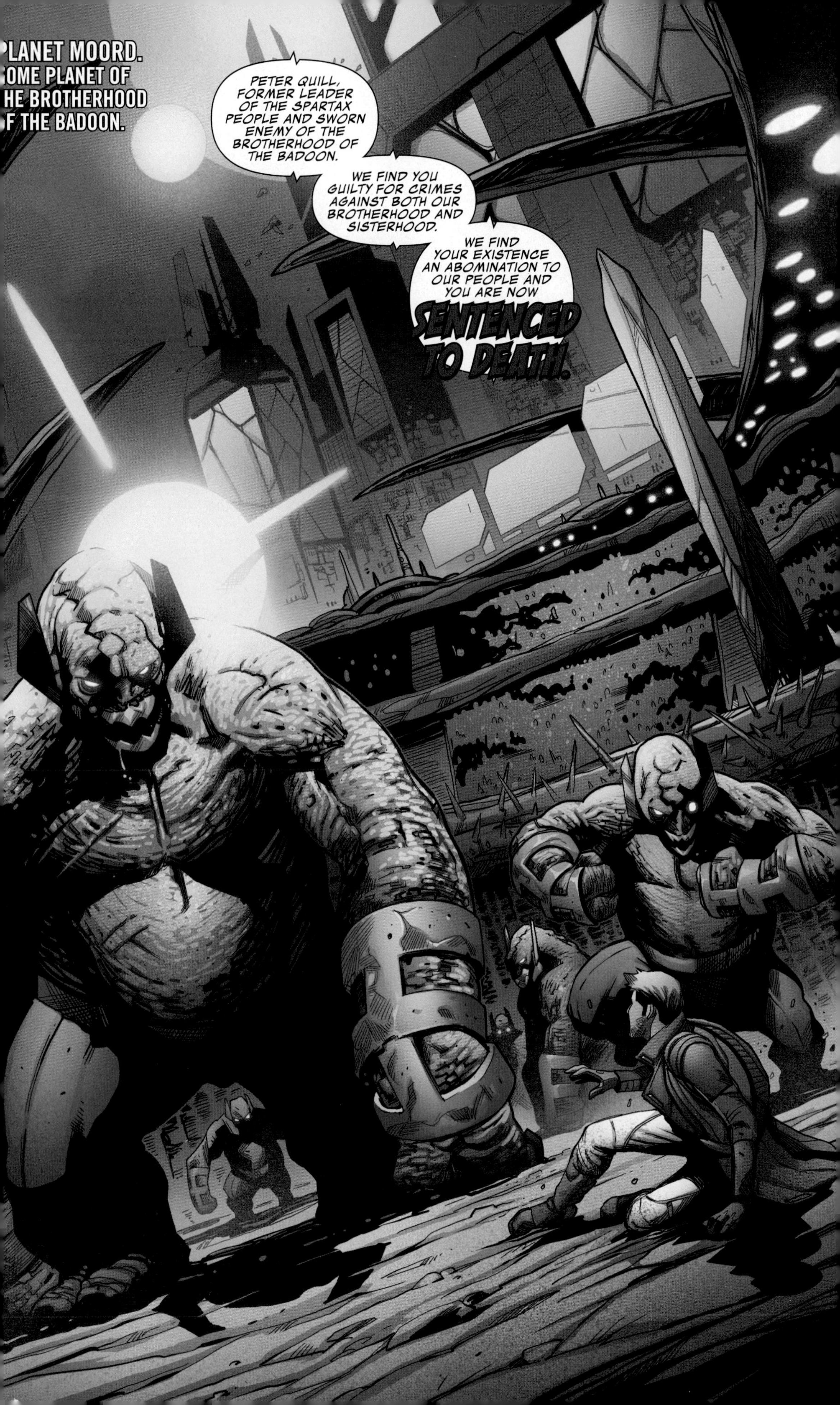

PLANET MOORD. HOME PLANET OF THE BROTHERHOOD OF THE BADOON.
PETER QUILL, FORMER LEADER OF THE SPARTAX PEOPLE AND SWORN ENEMY OF THE BROTHERHOOD OF THE BADOON.
WE FIND YOU GUILTY FOR CRIMES AGAINST BOTH OUR BROTHERHOOD AND SISTERHOOD.
WE FIND YOUR EXISTENCE AN ABOMINATION TO OUR PEOPLE AND YOU ARE NOW SENTENCED TO DEATH.

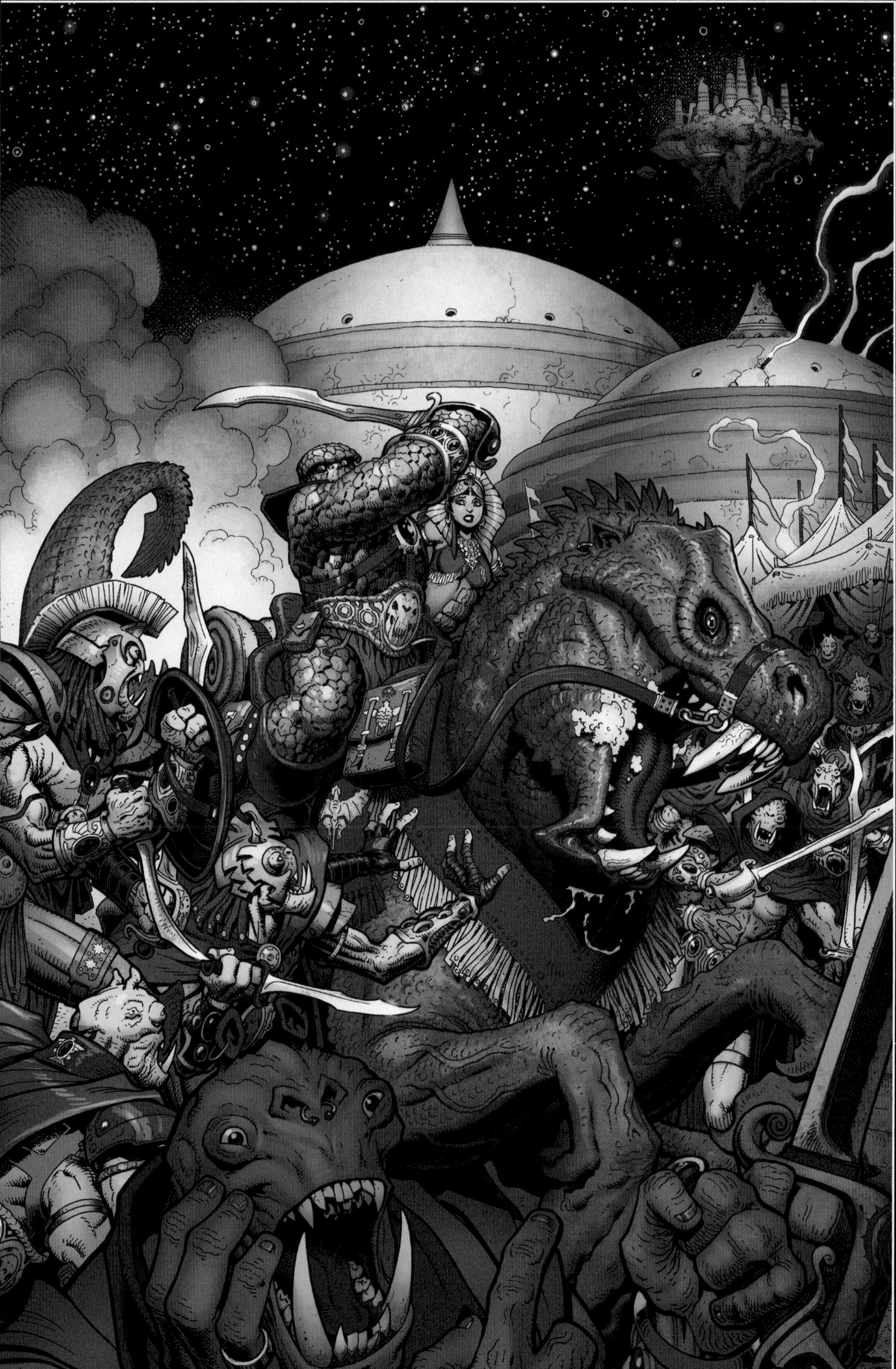
ARTHUR ADAMS 12-15 2015

7

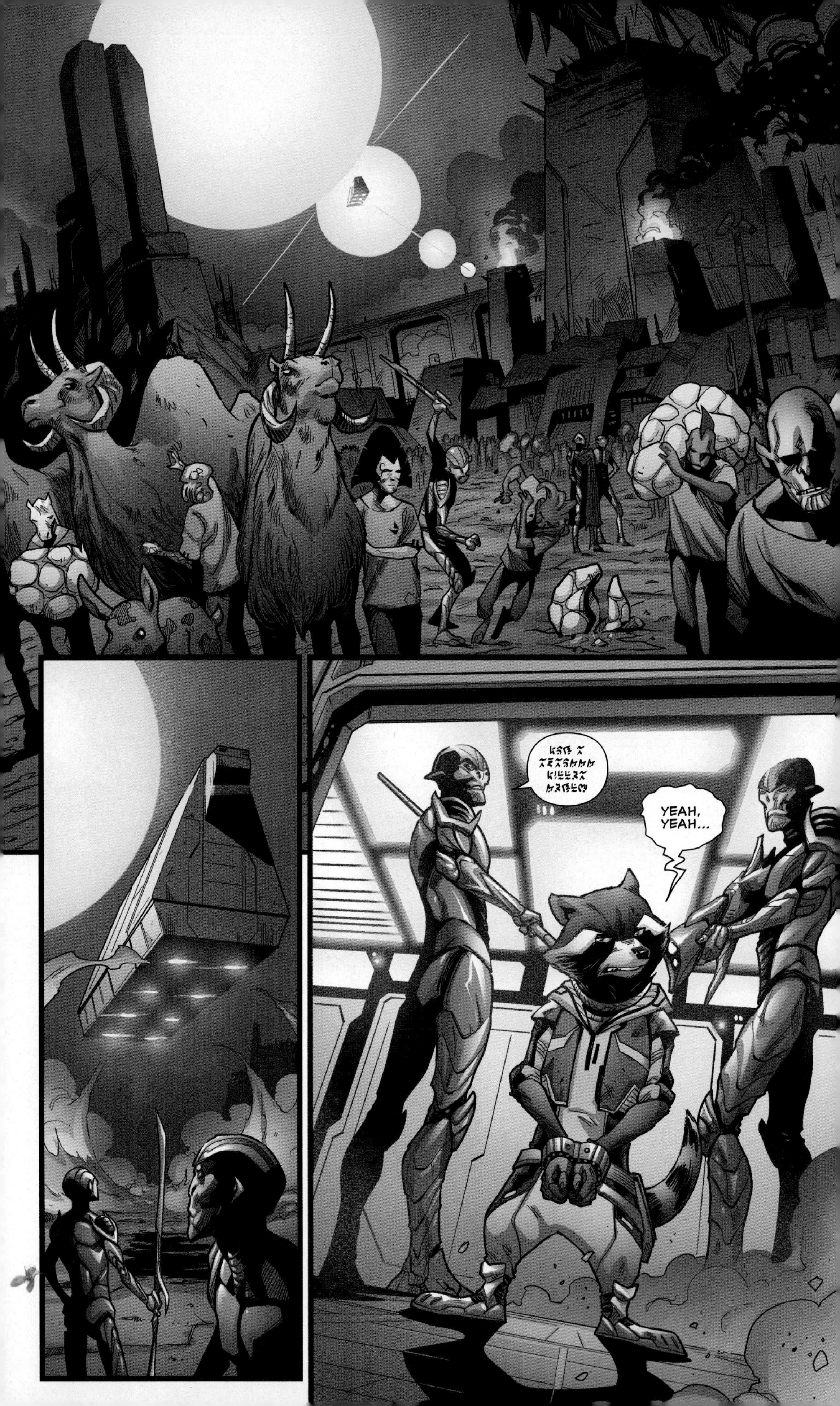
YEAH, YEAH...

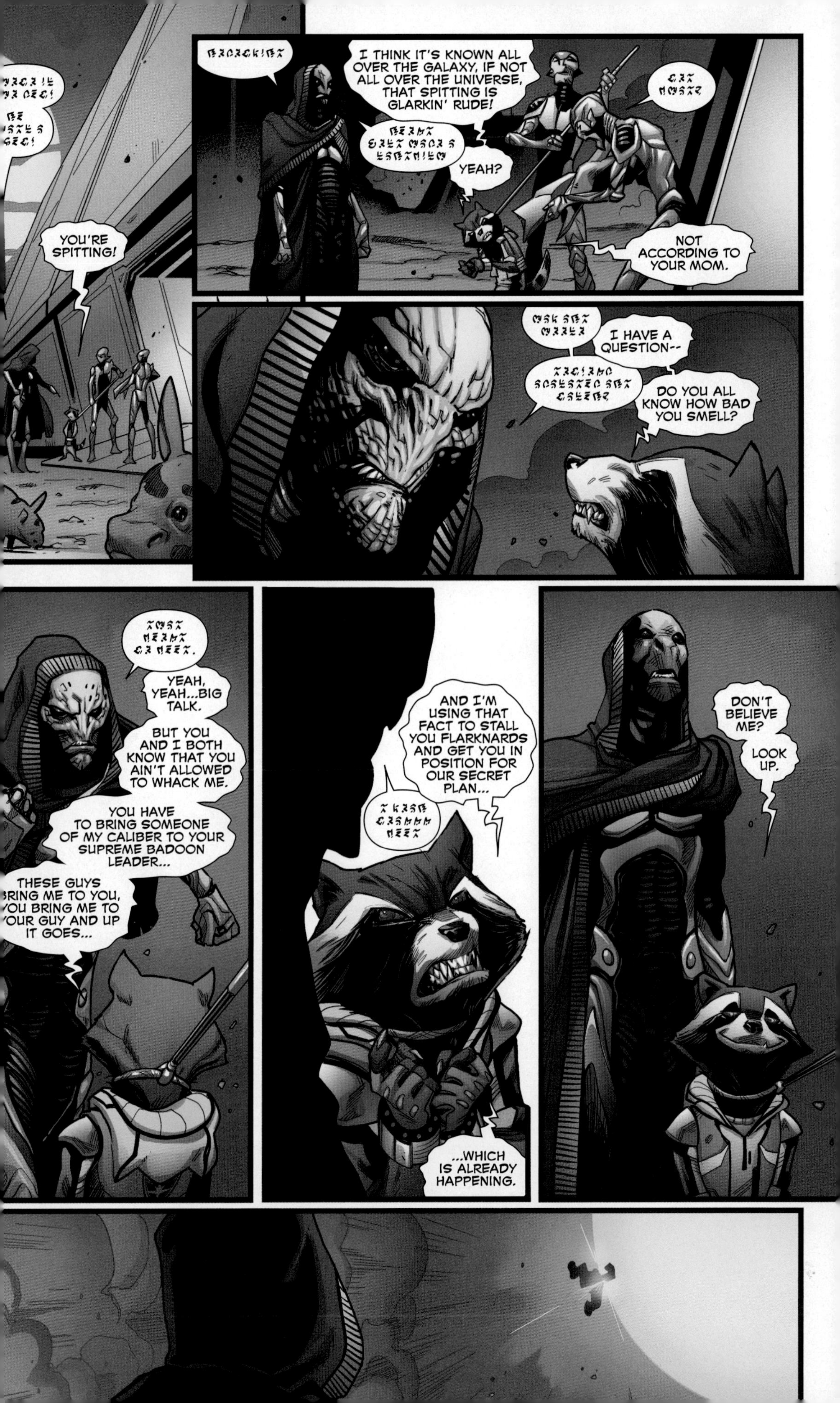

YOU'RE SPITTING!
I THINK IT'S KNOWN ALL OVER THE GALAXY, IF NOT ALL OVER THE UNIVERSE, THAT SPITTING IS GLARKIN' RUDE!
YEAH?
NOT ACCORDING TO YOUR MOM.
I HAVE A QUESTION--
DO YOU ALL KNOW HOW BAD YOU SMELL?
YEAH, YEAH...BIG TALK.
BUT YOU AND I BOTH KNOW THAT YOU AIN'T ALLOWED TO WHACK ME.
YOU HAVE TO BRING SOMEONE OF MY CALIBER TO YOUR SUPREME BADOON LEADER...
THESE GUYS BRING ME TO YOU, YOU BRING ME TO YOUR GUY AND UP IT GOES...
AND I'M USING THAT FACT TO STALL YOU FLARKNARDS AND GET YOU IN POSITION FOR OUR SECRET PLAN...
...WHICH IS ALREADY HAPPENING.
DON'T BELIEVE ME?
LOOK UP.

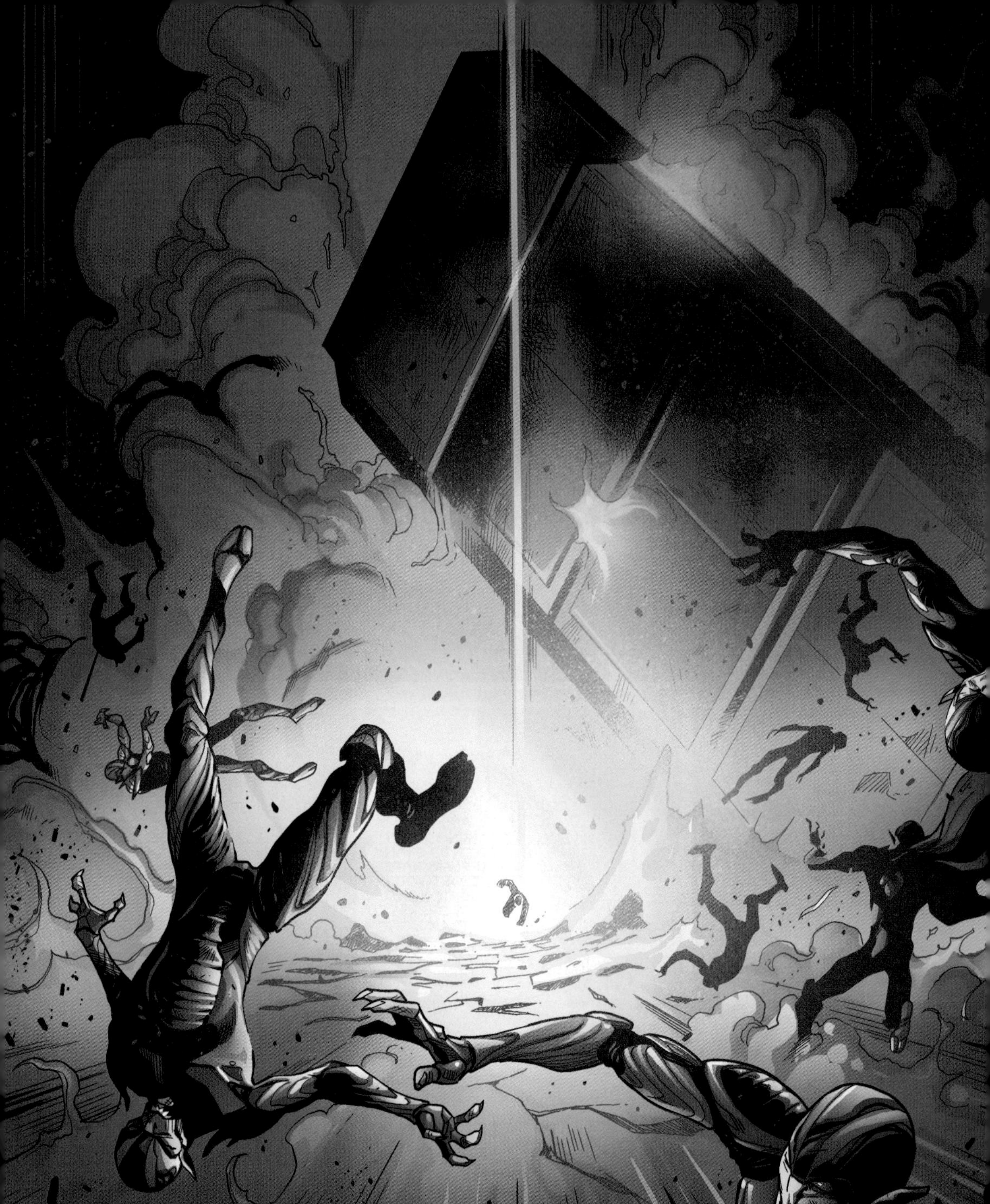

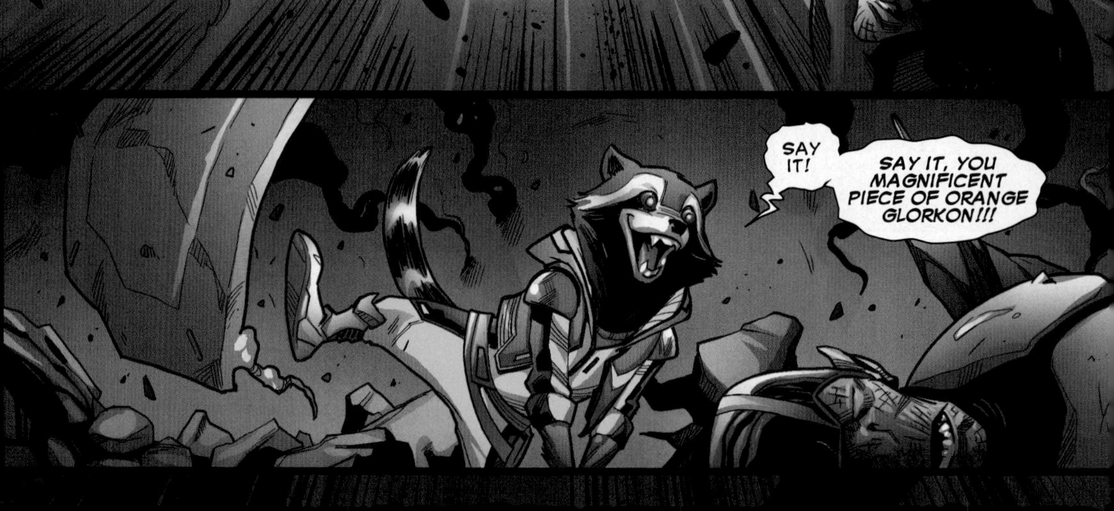

SAY IT!
SAY IT, YOU MAGNIFICENT PIECE OF ORANGE GLORKON!!!

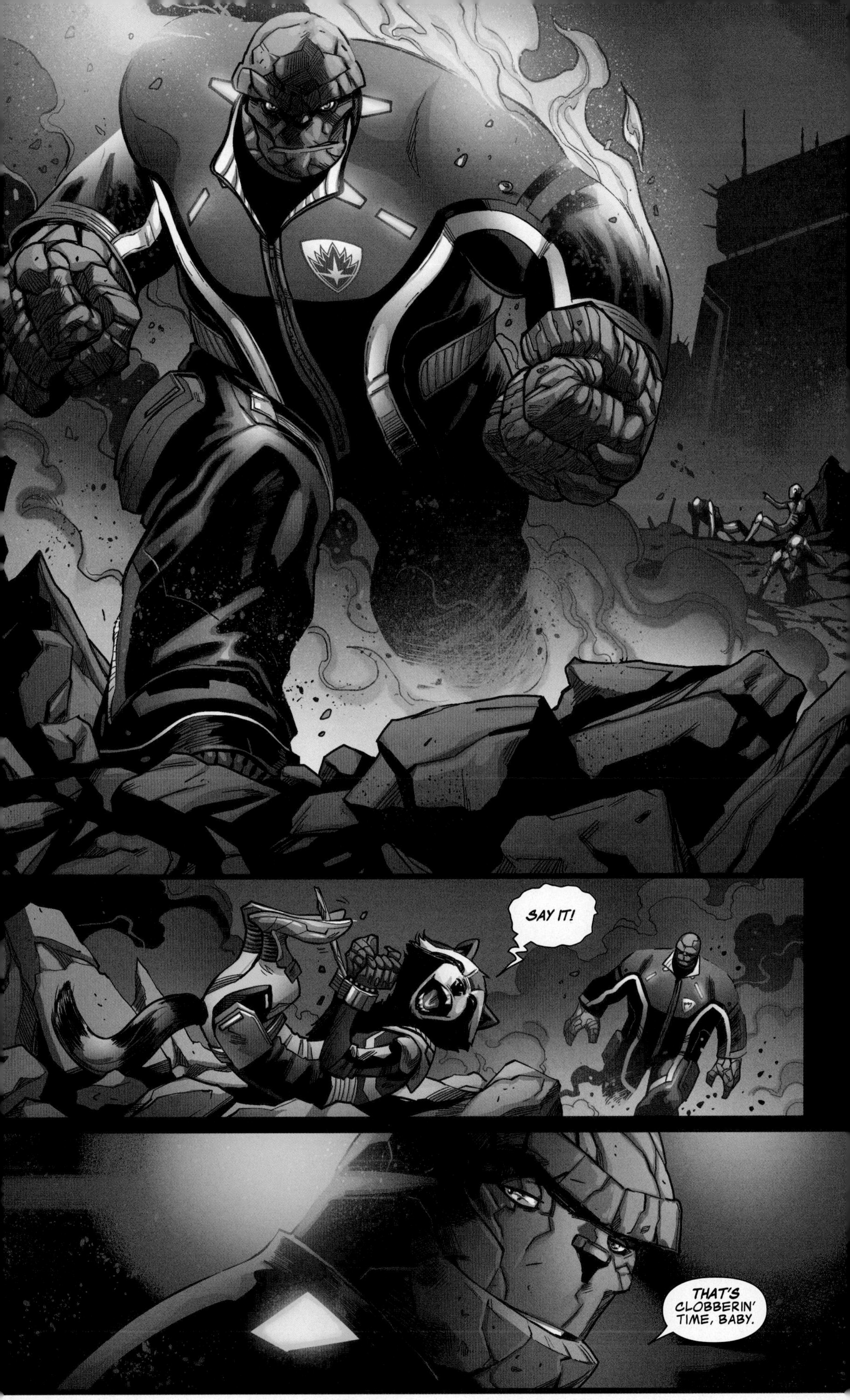
SAY IT!
THAT'S CLOBBERIN' TIME, BABY.

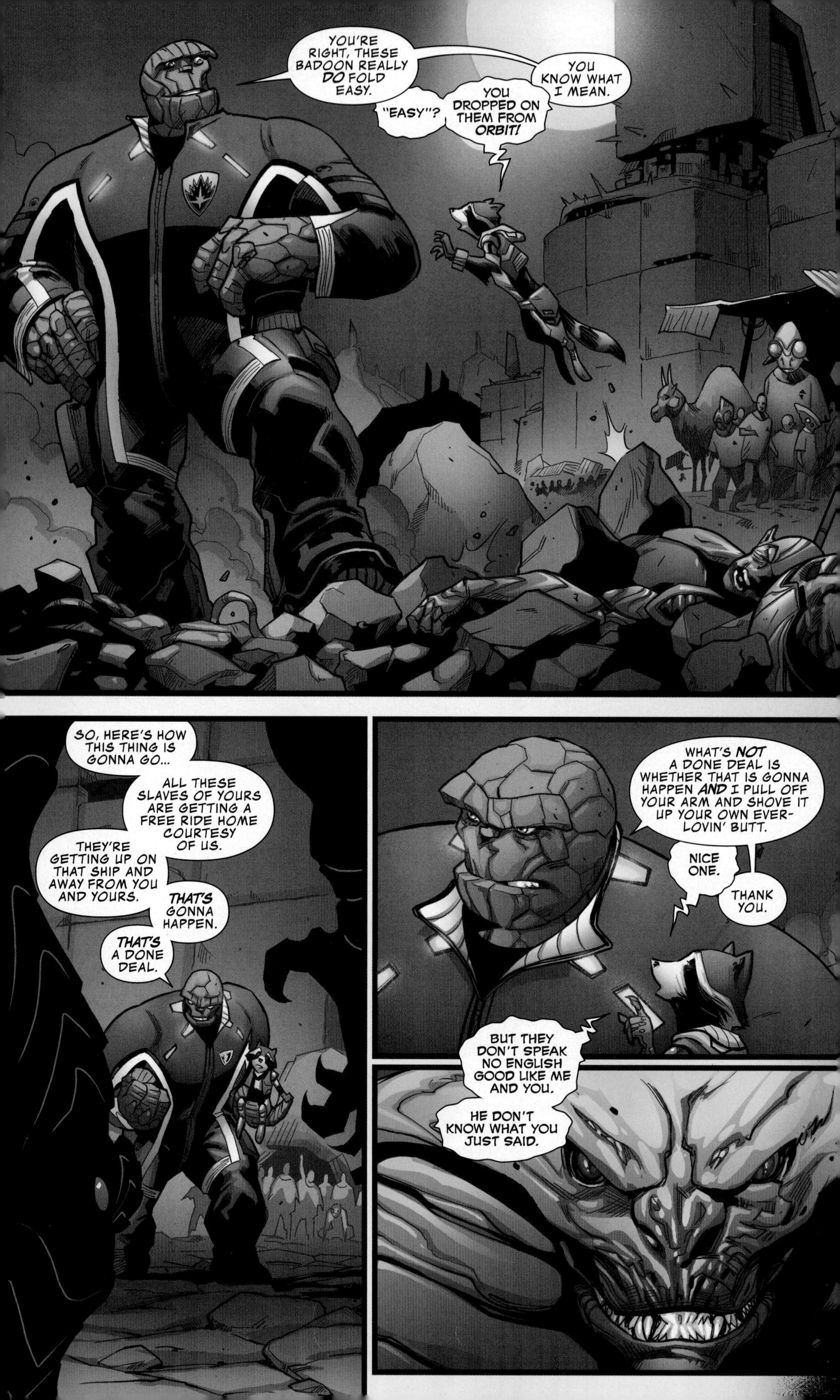

YOU'RE RIGHT, THESE BADOON REALLY DO FOLD EASY.
"EASY"?
YOU DROPPED ON THEM FROM ORBIT!
YOU KNOW WHAT I MEAN.
SO, HERE'S HOW THIS THING IS GONNA GO...
ALL THESE SLAVES OF YOURS ARE GETTING A FREE RIDE HOME COURTESY OF US.
THEY'RE GETTING UP ON THAT SHIP AND AWAY FROM YOU AND YOURS.
THAT'S GONNA HAPPEN.
THAT'S A DONE DEAL.
WHAT'S NOT A DONE DEAL IS WHETHER THAT IS GONNA HAPPEN AND I PULL OFF YOUR ARM AND SHOVE IT UP YOUR OWN EVER-LOVIN' BUTT.
NICE ONE.
THANK YOU.
BUT THEY DON'T SPEAK NO ENGLISH GOOD LIKE ME AND YOU.
HE DON'T KNOW WHAT YOU JUST SAID.

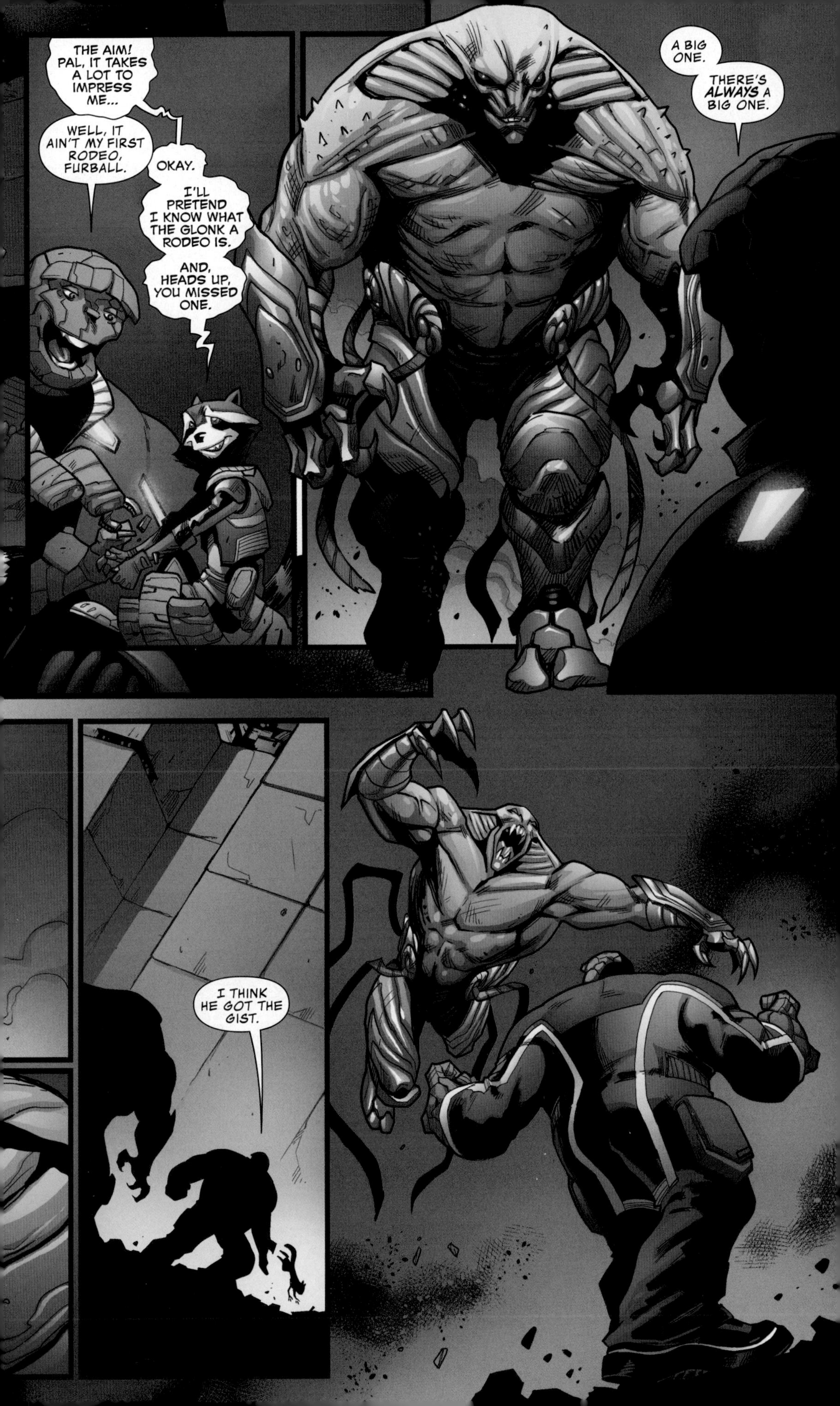
THE AIM! PAL, IT TAKES A LOT TO IMPRESS ME...
WELL, IT AIN'T MY FIRST RODEO, FURBALL.
OKAY.
I'LL PRETEND I KNOW WHAT THE GLONK A RODEO IS.
AND, HEADS UP, YOU MISSED ONE.
A BIG ONE.
THERE'S *ALWAYS* A BIG ONE.
I THINK HE GOT THE GIST.

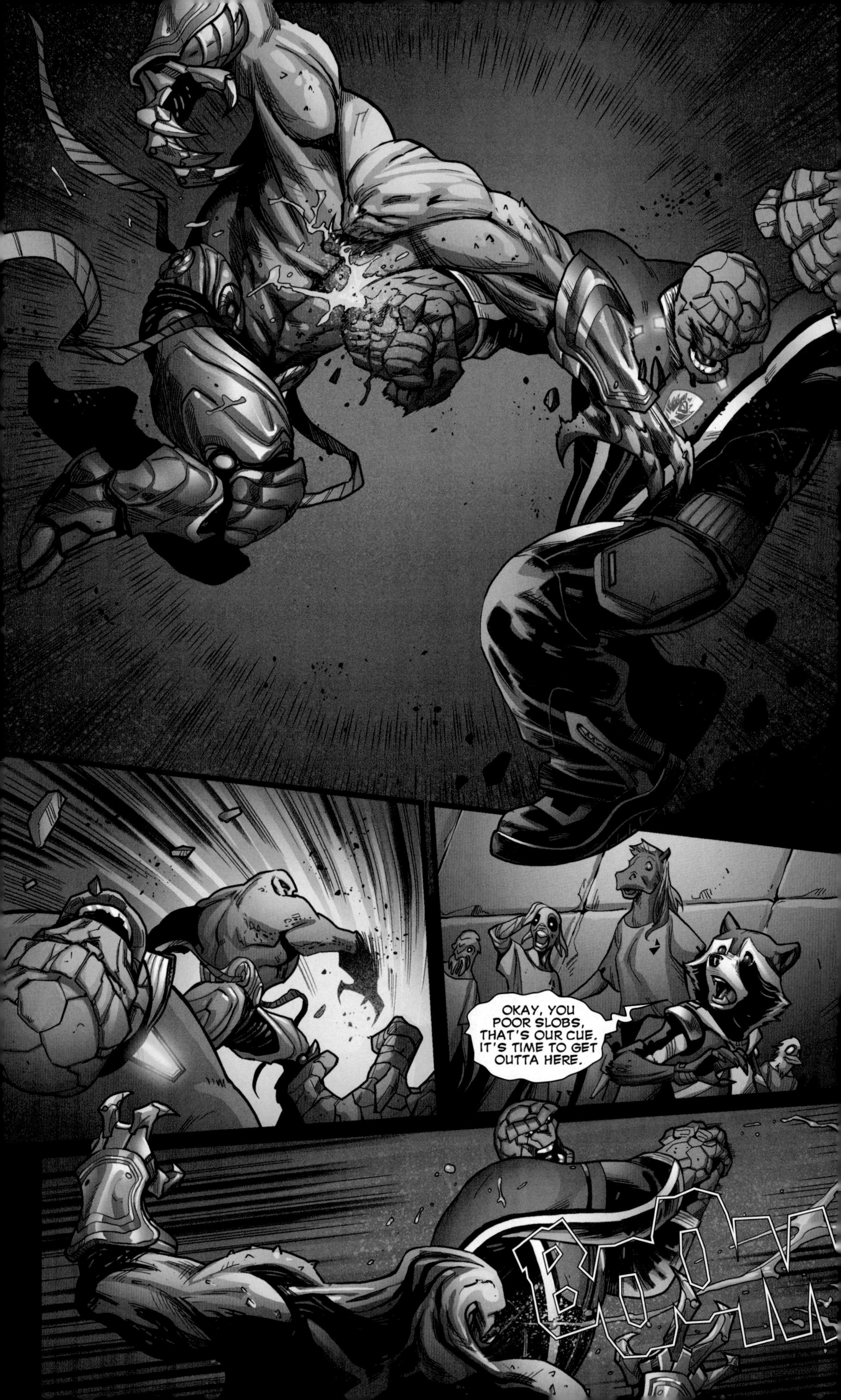
OKAY, YOU POOR SLOBS, THAT'S OUR CUE. IT'S TIME TO GET OUTTA HERE.
BOOM

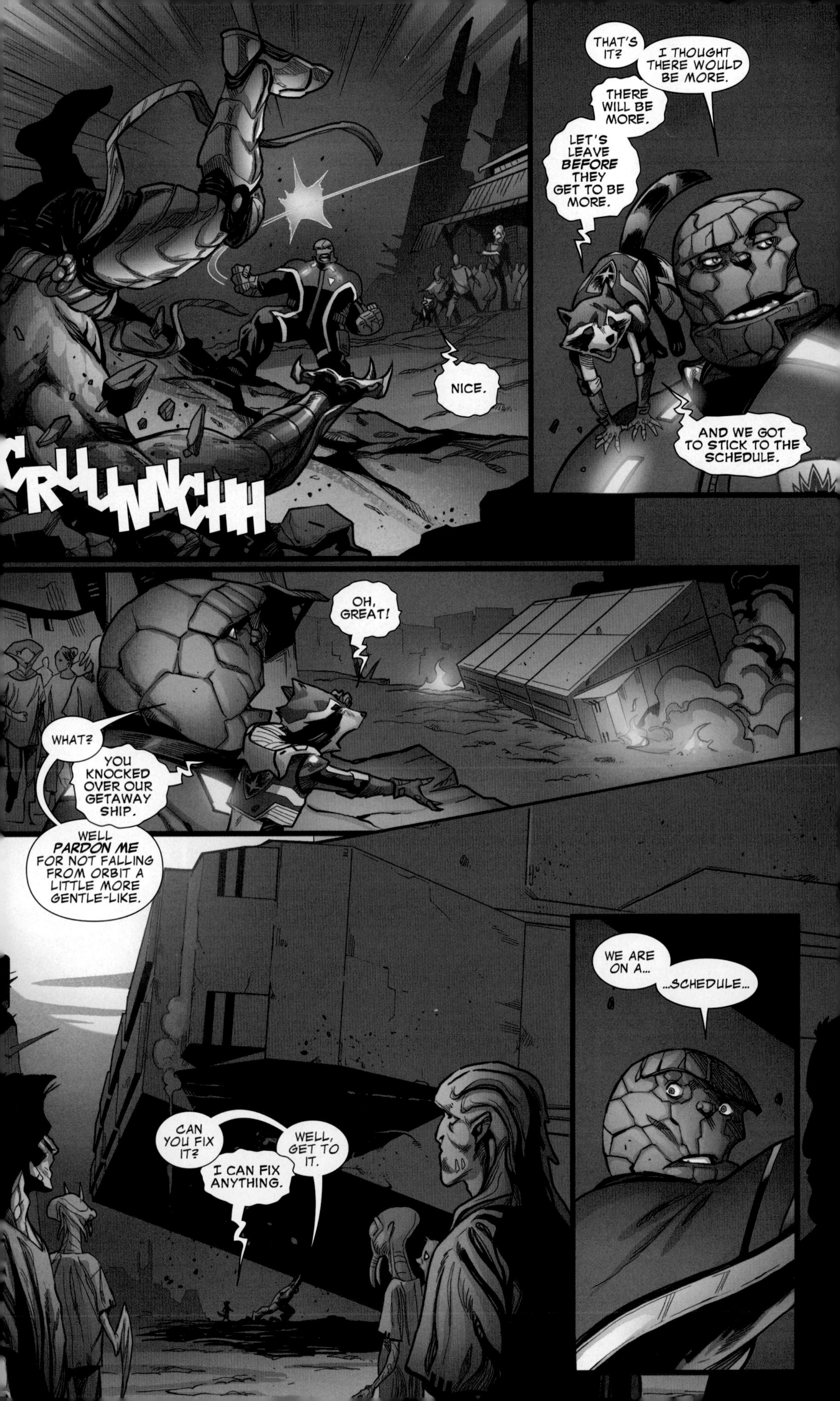
NICE.
CRUUNNCHH
THAT'S IT?
I THOUGHT THERE WOULD BE MORE.
THERE WILL BE MORE.
LET'S LEAVE BEFORE THEY GET TO BE MORE.
AND WE GOT TO STICK TO THE SCHEDULE.
OH, GREAT!
WHAT?
YOU KNOCKED OVER OUR GETAWAY SHIP.
WELL PARDON ME FOR NOT FALLING FROM ORBIT A LITTLE MORE GENTLE-LIKE.
CAN YOU FIX IT?
I CAN FIX ANYTHING.
WELL, GET TO IT.
WE ARE ON A...
...SCHEDULE...

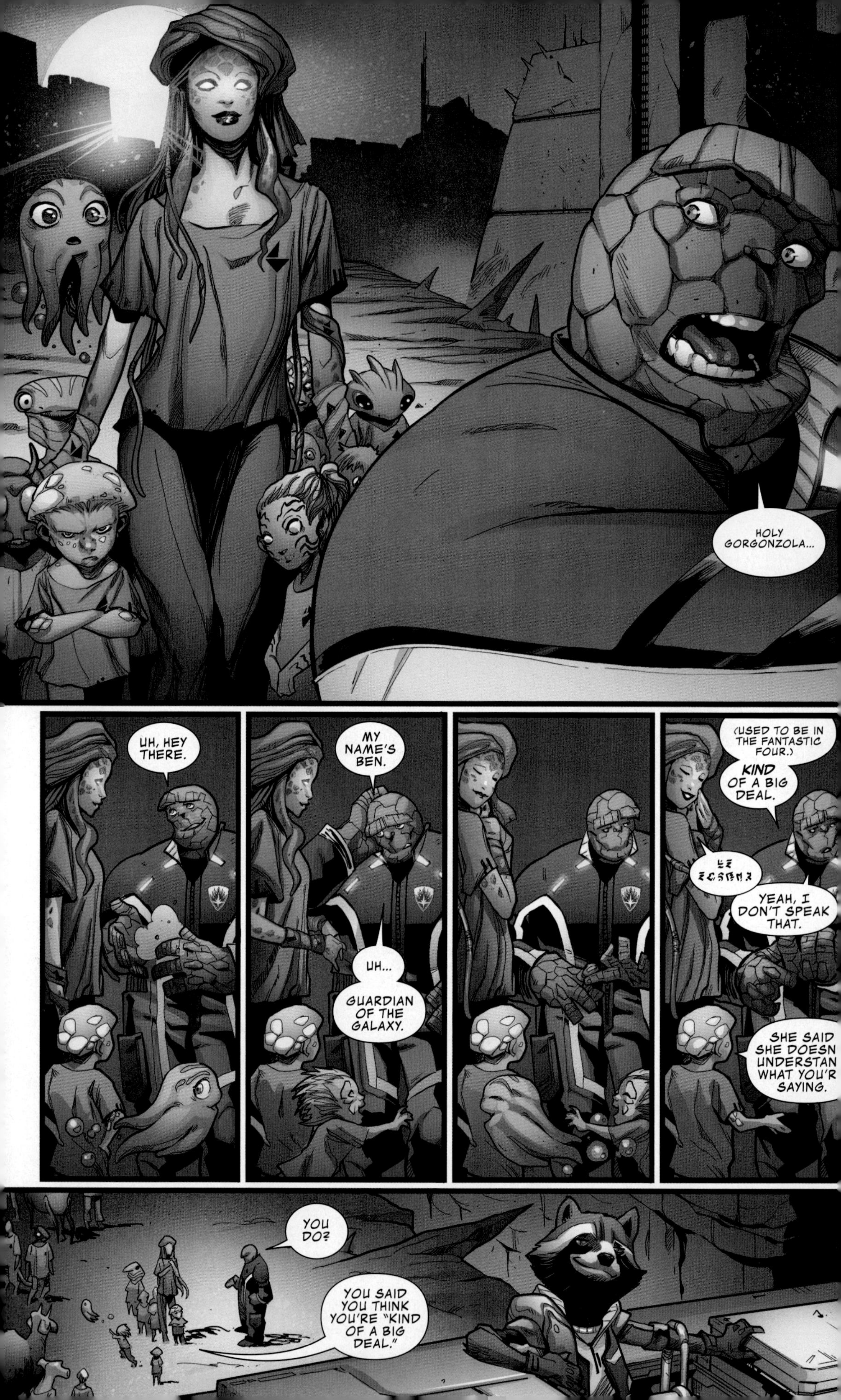

HOLY GORGONZOLA...
UH, HEY THERE.
MY NAME'S BEN.
UH...
GUARDIAN OF THE GALAXY.
(USED TO BE IN THE FANTASTIC FOUR.)
KIND OF A BIG DEAL.
YEAH, I DON'T SPEAK THAT.
SHE SAID SHE DOESN UNDERSTAN WHAT YOU'R SAYING.
YOU DO?
YOU SAID YOU THINK YOU'RE "KIND OF A BIG DEAL."

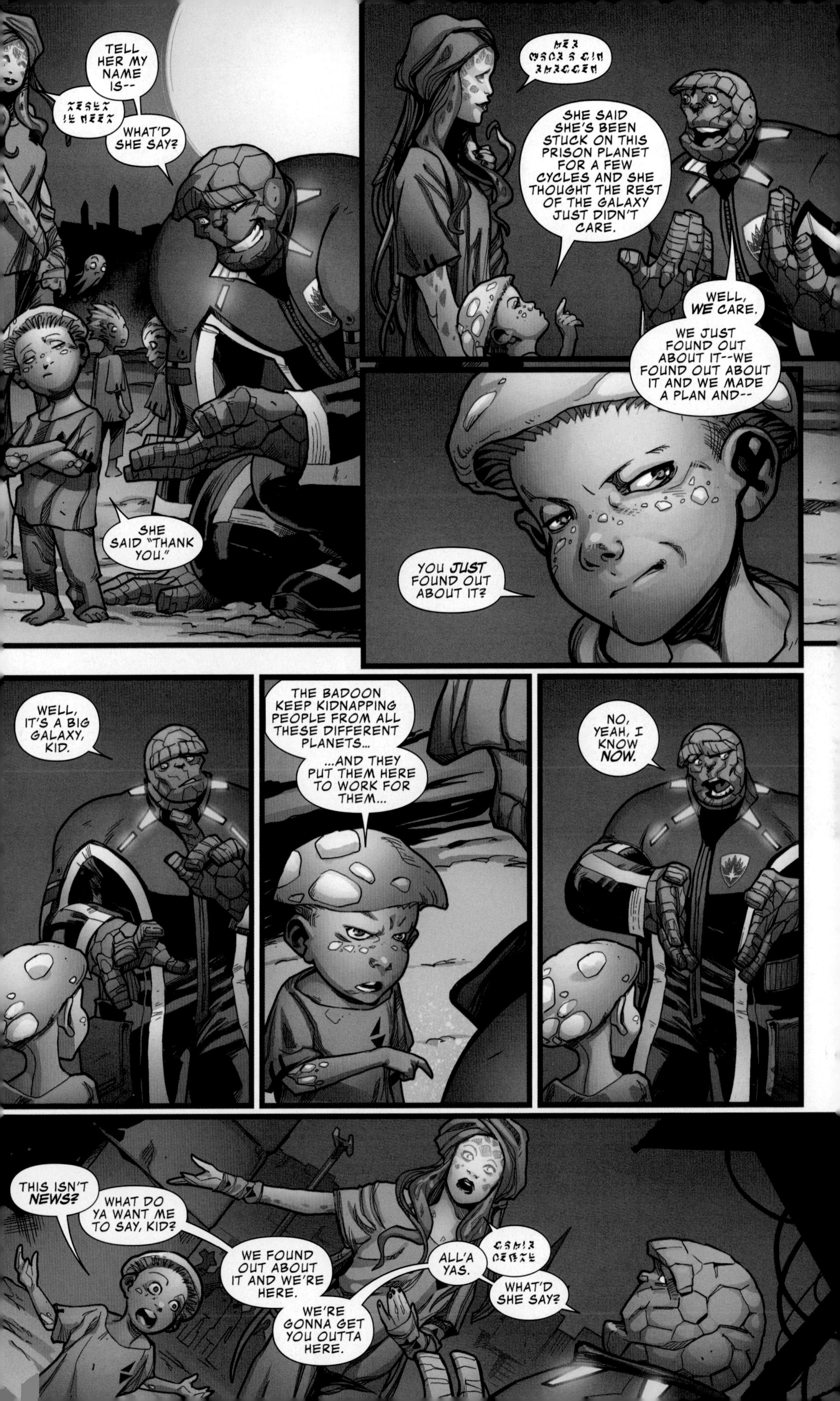
TELL HER MY NAME IS--
WHAT'D SHE SAY?
SHE SAID "THANK YOU."
SHE SAID SHE'S BEEN STUCK ON THIS PRISON PLANET FOR A FEW CYCLES AND SHE THOUGHT THE REST OF THE GALAXY JUST DIDN'T CARE.
WELL, WE CARE.
WE JUST FOUND OUT ABOUT IT--WE FOUND OUT ABOUT IT AND WE MADE A PLAN AND--
YOU JUST FOUND OUT ABOUT IT?
WELL, IT'S A BIG GALAXY, KID.
THE BADOON KEEP KIDNAPPING PEOPLE FROM ALL THESE DIFFERENT PLANETS...
...AND THEY PUT THEM HERE TO WORK FOR THEM...
NO, YEAH, I KNOW NOW.
THIS ISN'T NEWS?
WHAT DO YA WANT ME TO SAY, KID?
WE FOUND OUT ABOUT IT AND WE'RE HERE.
WE'RE GONNA GET YOU OUTTA HERE.
ALL'A YAS.
WHAT'D SHE SAY?

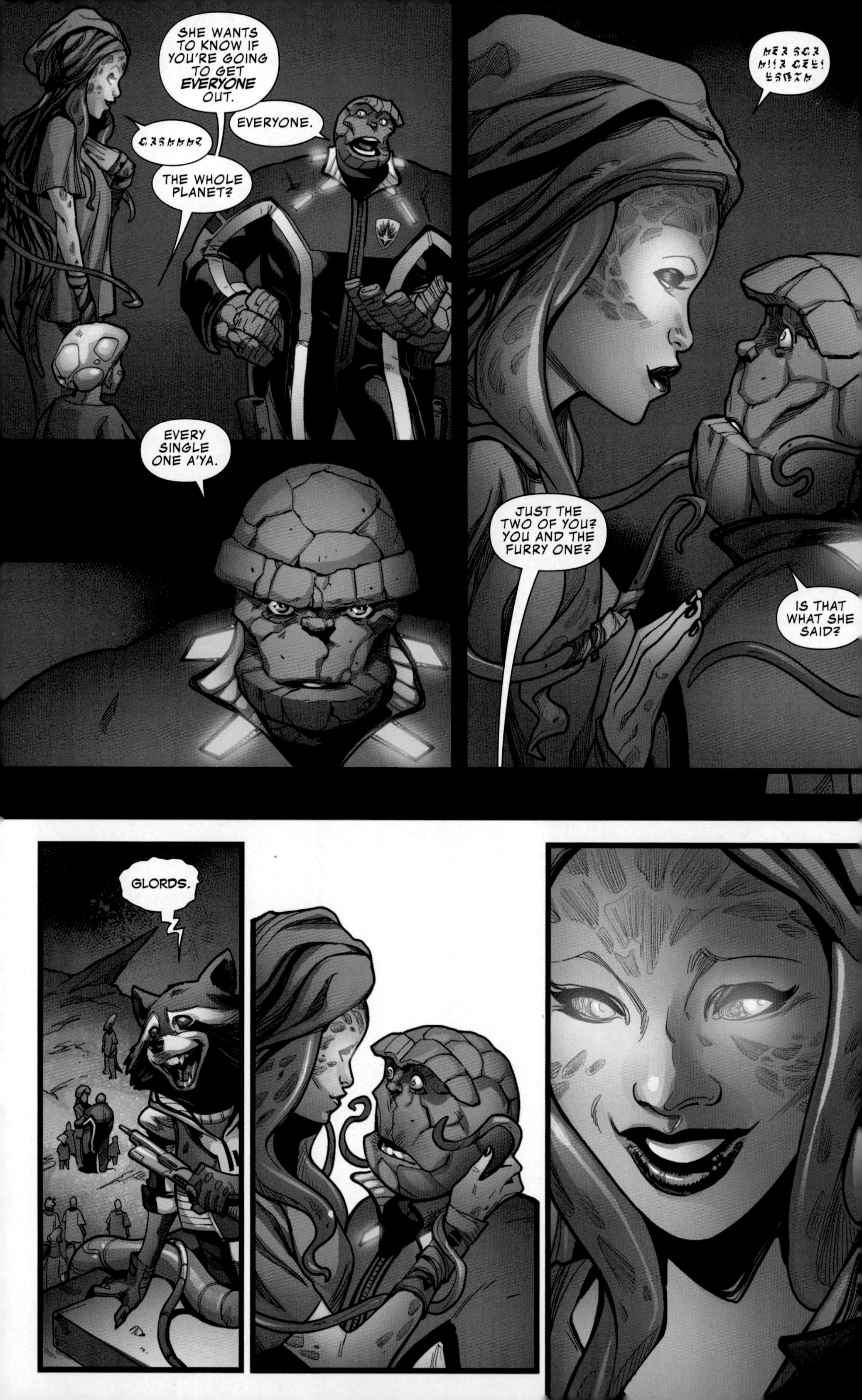
SHE WANTS TO KNOW IF YOU'RE GOING TO GET **EVERYONE** OUT.
THE WHOLE PLANET?
EVERYONE.
EVERY SINGLE ONE A'YA.
JUST THE TWO OF YOU? YOU AND THE FURRY ONE?
IS THAT WHAT SHE SAID?
GLORDS.

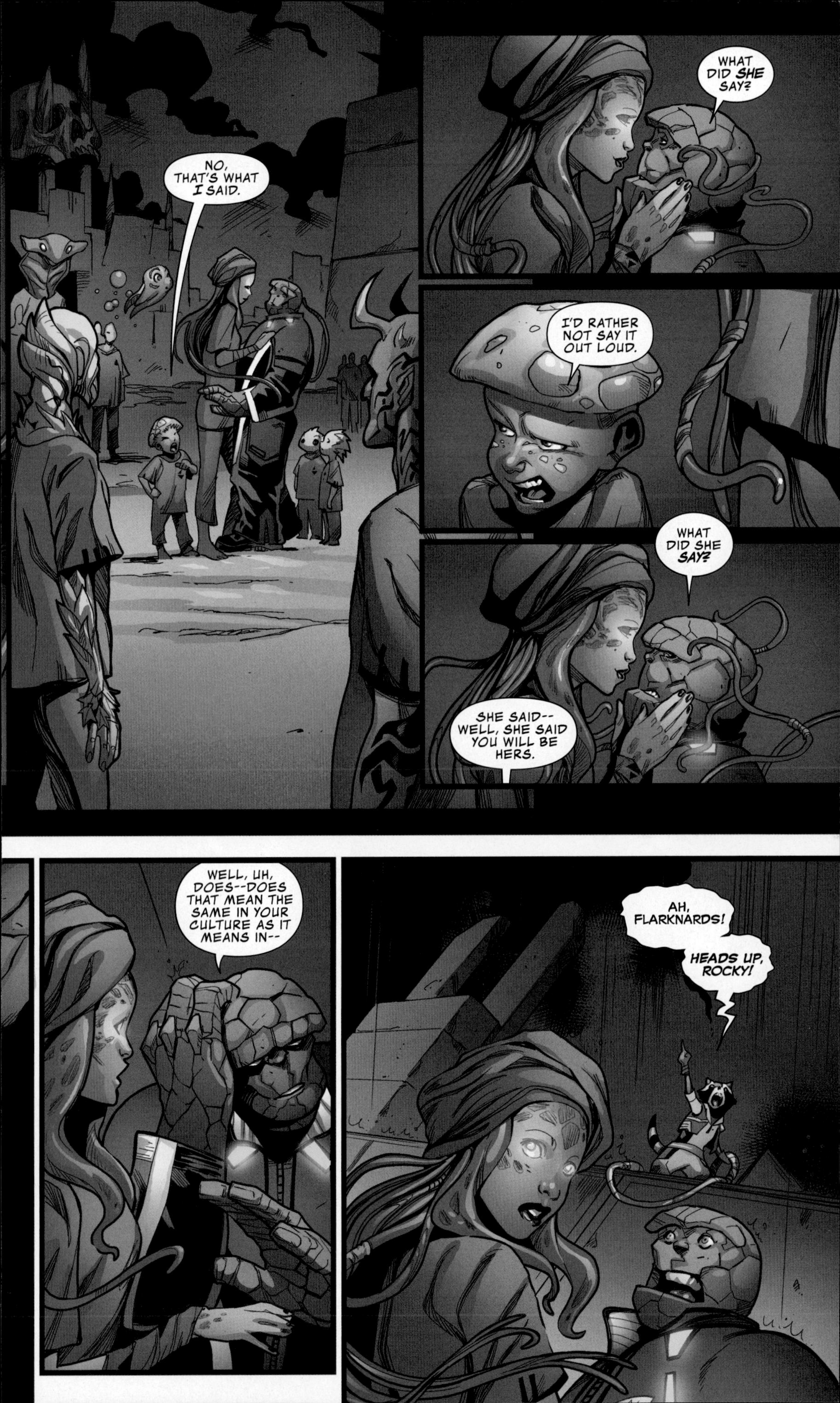

NO, THAT'S WHAT I SAID.
WHAT DID SHE SAY?
I'D RATHER NOT SAY IT OUT LOUD.
WHAT DID SHE SAY?
SHE SAID-- WELL, SHE SAID YOU WILL BE HERS.
WELL, UH, DOES--DOES THAT MEAN THE SAME IN YOUR CULTURE AS IT MEANS IN--
AH, FLARKNARDS!
HEADS UP, ROCKY!

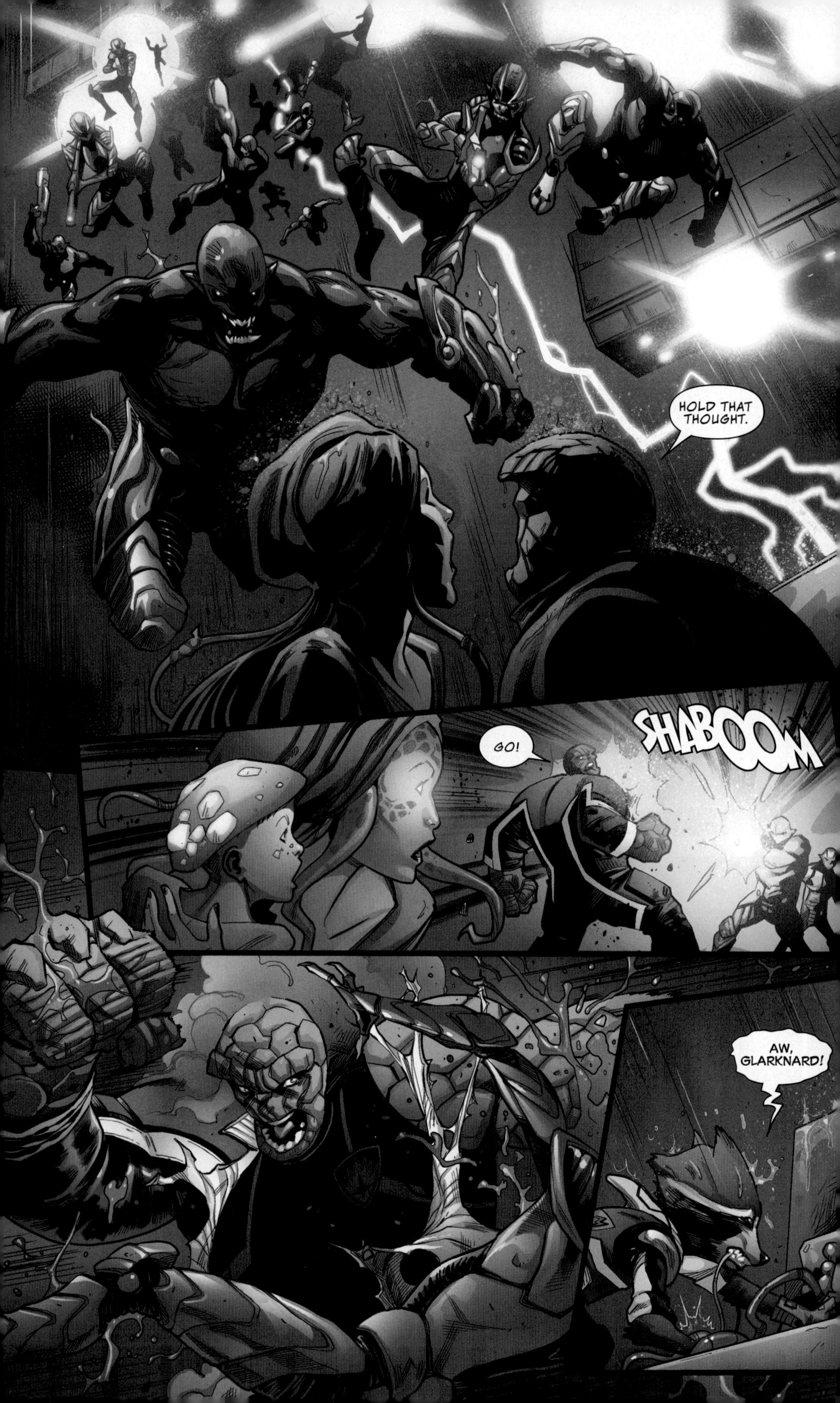
HOLD THAT THOUGHT.
GO!
SHABOOM
AW, GLARKNARD!

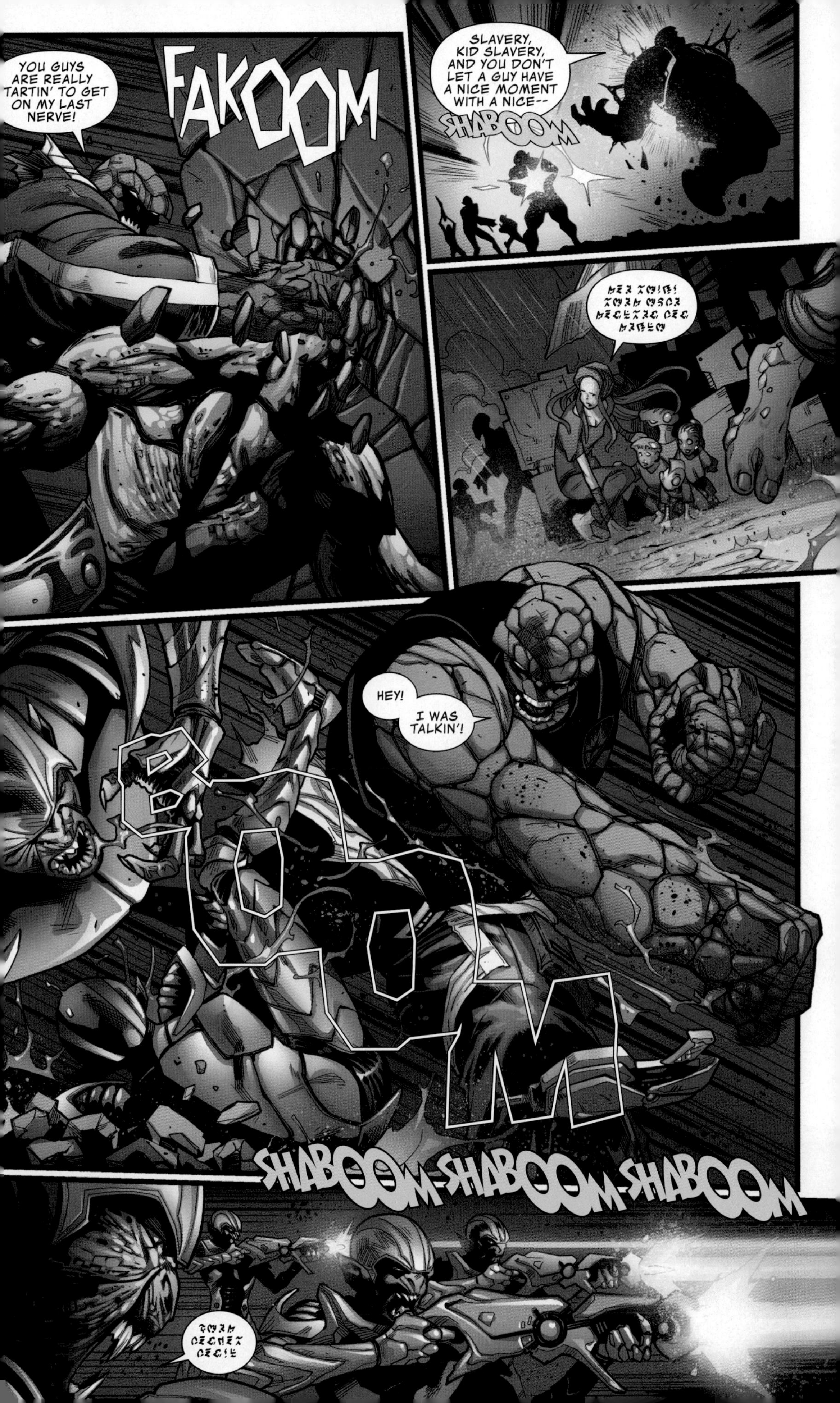
YOU GUYS ARE REALLY TARTIN' TO GET ON MY LAST NERVE!
FAKOOM
SLAVERY, KID SLAVERY, AND YOU DON'T LET A GUY HAVE A NICE MOMENT WITH A NICE--
SHABOOM
HEY!
I WAS TALKIN'!
BOOM
SHABOOM-SHABOOM-SHABOOM

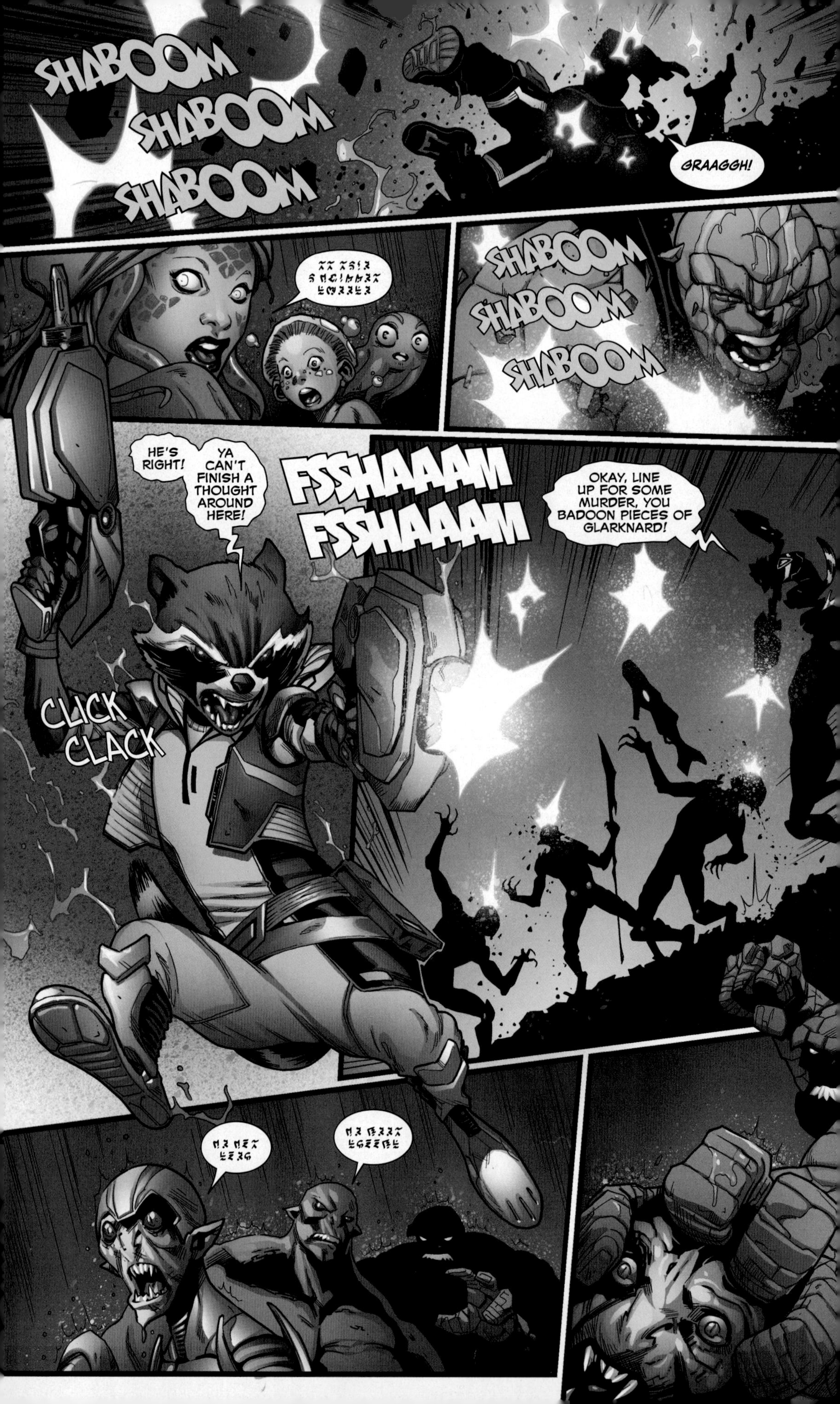
SHABOOM
SHABOOM
SHABOOM
GRAAGGH!
SHABOOM
SHABOOM
SHABOOM
HE'S RIGHT!
YA CAN'T FINISH A THOUGHT AROUND HERE!
FSSHAAAM
FSSHAAAM
OKAY, LINE UP FOR SOME MURDER, YOU BADOON PIECES OF GLARKNARD!
CLICK
CLACK

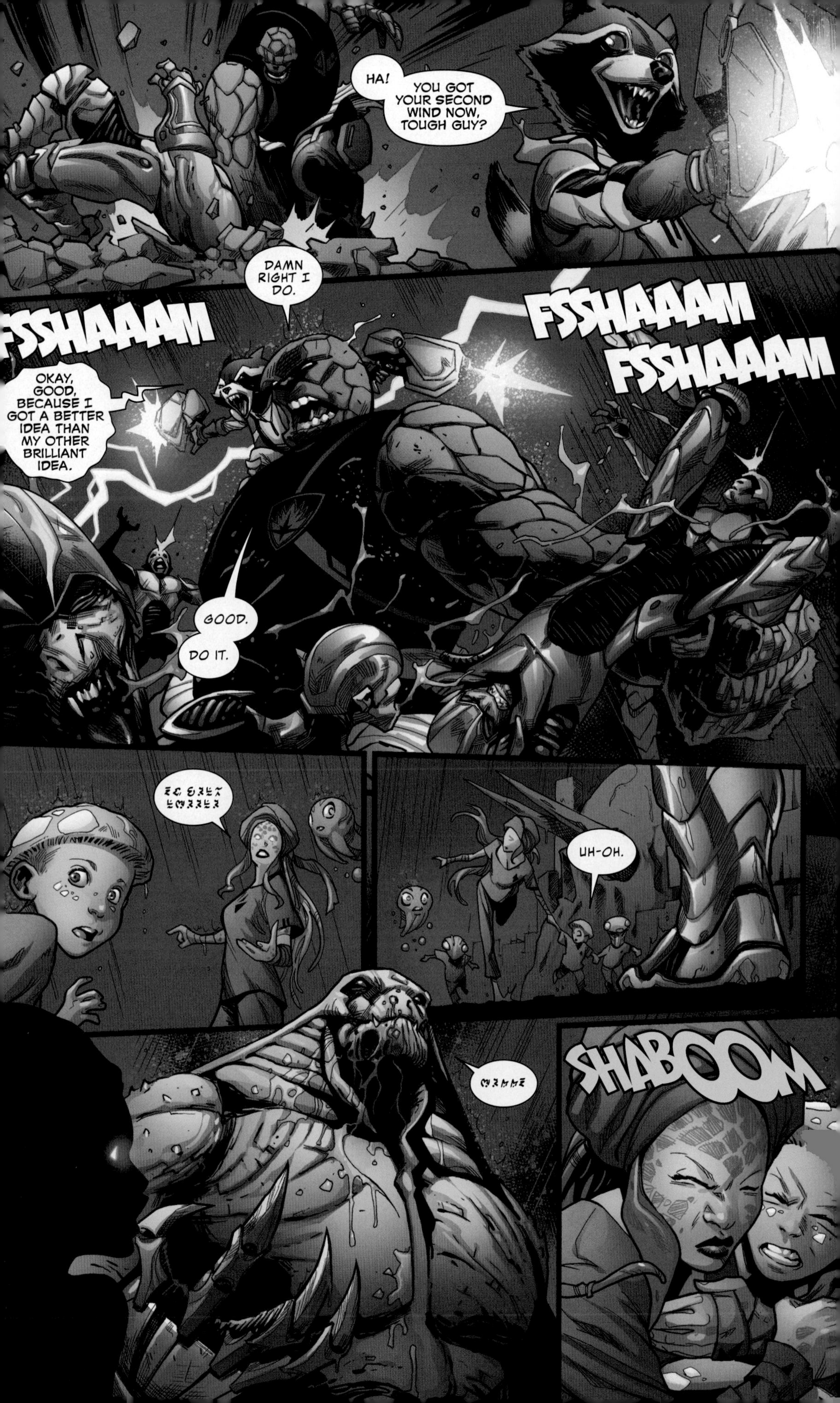
HA!
YOU GOT YOUR SECOND WIND NOW, TOUGH GUY?
DAMN RIGHT I DO.
FSSHAAAM
OKAY, GOOD, BECAUSE I GOT A BETTER IDEA THAN MY OTHER BRILLIANT IDEA.
FSSHAAAM
FSSHAAAM
GOOD.
DO IT.
UH-OH.
SHABOOM

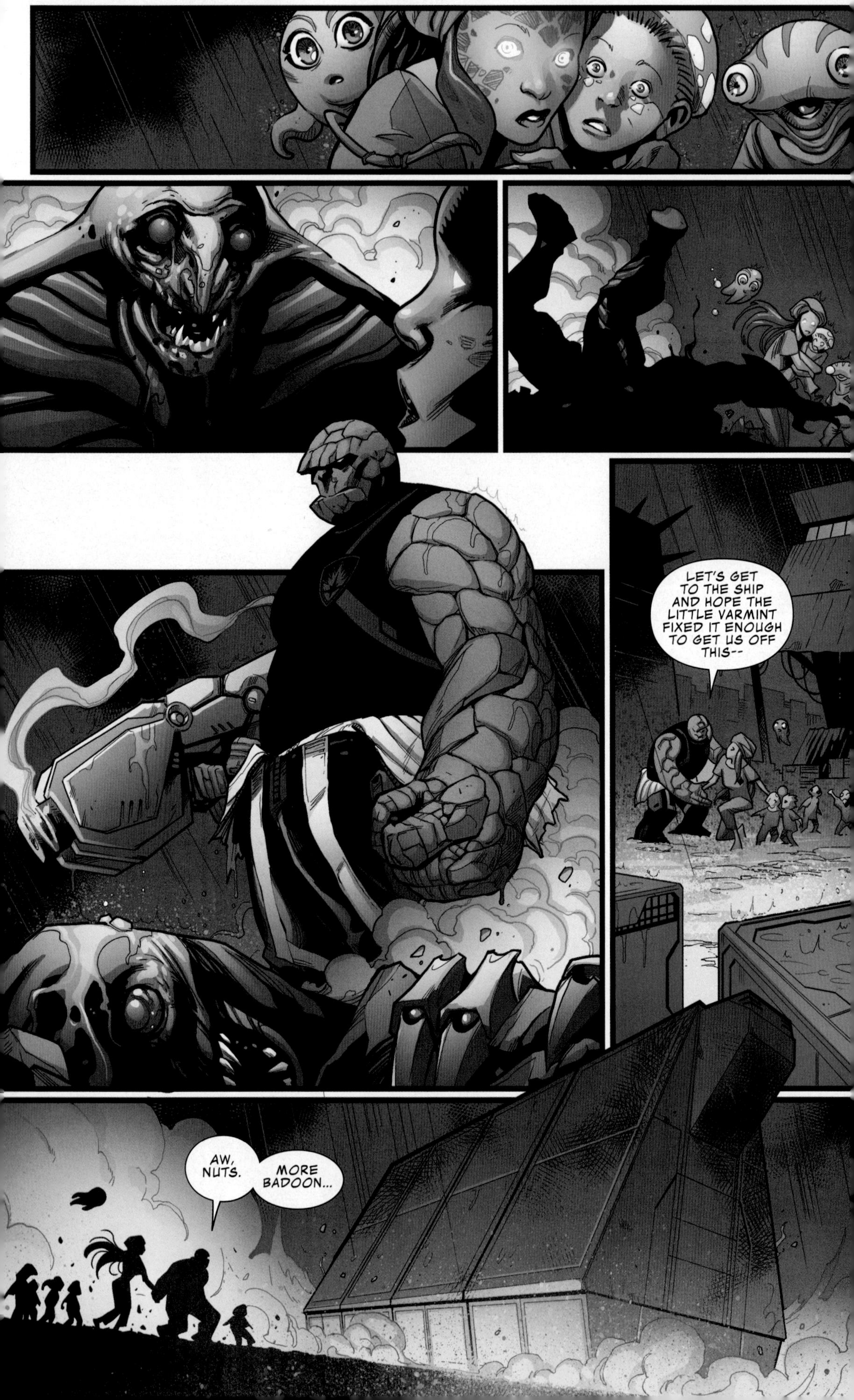
LET'S GET TO THE SHIP AND HOPE THE LITTLE VARMINT FIXED IT ENOUGH TO GET US OFF THIS--
AW, NUTS.
MORE BADOON...

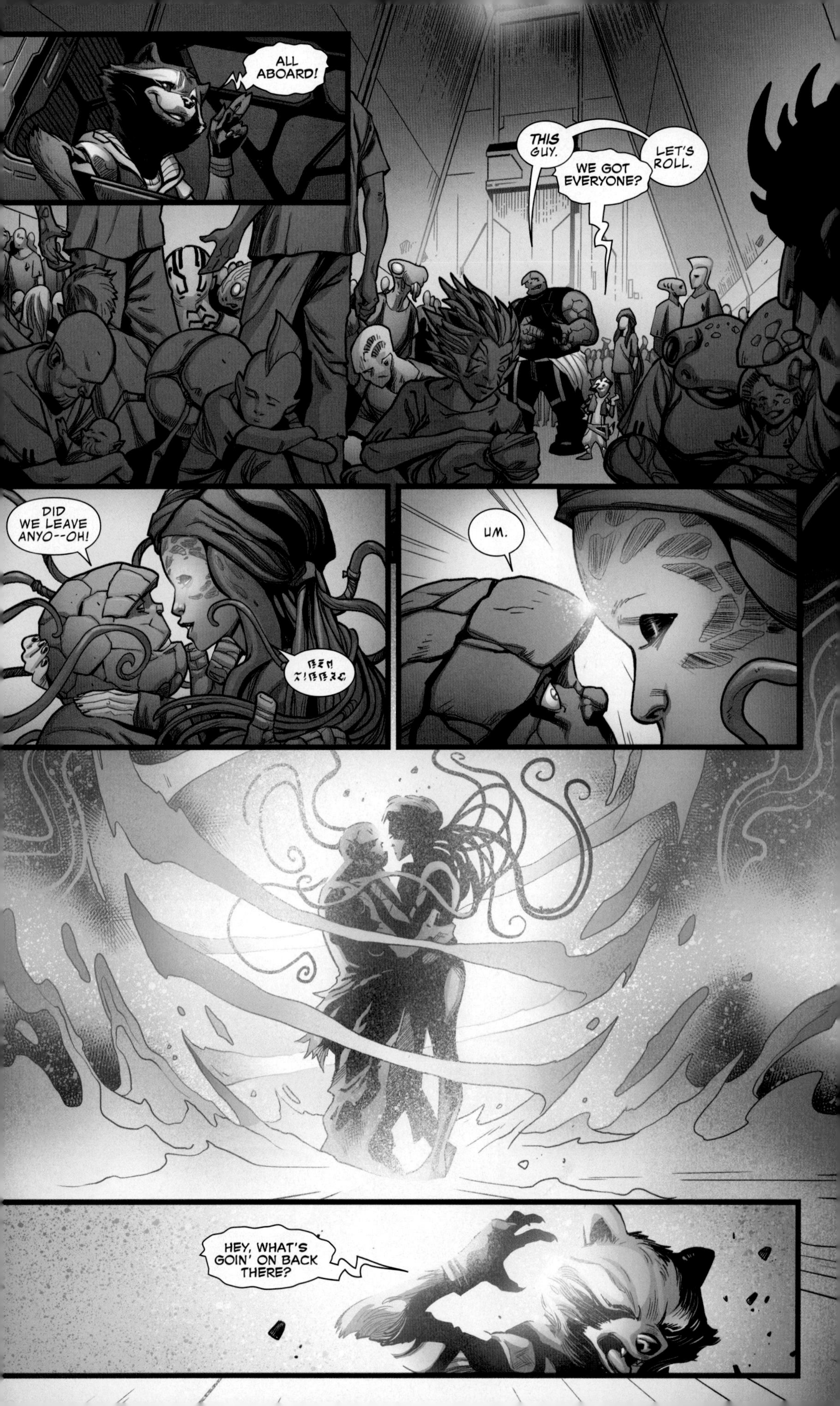
ALL ABOARD!
THIS GUY.
WE GOT EVERYONE?
LET'S ROLL.
DID WE LEAVE ANYO--OH!
UM.
HEY, WHAT'S GOIN' ON BACK THERE?

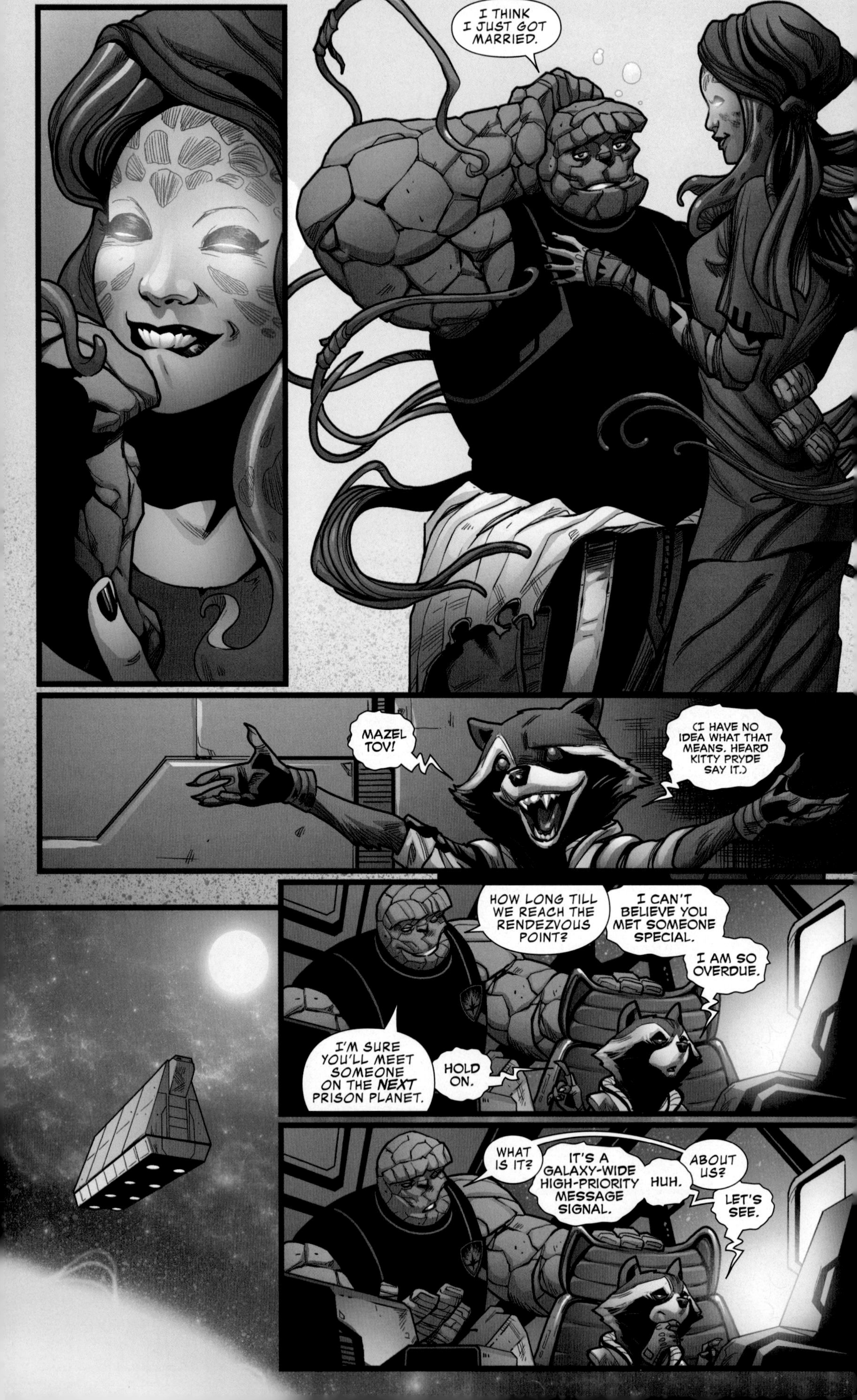
I THINK I JUST GOT MARRIED.
MAZEL TOV!
(I HAVE NO IDEA WHAT THAT MEANS. HEARD KITTY PRYDE SAY IT.)
HOW LONG TILL WE REACH THE RENDEZVOUS POINT?
I CAN'T BELIEVE YOU MET SOMEONE SPECIAL.
I AM SO OVERDUE.
I'M SURE YOU'LL MEET SOMEONE ON THE NEXT PRISON PLANET.
HOLD ON.
WHAT IS IT?
IT'S A GALAXY-WIDE HIGH-PRIORITY MESSAGE SIGNAL.
HUH.
ABOUT US?
LET'S SEE.

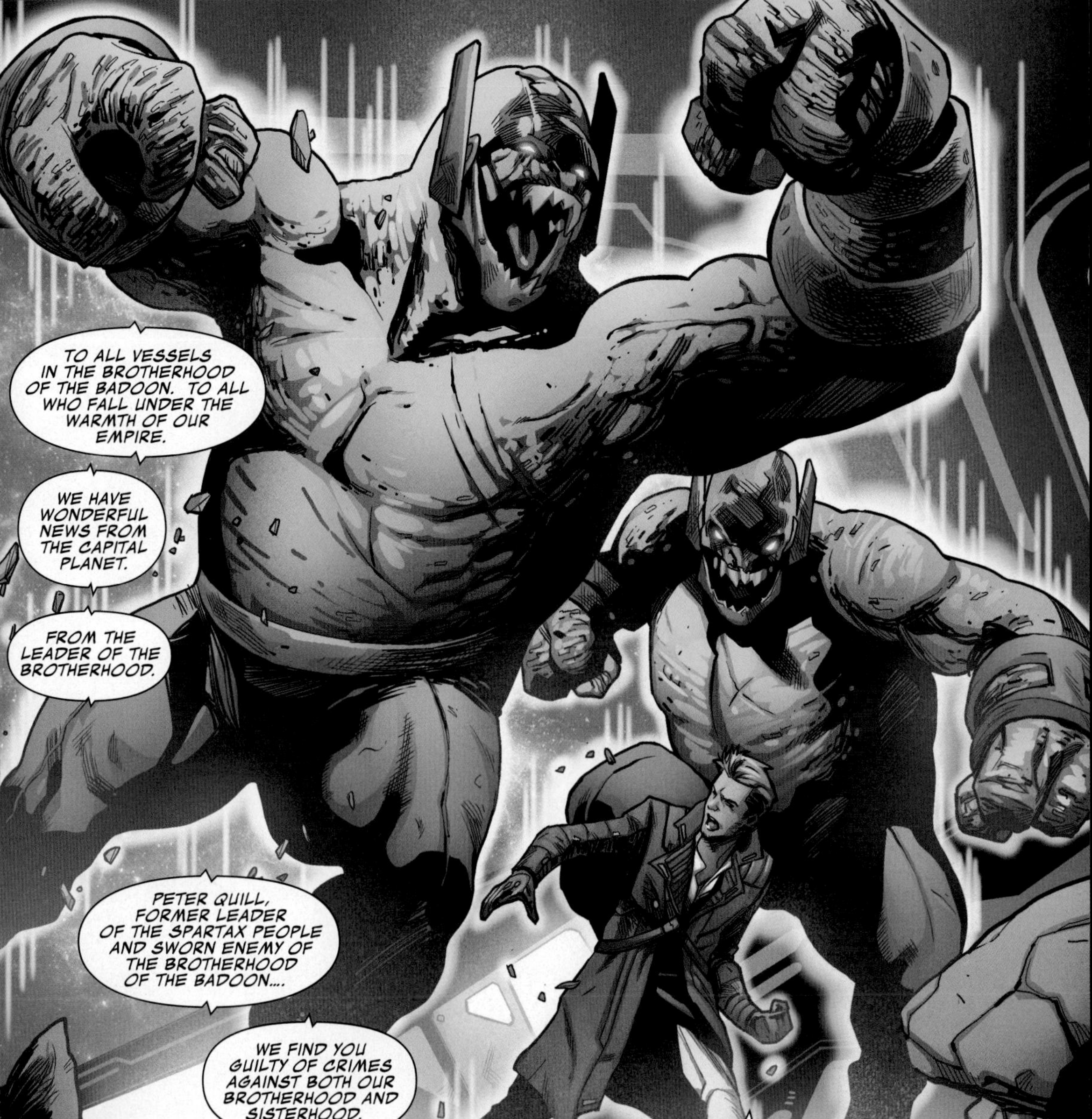
TO ALL VESSELS IN THE BROTHERHOOD OF THE BADOON. TO ALL WHO FALL UNDER THE WARMTH OF OUR EMPIRE.
WE HAVE WONDERFUL NEWS FROM THE CAPITAL PLANET.
FROM THE LEADER OF THE BROTHERHOOD.
PETER QUILL, FORMER LEADER OF THE SPARTAX PEOPLE AND SWORN ENEMY OF THE BROTHERHOOD OF THE BADOON....
WE FIND YOU GUILTY OF CRIMES AGAINST BOTH OUR BROTHERHOOD AND SISTERHOOD.
WE FIND YOUR EXISTENCE AN ABOMINATION TO OUR PEOPLE AND YOU ARE NOW SENTENCED TO DEATH.
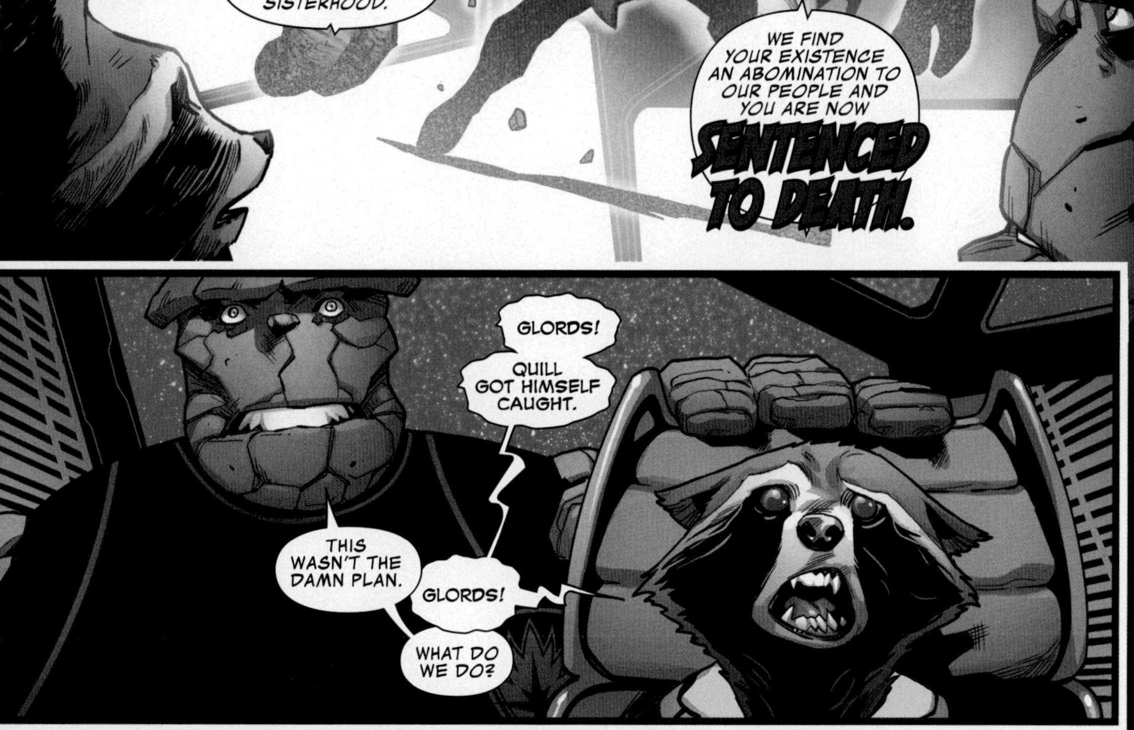
GLORDS!
QUILL GOT HIMSELF CAUGHT.
THIS WASN'T THE DAMN PLAN.
GLORDS!
WHAT DO WE DO?

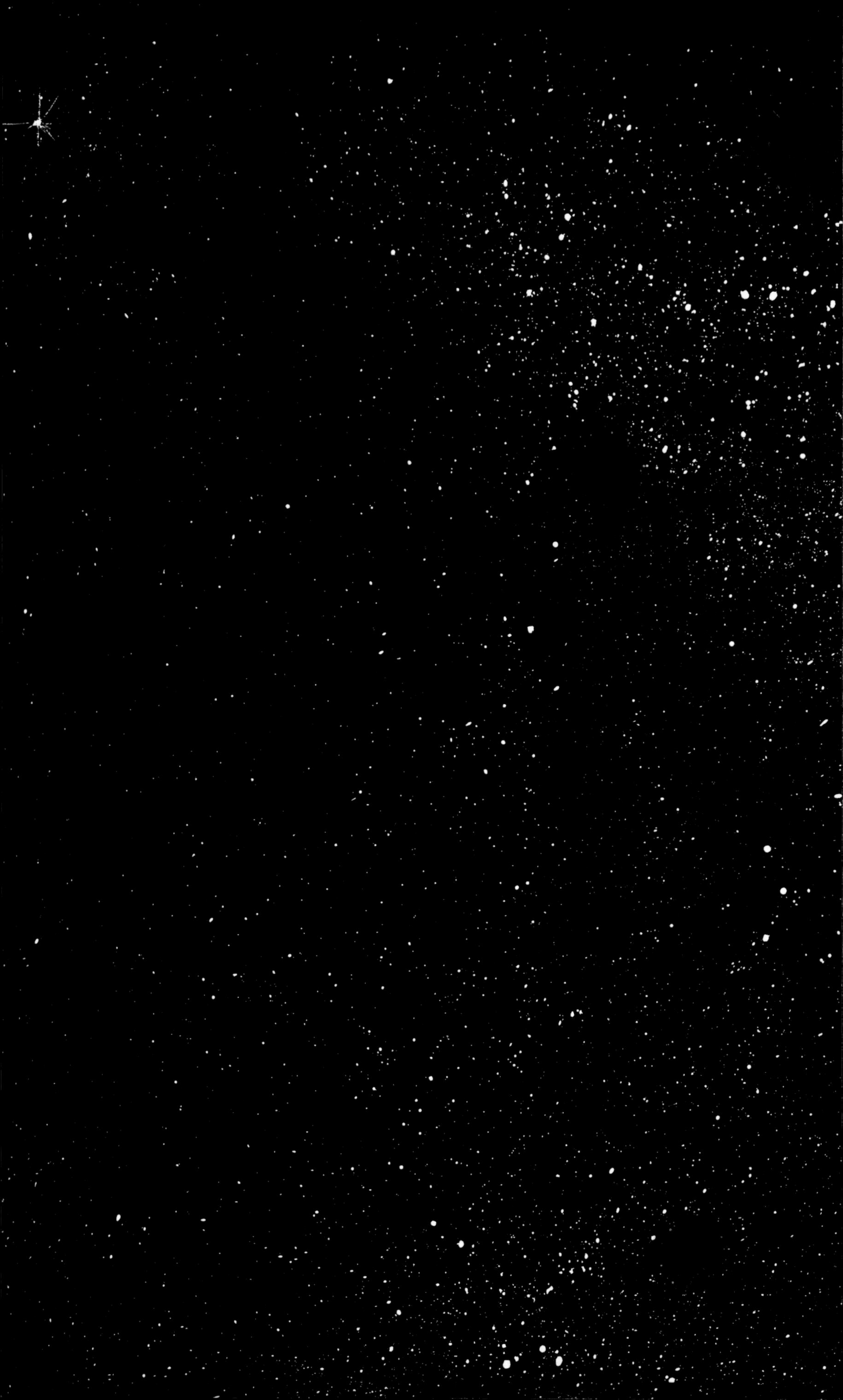

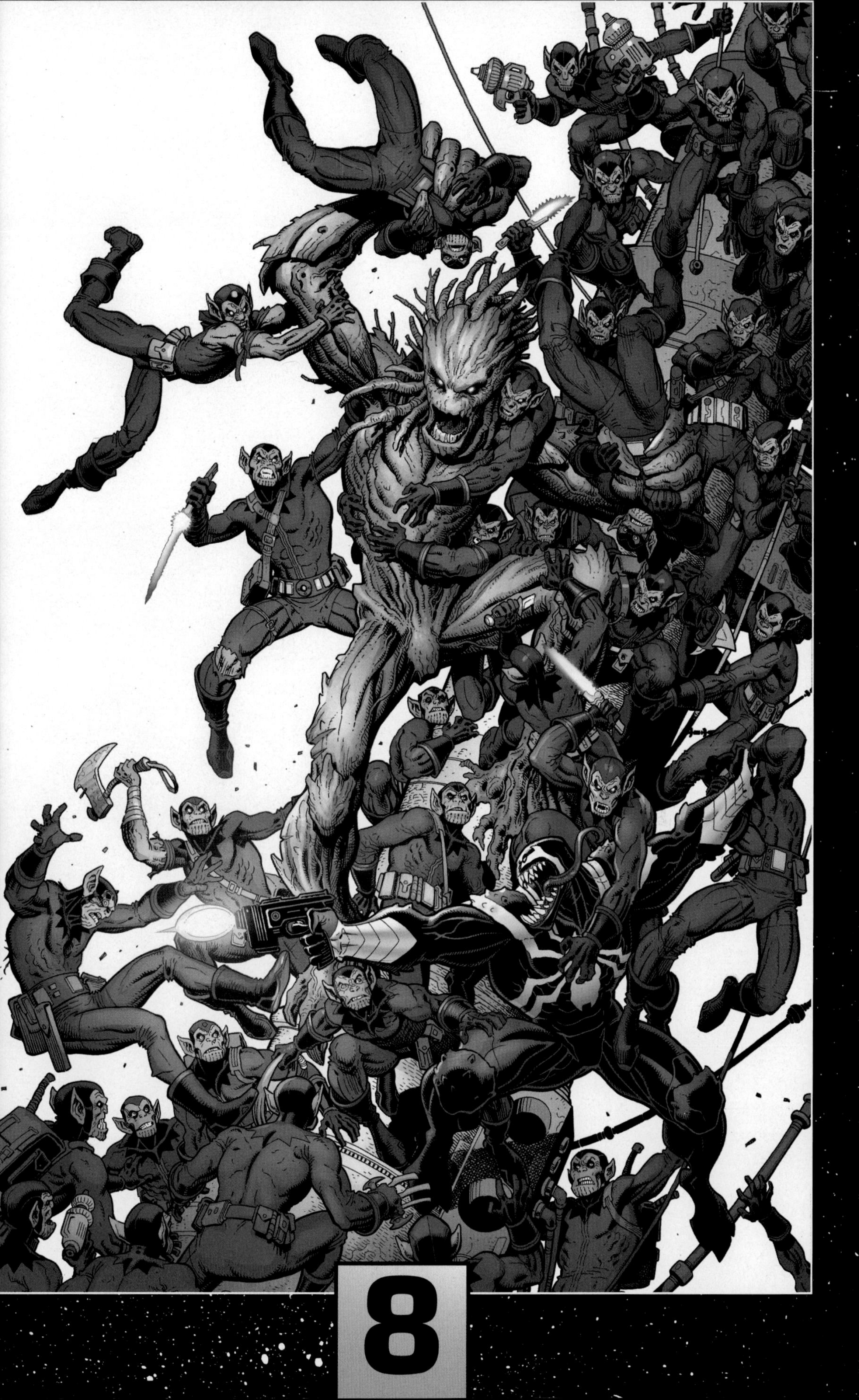

8

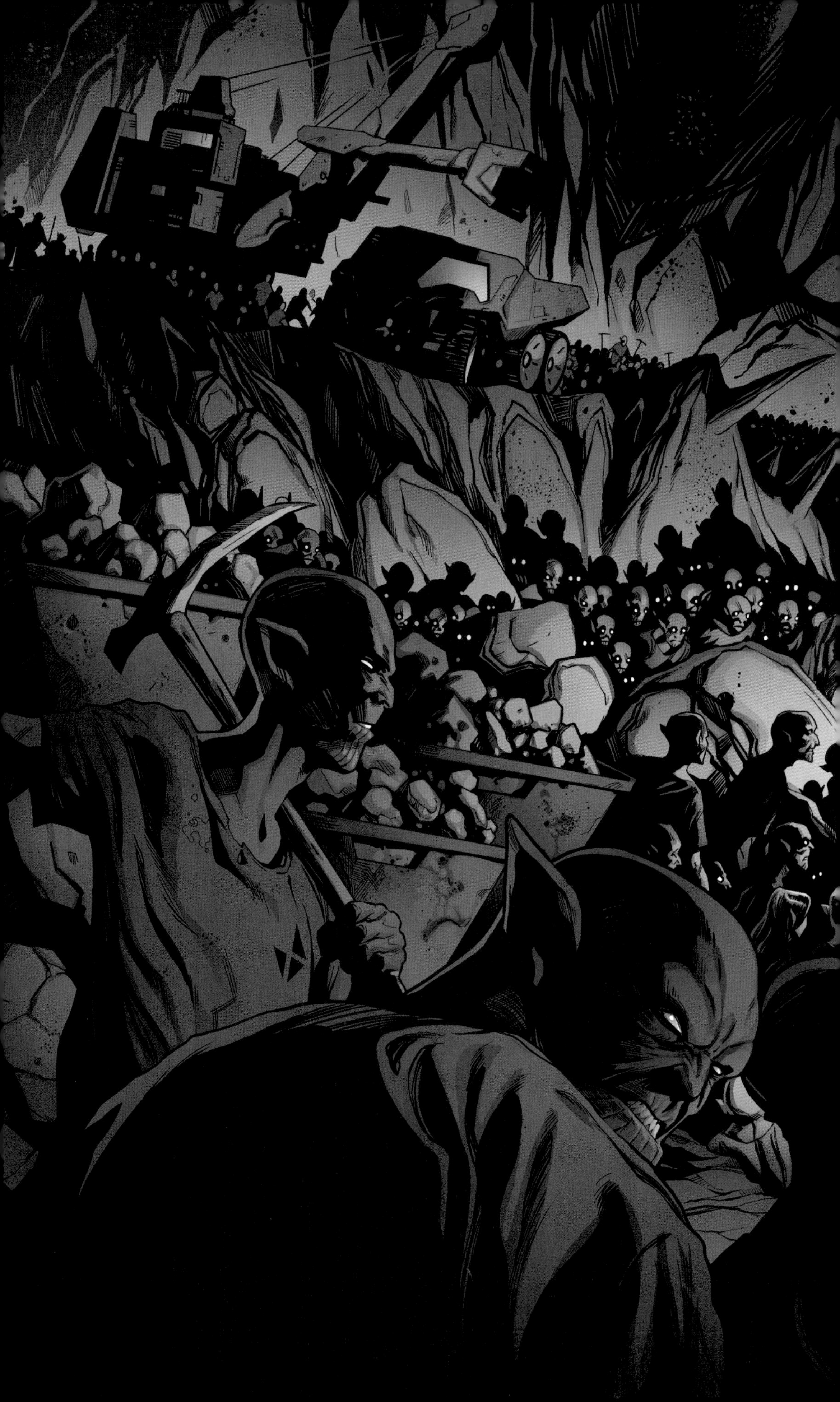

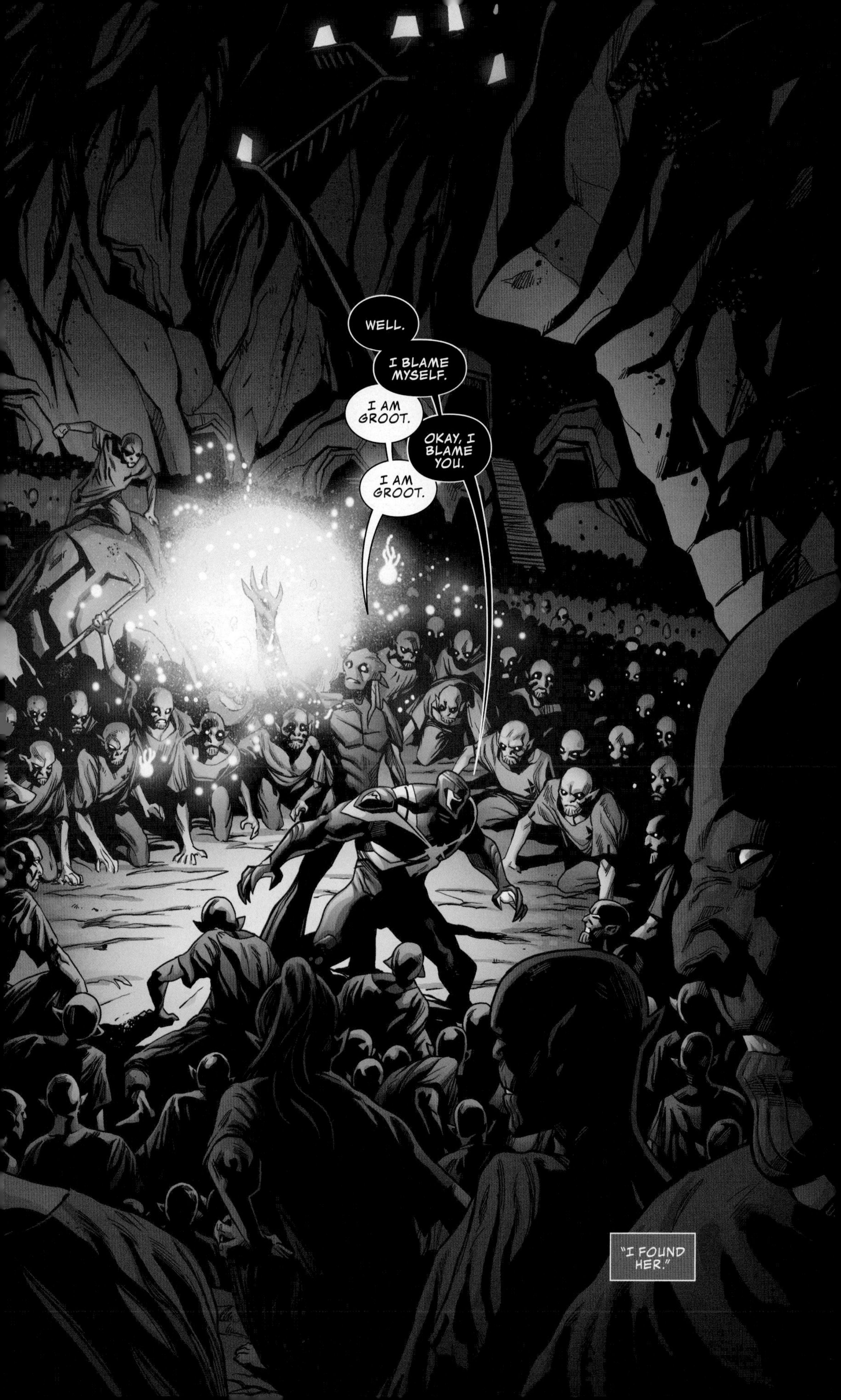
WELL.
I BLAME MYSELF.
I AM GROOT.
OKAY, I BLAME YOU.
I AM GROOT.
"I FOUND HER."

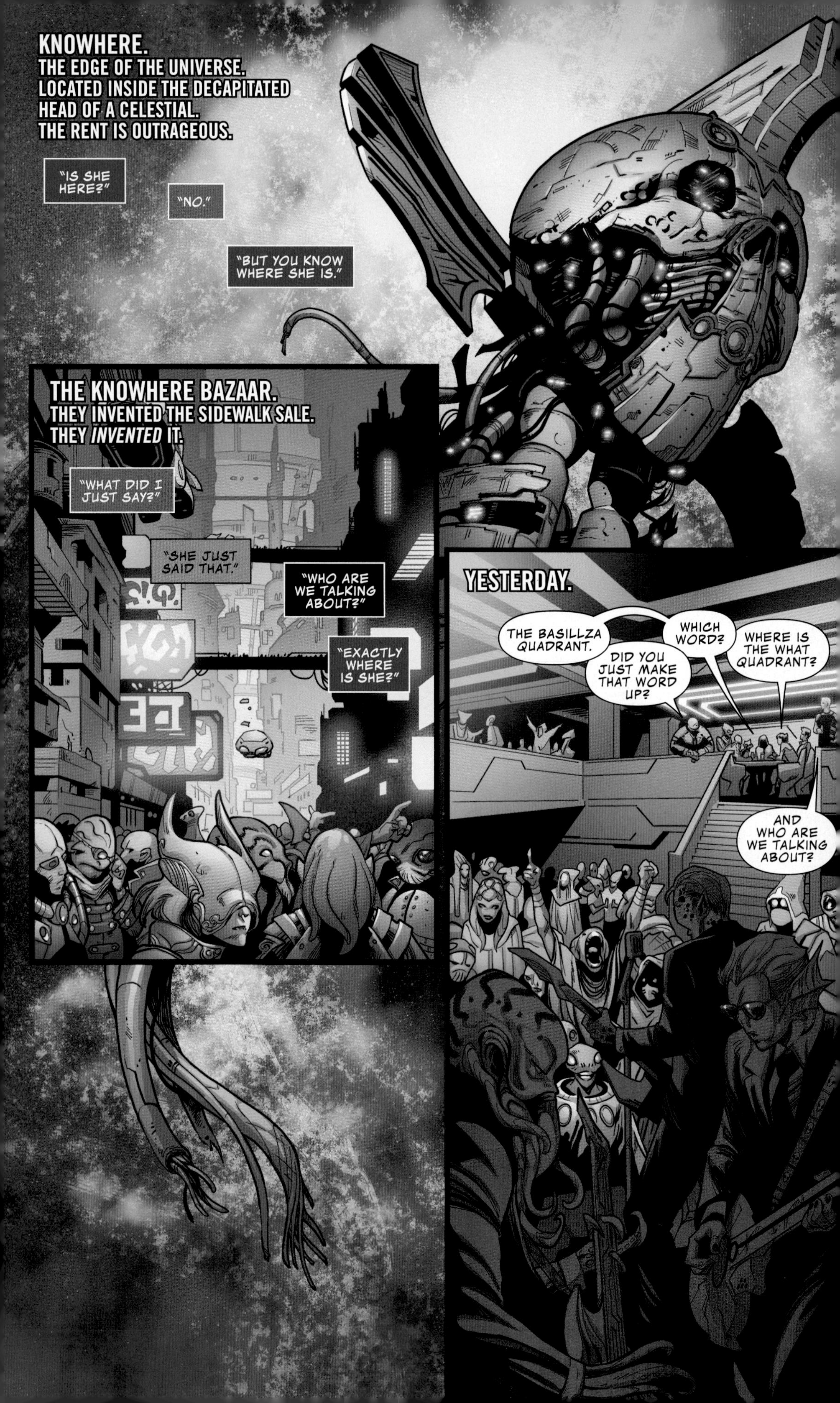

KNOWHERE.
THE EDGE OF THE UNIVERSE.
LOCATED INSIDE THE DECAPITATED
HEAD OF A CELESTIAL.
THE RENT IS OUTRAGEOUS.
"IS SHE HERE?"
"NO."
"BUT YOU KNOW WHERE SHE IS."
THE KNOWHERE BAZAAR.
THEY INVENTED THE SIDEWALK SALE.
THEY *INVENTED* IT.
"WHAT DID I JUST SAY?"
"SHE JUST SAID THAT."
"WHO ARE WE TALKING ABOUT?"
"EXACTLY WHERE IS SHE?"
YESTERDAY.
THE BASILLZA QUADRANT.
WHICH WORD?
DID YOU JUST MAKE THAT WORD UP?
WHERE IS THE WHAT QUADRANT?
AND WHO ARE WE TALKING ABOUT?

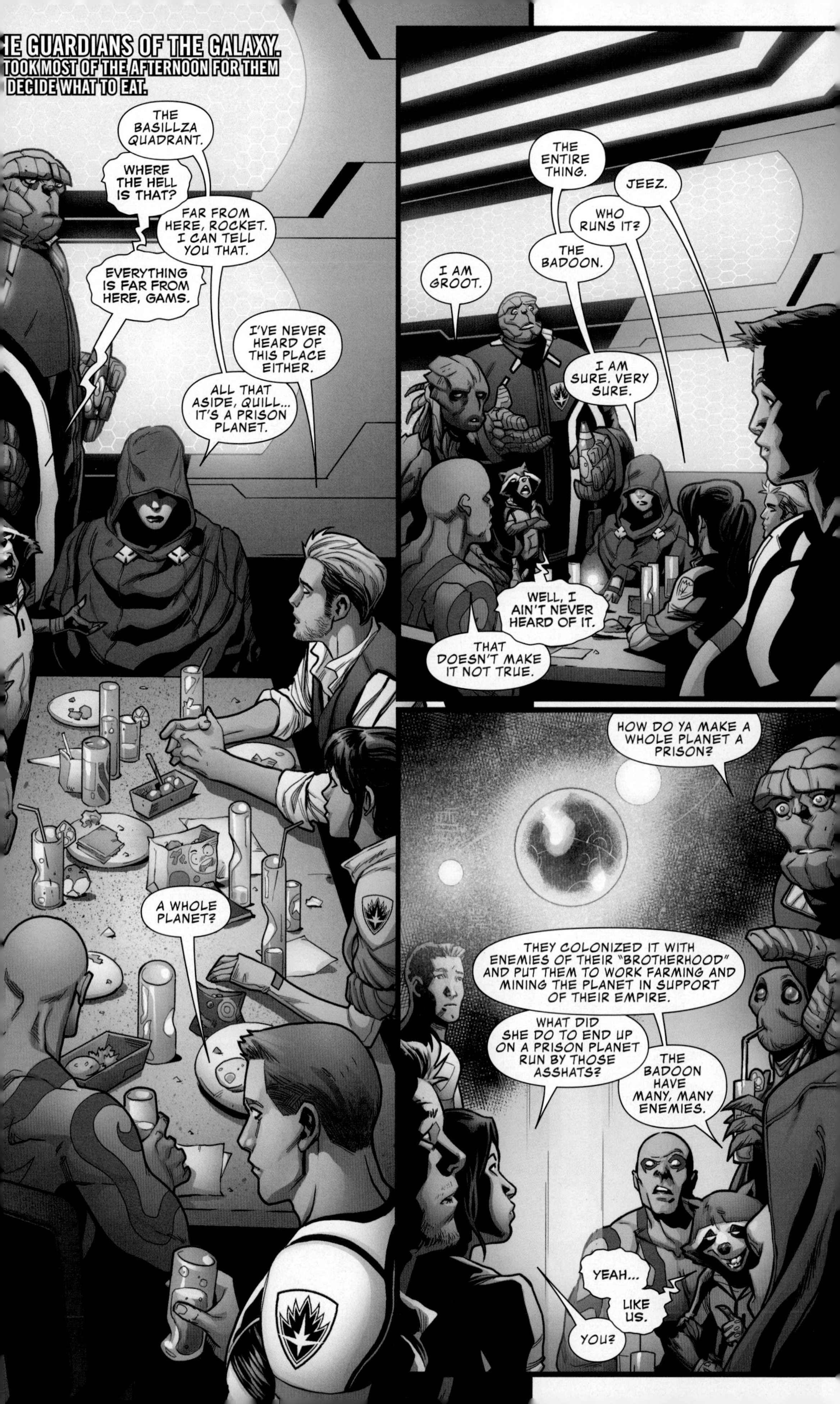

...HE GUARDIANS OF THE GALAXY. ...TOOK MOST OF THE AFTERNOON FOR THEM ...DECIDE WHAT TO EAT.
THE BASILLZA QUADRANT.
WHERE THE HELL IS THAT?
FAR FROM HERE, ROCKET. I CAN TELL YOU THAT.
EVERYTHING IS FAR FROM HERE, GAMS.
I'VE NEVER HEARD OF THIS PLACE EITHER.
ALL THAT ASIDE, QUILL... IT'S A PRISON PLANET.
A WHOLE PLANET?
THE ENTIRE THING.
JEEZ.
WHO RUNS IT?
THE BADOON.
I AM GROOT.
I AM SURE. VERY SURE.
WELL, I AIN'T NEVER HEARD OF IT.
THAT DOESN'T MAKE IT NOT TRUE.
HOW DO YA MAKE A WHOLE PLANET A PRISON?
THEY COLONIZED IT WITH ENEMIES OF THEIR "BROTHERHOOD" AND PUT THEM TO WORK FARMING AND MINING THE PLANET IN SUPPORT OF THEIR EMPIRE.
WHAT DID SHE DO TO END UP ON A PRISON PLANET RUN BY THOSE ASSHATS?
THE BADOON HAVE MANY, MANY ENEMIES.
YEAH...
LIKE US.
YOU?

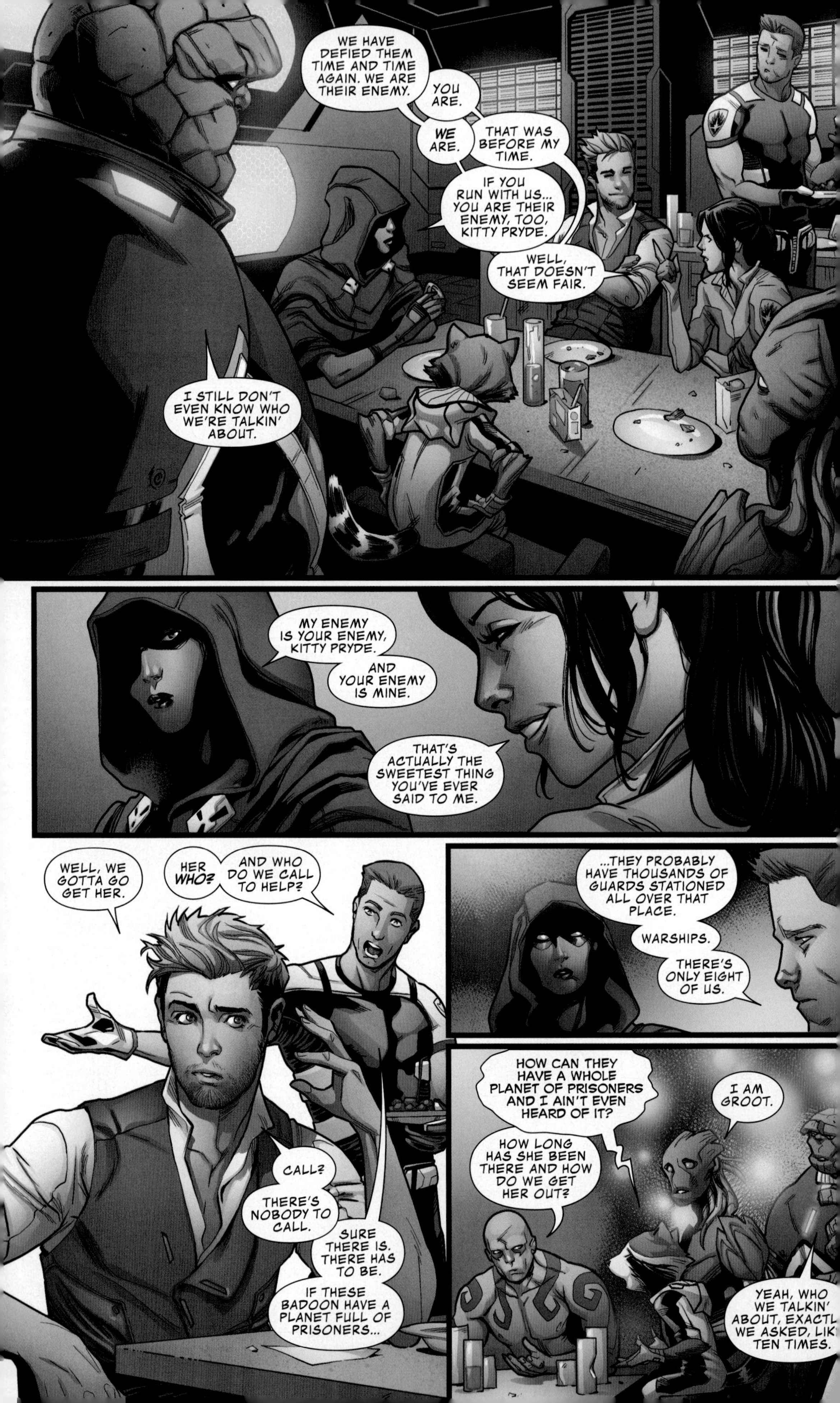
WE HAVE DEFIED THEM TIME AND TIME AGAIN. WE ARE THEIR ENEMY.
YOU ARE.
WE ARE.
THAT WAS BEFORE MY TIME.
IF YOU RUN WITH US... YOU ARE THEIR ENEMY, TOO, KITTY PRYDE.
WELL, THAT DOESN'T SEEM FAIR.
I STILL DON'T EVEN KNOW WHO WE'RE TALKIN' ABOUT.
MY ENEMY IS YOUR ENEMY, KITTY PRYDE.
AND YOUR ENEMY IS MINE.
THAT'S ACTUALLY THE SWEETEST THING YOU'VE EVER SAID TO ME.
WELL, WE GOTTA GO GET HER.
HER WHO?
AND WHO DO WE CALL TO HELP?
CALL?
THERE'S NOBODY TO CALL.
SURE THERE IS. THERE HAS TO BE.
IF THESE BADOON HAVE A PLANET FULL OF PRISONERS...
...THEY PROBABLY HAVE THOUSANDS OF GUARDS STATIONED ALL OVER THAT PLACE.
WARSHIPS.
THERE'S ONLY EIGHT OF US.
HOW CAN THEY HAVE A WHOLE PLANET OF PRISONERS AND I AIN'T EVEN HEARD OF IT?
HOW LONG HAS SHE BEEN THERE AND HOW DO WE GET HER OUT?
I AM GROOT.
YEAH, WHO WE TALKIN' ABOUT, EXACTL WE ASKED, LIK TEN TIMES.

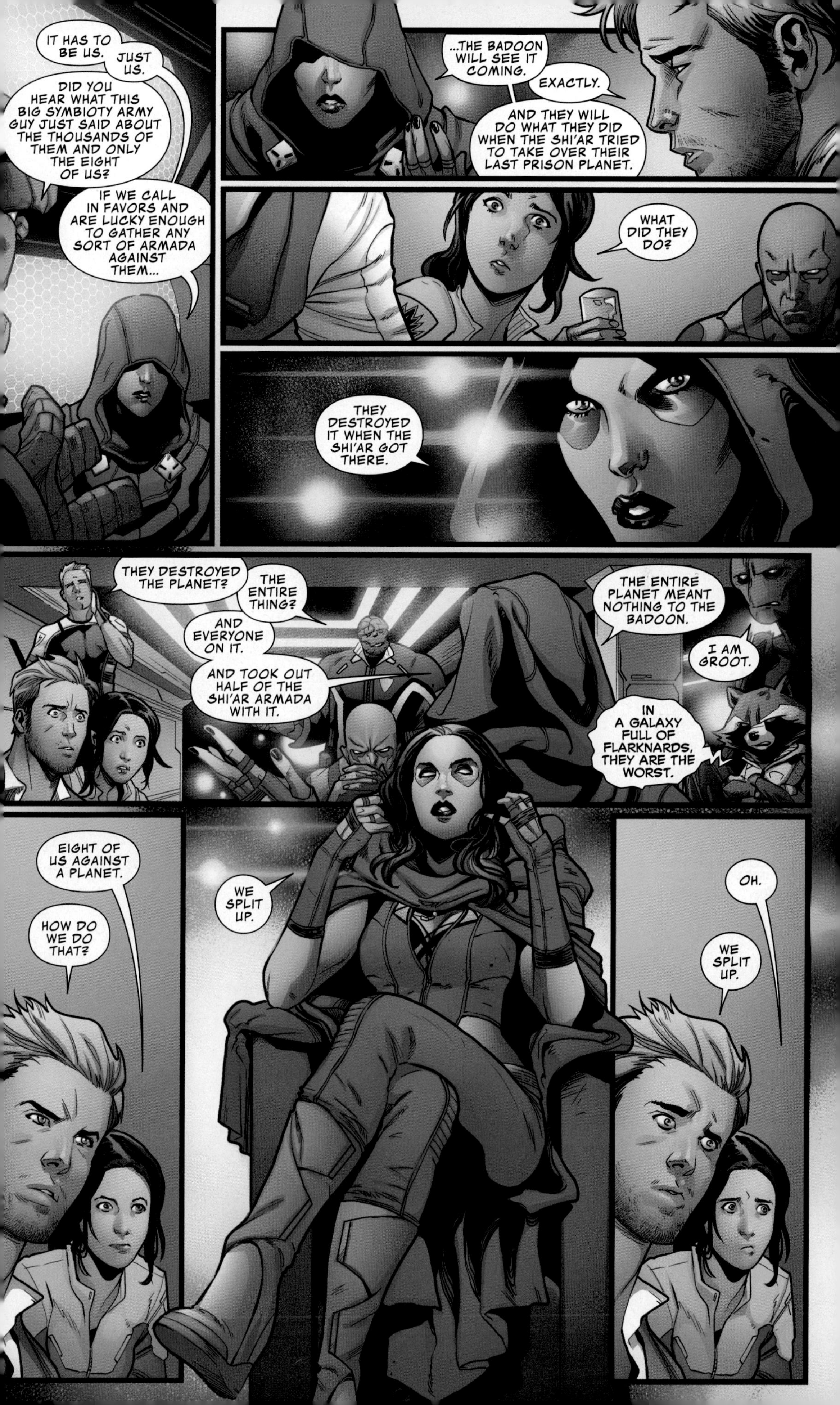
IT HAS TO BE US.
JUST US.
DID YOU HEAR WHAT THIS BIG SYMBIOTY ARMY GUY JUST SAID ABOUT THE THOUSANDS OF THEM AND ONLY THE EIGHT OF US?
IF WE CALL IN FAVORS AND ARE LUCKY ENOUGH TO GATHER ANY SORT OF ARMADA AGAINST THEM...
...THE BADOON WILL SEE IT COMING.
EXACTLY.
AND THEY WILL DO WHAT THEY DID WHEN THE SHI'AR TRIED TO TAKE OVER THEIR LAST PRISON PLANET.
WHAT DID THEY DO?
THEY DESTROYED IT WHEN THE SHI'AR GOT THERE.
THEY DESTROYED THE PLANET?
THE ENTIRE THING?
AND EVERYONE ON IT.
AND TOOK OUT HALF OF THE SHI'AR ARMADA WITH IT.
THE ENTIRE PLANET MEANT NOTHING TO THE BADOON.
I AM GROOT.
IN A GALAXY FULL OF FLARKNARDS, THEY ARE THE WORST.
EIGHT OF US AGAINST A PLANET.
HOW DO WE DO THAT?
WE SPLIT UP.
OH.
WE SPLIT UP.

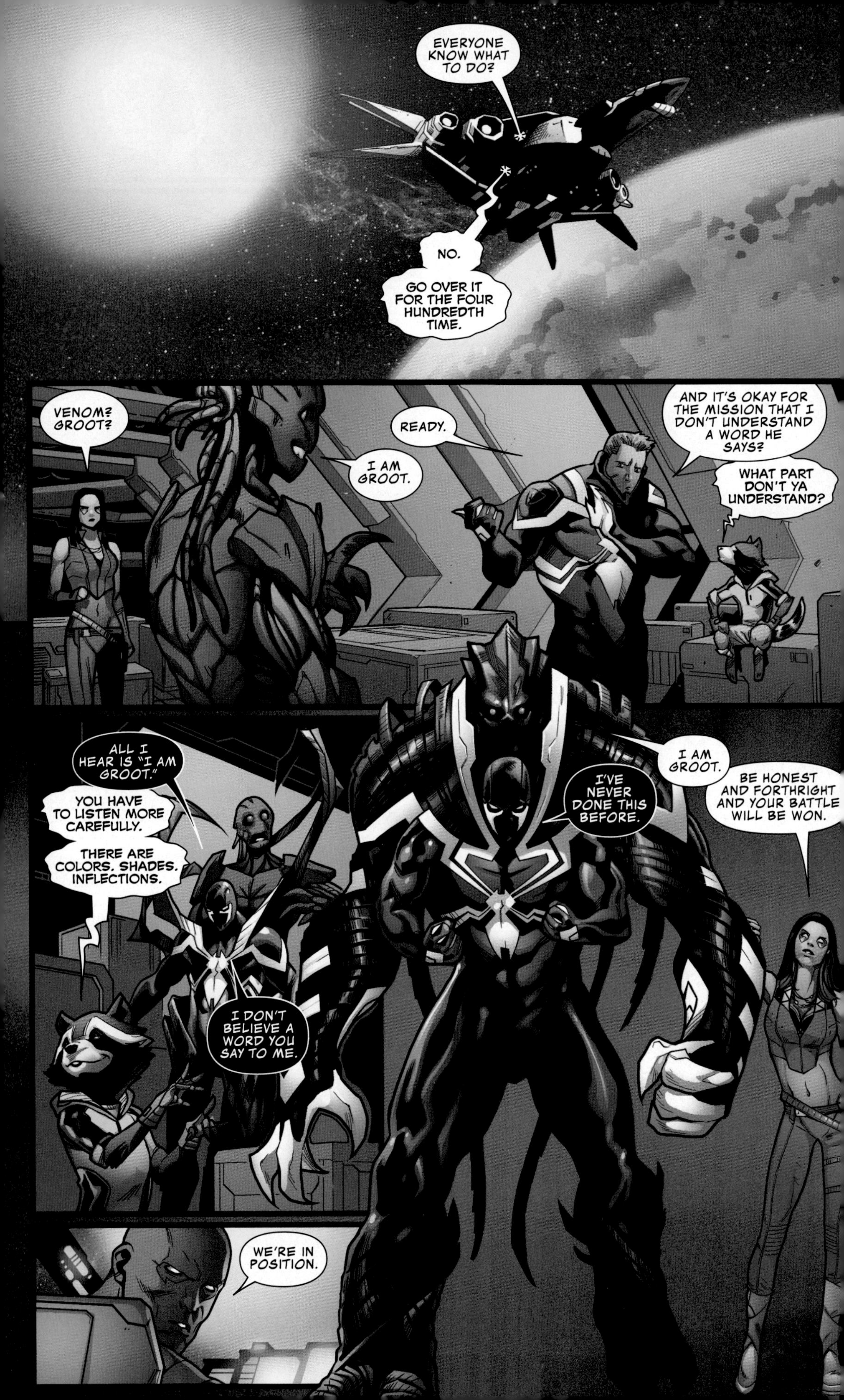
EVERYONE KNOW WHAT TO DO?
NO.
GO OVER IT FOR THE FOUR HUNDREDTH TIME.
VENOM? GROOT?
I AM GROOT.
READY.
AND IT'S OKAY FOR THE MISSION THAT I DON'T UNDERSTAND A WORD HE SAYS?
WHAT PART DON'T YA UNDERSTAND?
ALL I HEAR IS "I AM GROOT."
YOU HAVE TO LISTEN MORE CAREFULLY.
THERE ARE COLORS. SHADES. INFLECTIONS.
I DON'T BELIEVE A WORD YOU SAY TO ME.
I'VE NEVER DONE THIS BEFORE.
I AM GROOT.
BE HONEST AND FORTHRIGHT AND YOUR BATTLE WILL BE WON.
WE'RE IN POSITION.

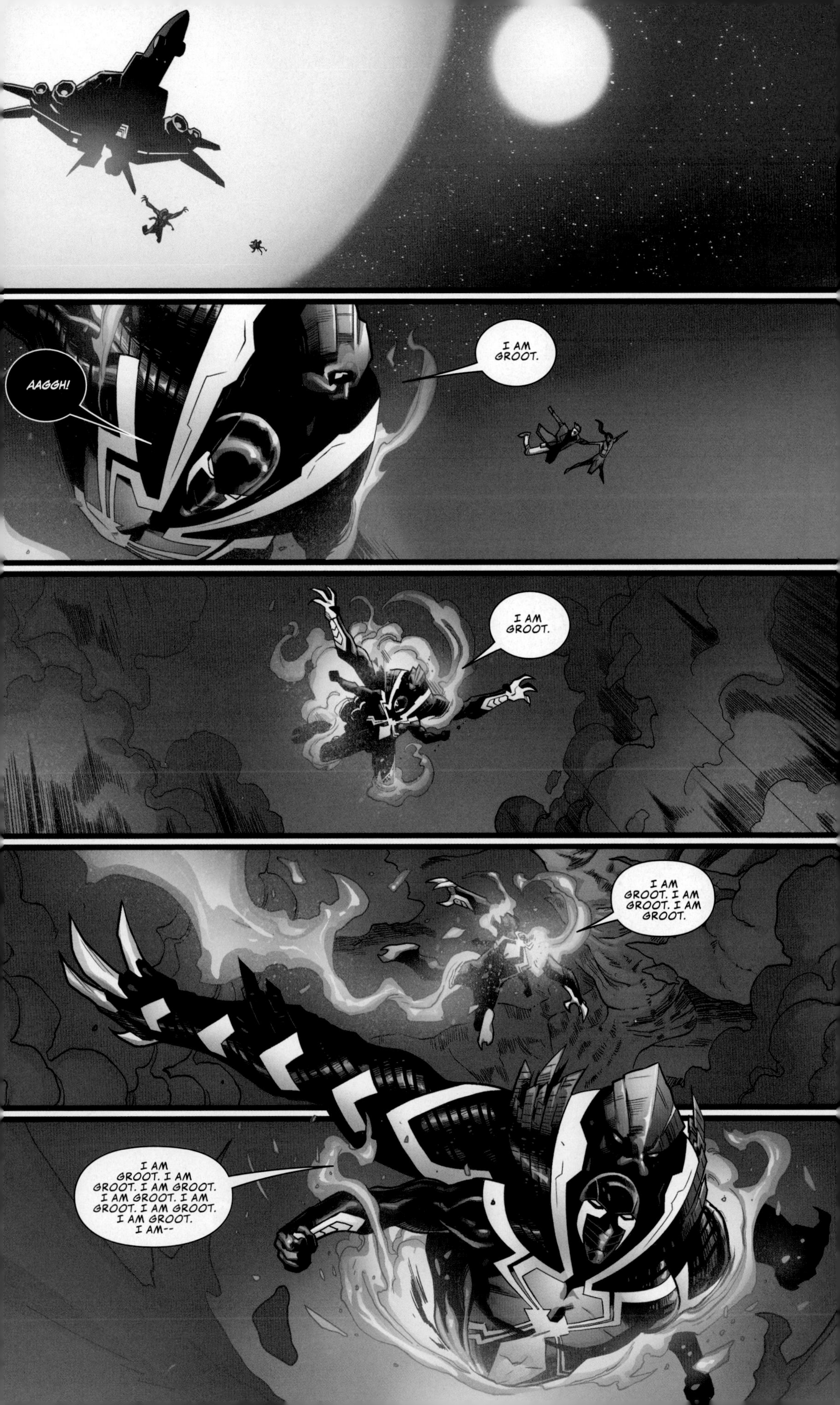
AAGGH!
I AM GROOT.
I AM GROOT.
I AM GROOT. I AM GROOT. I AM GROOT.
I AM GROOT. I AM GROOT. I AM GROOT. I AM GROOT. I AM GROOT. I AM GROOT. I AM GROOT. I AM--

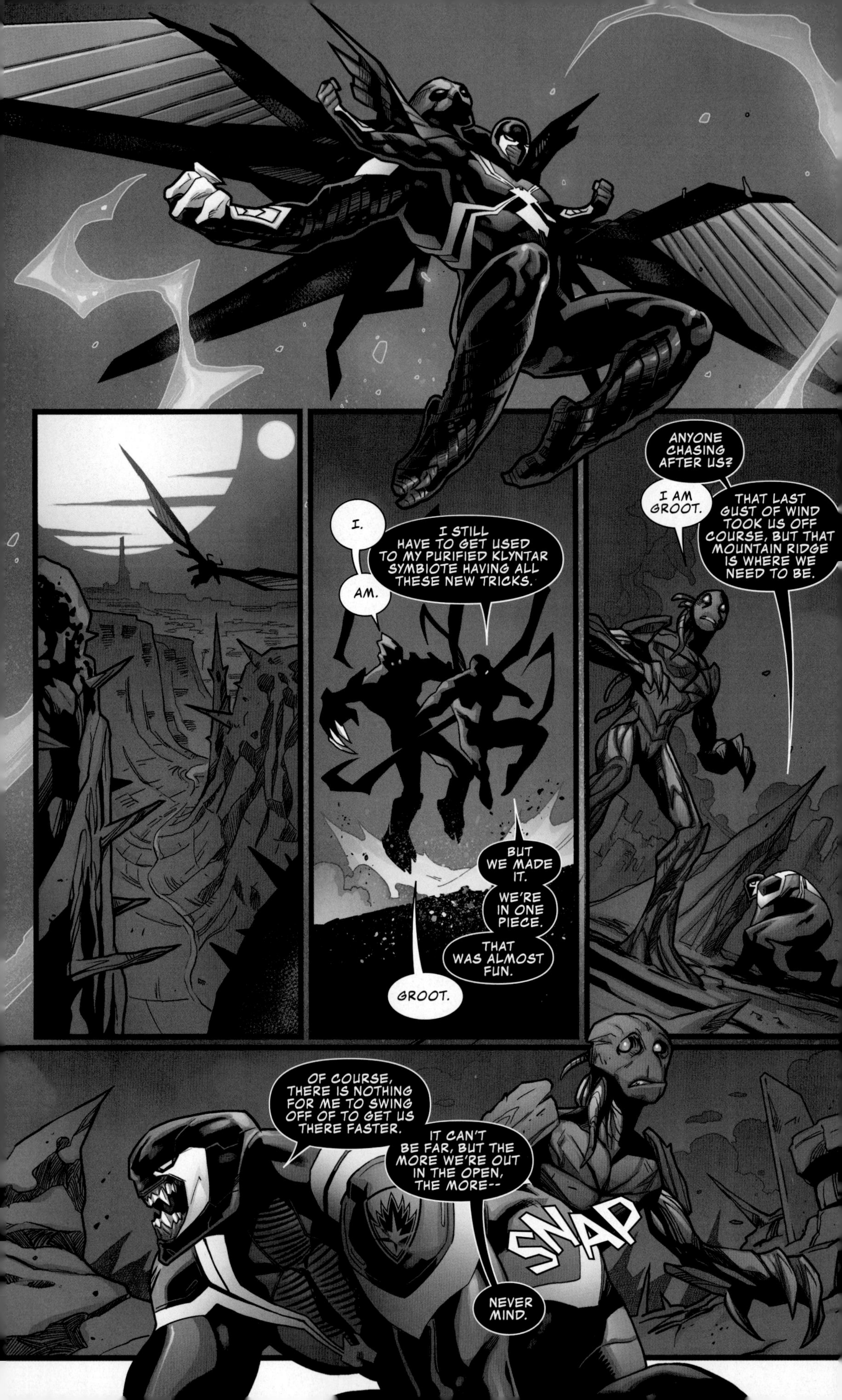
I.
I STILL HAVE TO GET USED TO MY PURIFIED KLYNTAR SYMBIOTE HAVING ALL THESE NEW TRICKS.
AM.
BUT WE MADE IT.
WE'RE IN ONE PIECE.
THAT WAS ALMOST FUN.
GROOT.
ANYONE CHASING AFTER US?
I AM GROOT.
THAT LAST GUST OF WIND TOOK US OFF COURSE, BUT THAT MOUNTAIN RIDGE IS WHERE WE NEED TO BE.
OF COURSE, THERE IS NOTHING FOR ME TO SWING OFF OF TO GET US THERE FASTER.
IT CAN'T BE FAR, BUT THE MORE WE'RE OUT IN THE OPEN, THE MORE--
SNAP
NEVER MIND.

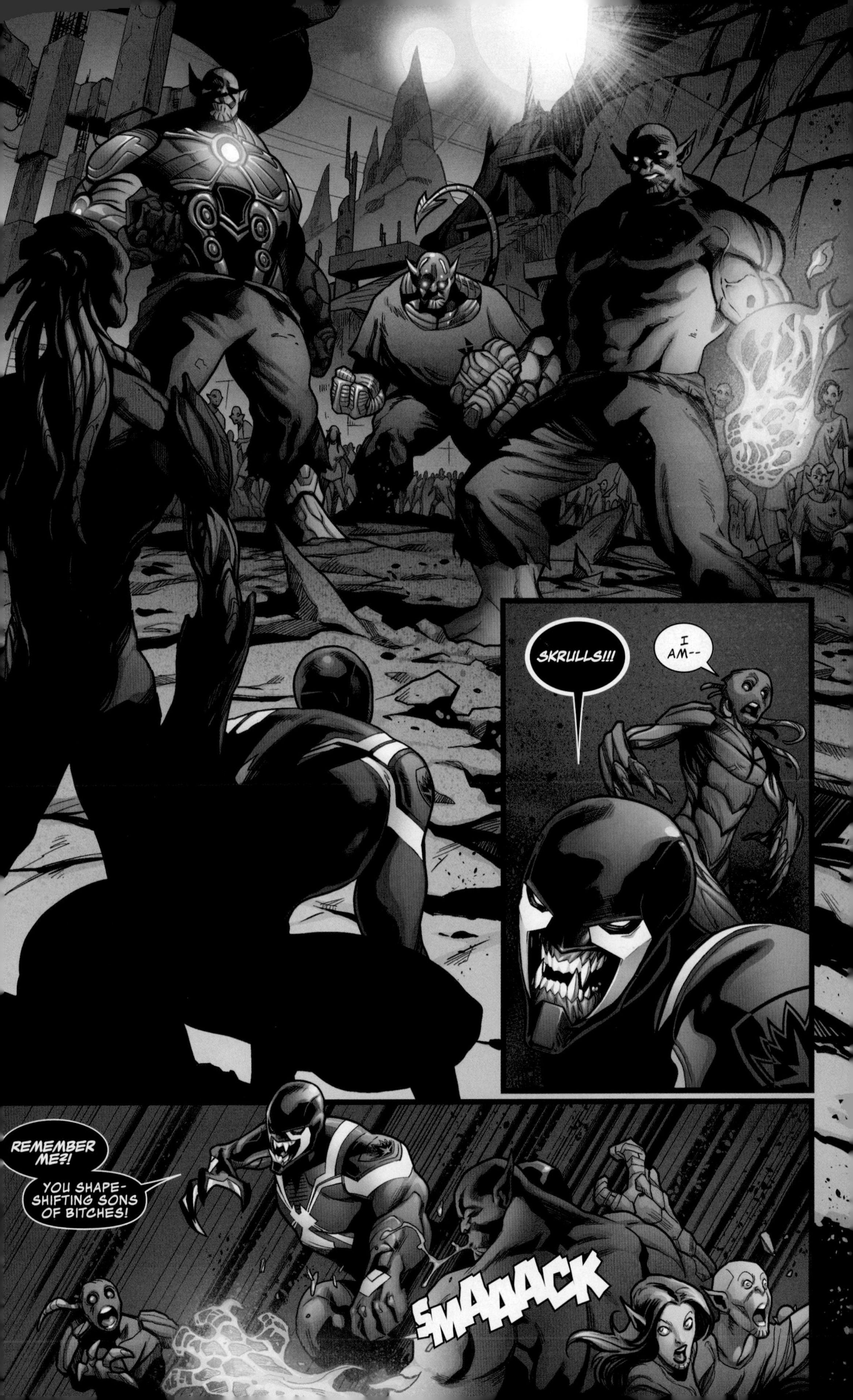
SKRULLS!!!
I AM--
REMEMBER ME?!
YOU SHAPE-SHIFTING SONS OF BITCHES!
SMAAACK

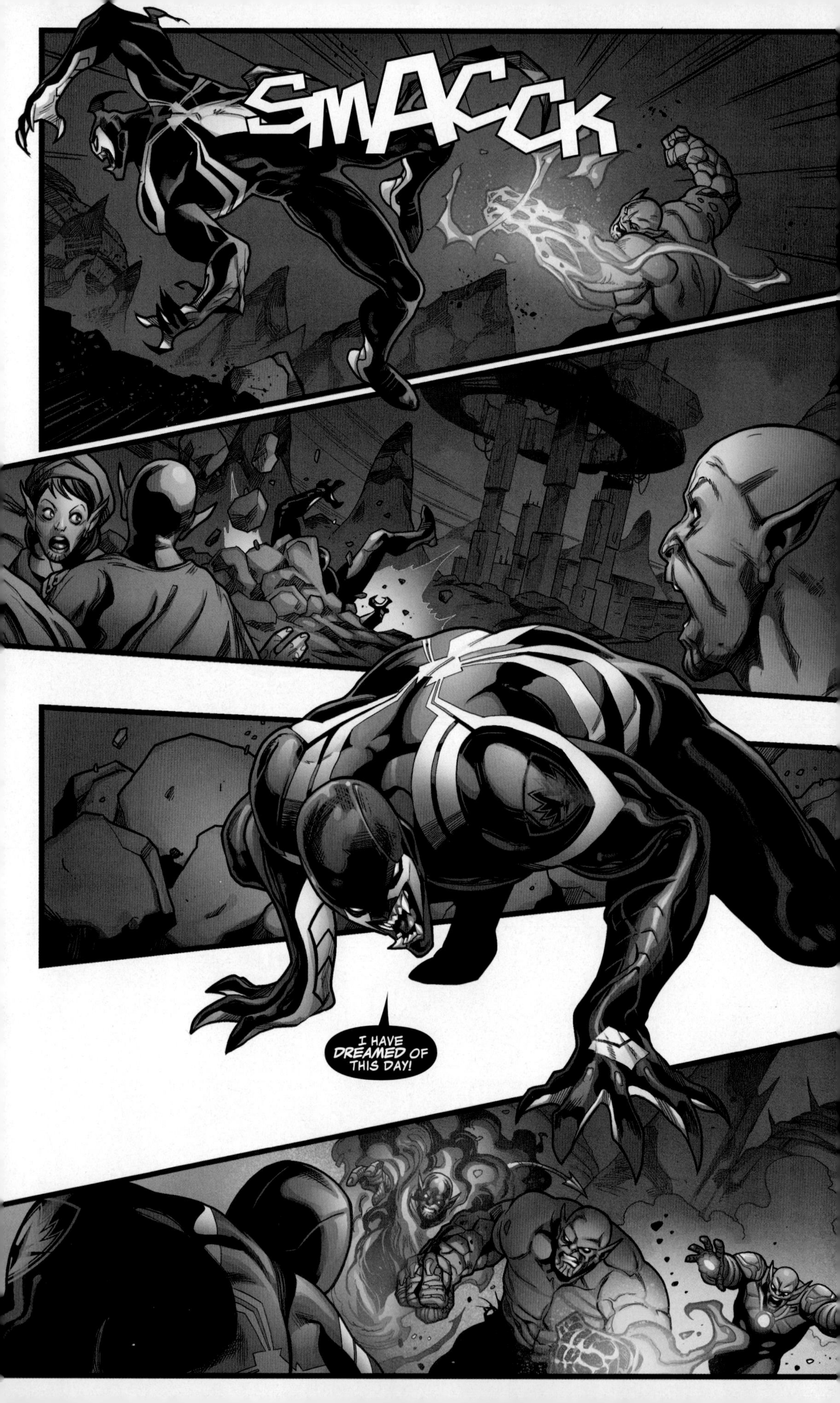
SMACCK
I HAVE DREAMED OF THIS DAY!

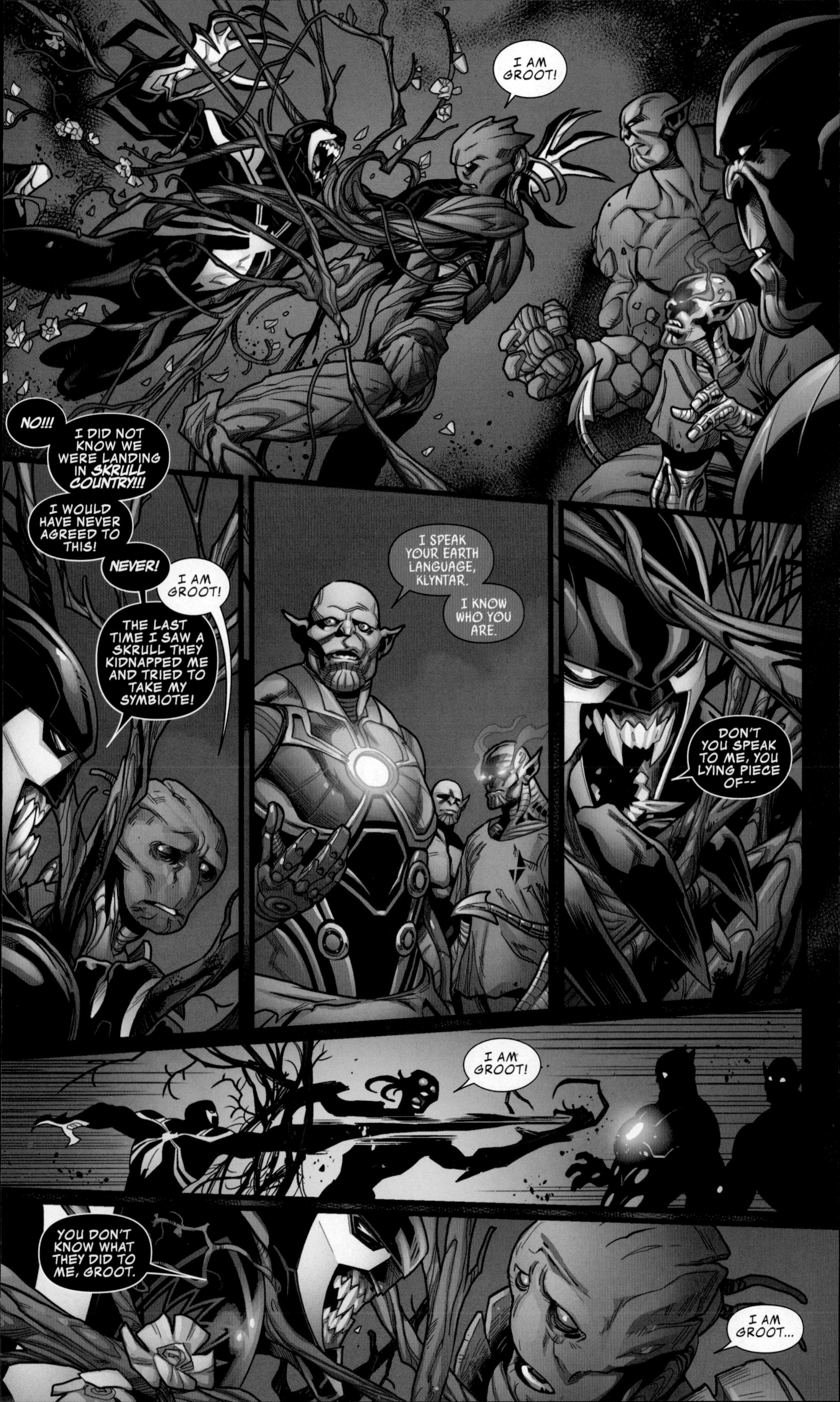
I AM GROOT!
NO!!!
I DID NOT KNOW WE WERE LANDING IN SKRULL COUNTRY!!!
I WOULD HAVE NEVER AGREED TO THIS!
NEVER!
I AM GROOT!
THE LAST TIME I SAW A SKRULL THEY KIDNAPPED ME AND TRIED TO TAKE MY SYMBIOTE!
I SPEAK YOUR EARTH LANGUAGE, KLYNTAR.
I KNOW WHO YOU ARE.
DON'T YOU SPEAK TO ME, YOU LYING PIECE OF--
I AM GROOT!
YOU DON'T KNOW WHAT THEY DID TO ME, GROOT.
I AM GROOT...

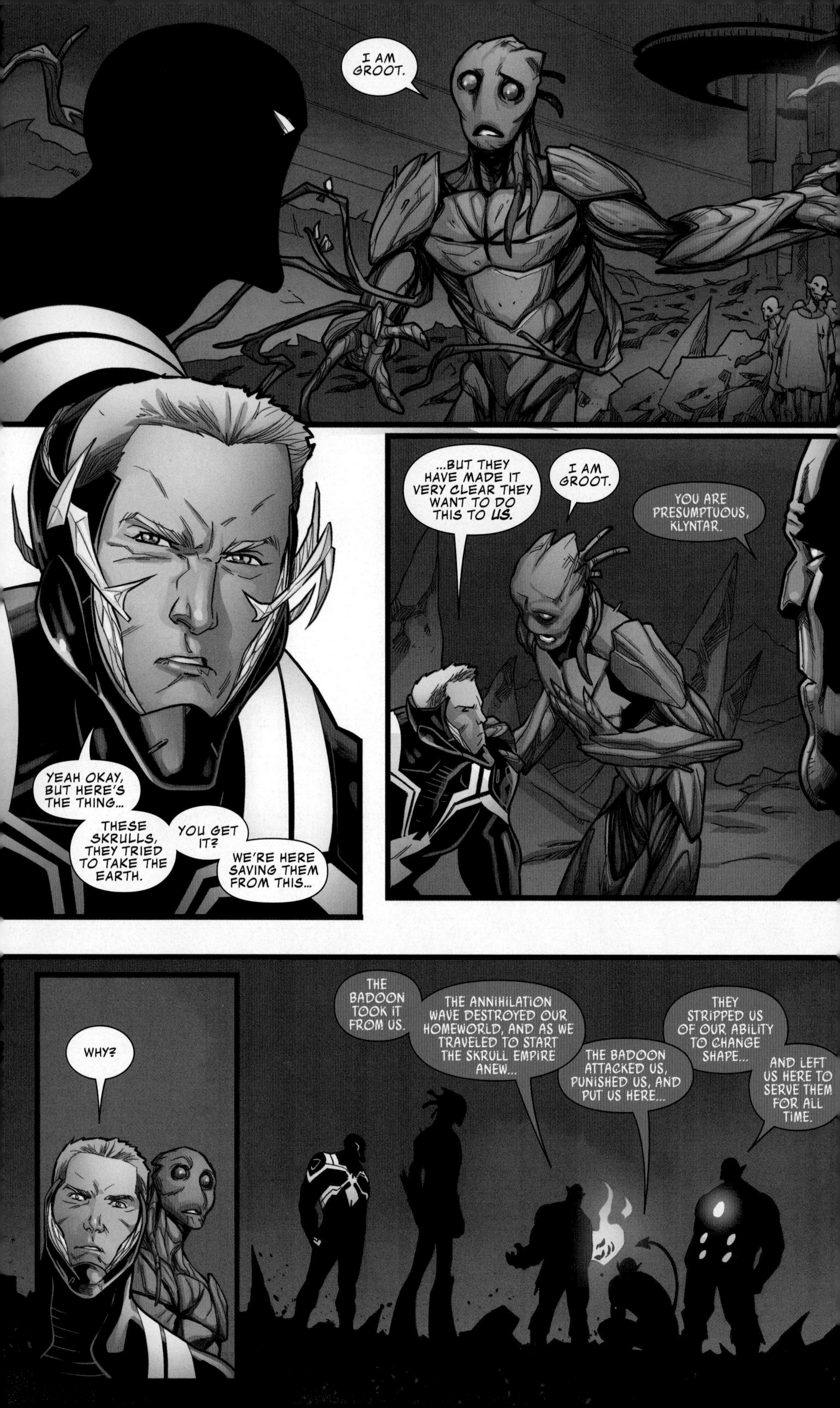

I AM GROOT.
YEAH OKAY, BUT HERE'S THE THING...
THESE SKRULLS, THEY TRIED TO TAKE THE EARTH.
YOU GET IT?
WE'RE HERE SAVING THEM FROM THIS...
...BUT THEY HAVE MADE IT VERY CLEAR THEY WANT TO DO THIS TO *US.*
I AM GROOT.
YOU ARE PRESUMPTUOUS, KLYNTAR.
WHY?
THE BADOON TOOK IT FROM US.
THE ANNIHILATION WAVE DESTROYED OUR HOMEWORLD, AND AS WE TRAVELED TO START THE SKRULL EMPIRE ANEW...
THE BADOON ATTACKED US, PUNISHED US, AND PUT US HERE...
THEY STRIPPED US OF OUR ABILITY TO CHANGE SHAPE...
AND LEFT US HERE TO SERVE THEM FOR ALL TIME.

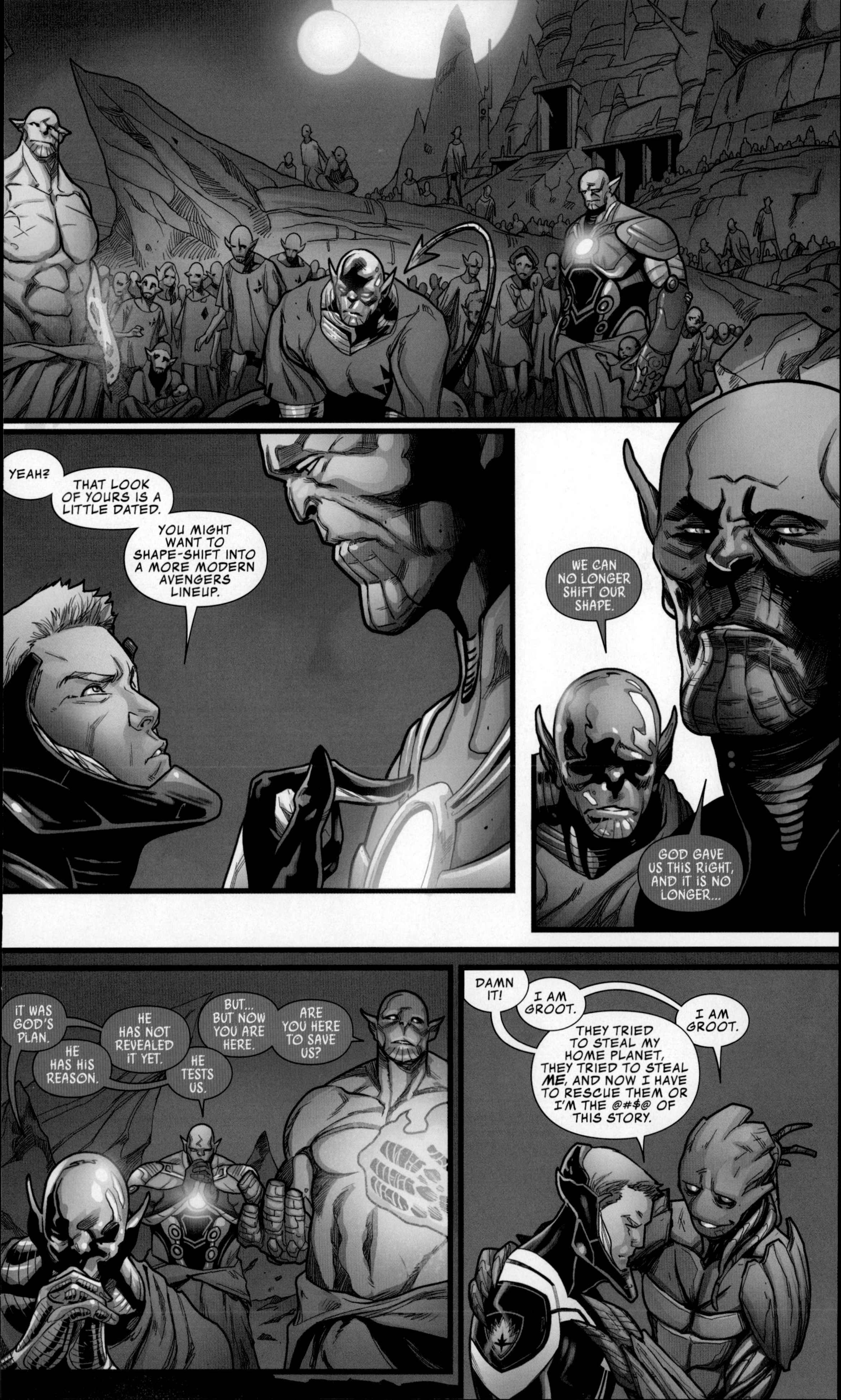
YEAH?
THAT LOOK OF YOURS IS A LITTLE DATED.
YOU MIGHT WANT TO SHAPE-SHIFT INTO A MORE MODERN AVENGERS LINEUP.
WE CAN NO LONGER SHIFT OUR SHAPE.
GOD GAVE US THIS RIGHT, AND IT IS NO LONGER...
IT WAS GOD'S PLAN.
HE HAS HIS REASON.
HE HAS NOT REVEALED IT YET.
HE TESTS US.
BUT... BUT NOW YOU ARE HERE.
ARE YOU HERE TO SAVE US?
DAMN IT!
I AM GROOT.
I AM GROOT.
THEY TRIED TO STEAL MY HOME PLANET, THEY TRIED TO STEAL **ME**, AND NOW I HAVE TO RESCUE THEM OR I'M THE @#$@ OF THIS STORY.

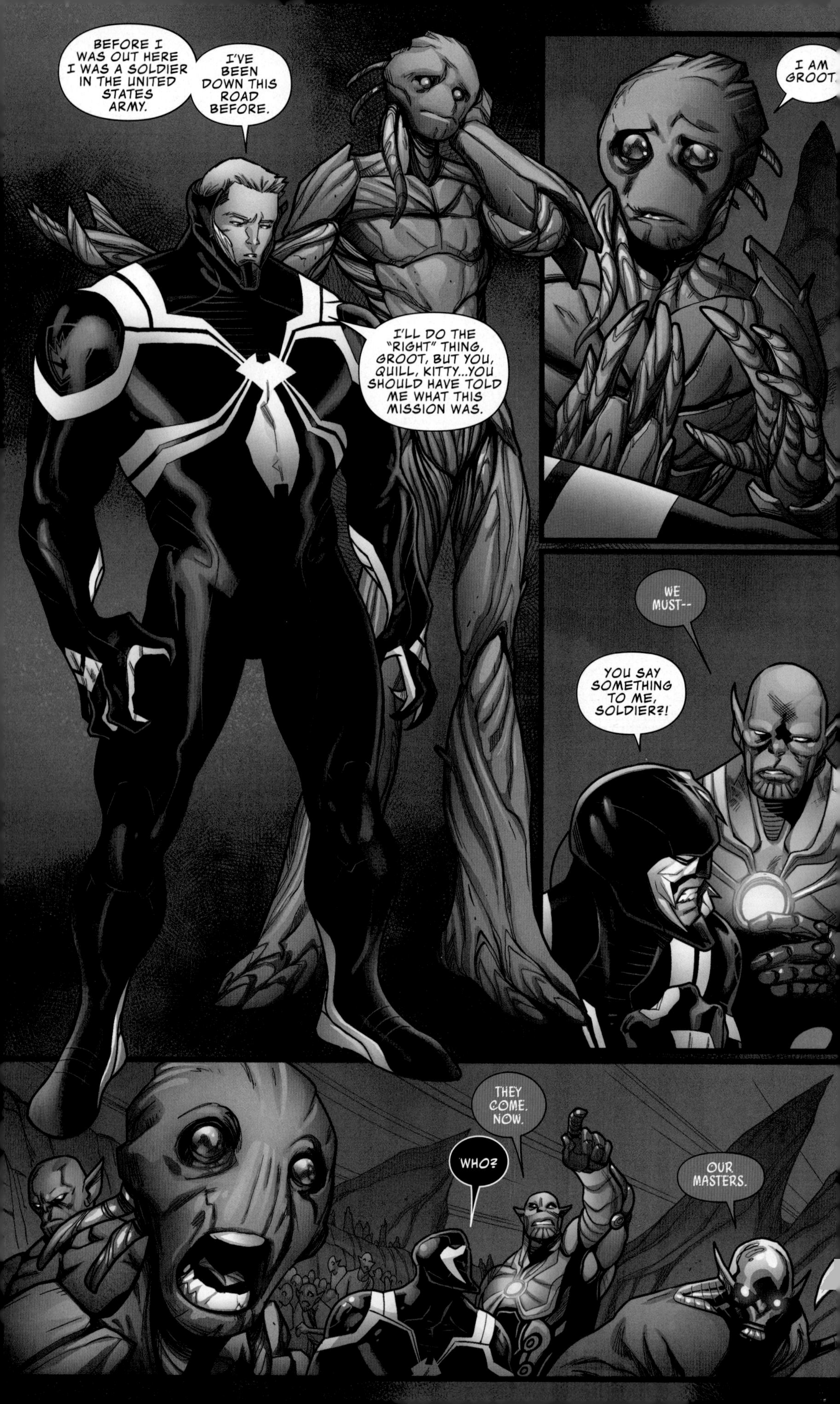
BEFORE I WAS OUT HERE I WAS A SOLDIER IN THE UNITED STATES ARMY.
I'VE BEEN DOWN THIS ROAD BEFORE.
I'LL DO THE "RIGHT" THING, GROOT, BUT YOU, QUILL, KITTY...YOU SHOULD HAVE TOLD ME WHAT THIS MISSION WAS.
I AM GROOT.
WE MUST--
YOU SAY SOMETHING TO ME, SOLDIER?!
THEY COME. NOW.
WHO?
OUR MASTERS.

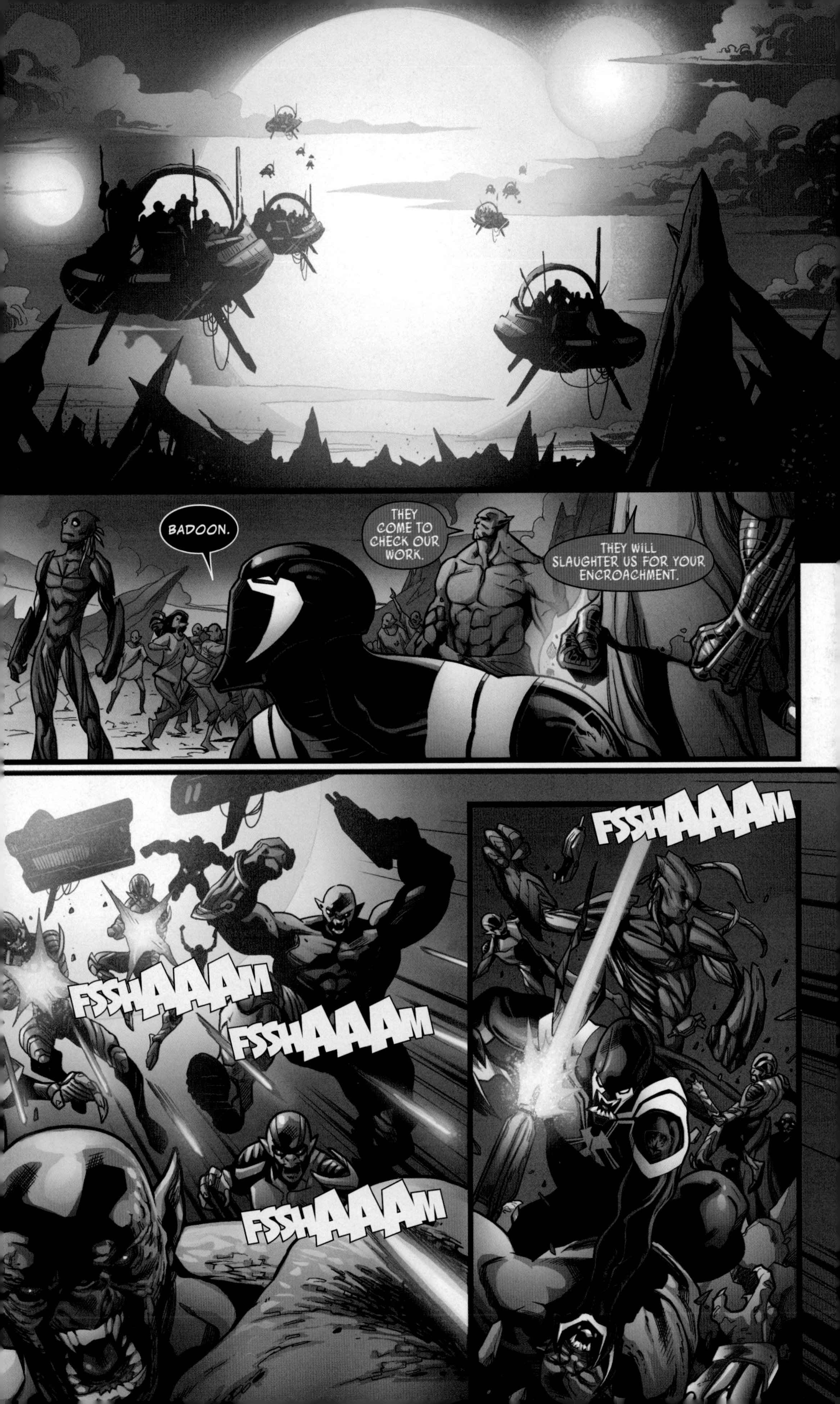
BADOON.
THEY COME TO CHECK OUR WORK.
THEY WILL SLAUGHTER US FOR YOUR ENCROACHMENT.
FSSHAAAM
FSSHAAAM
FSSHAAAM
FSSHAAAM

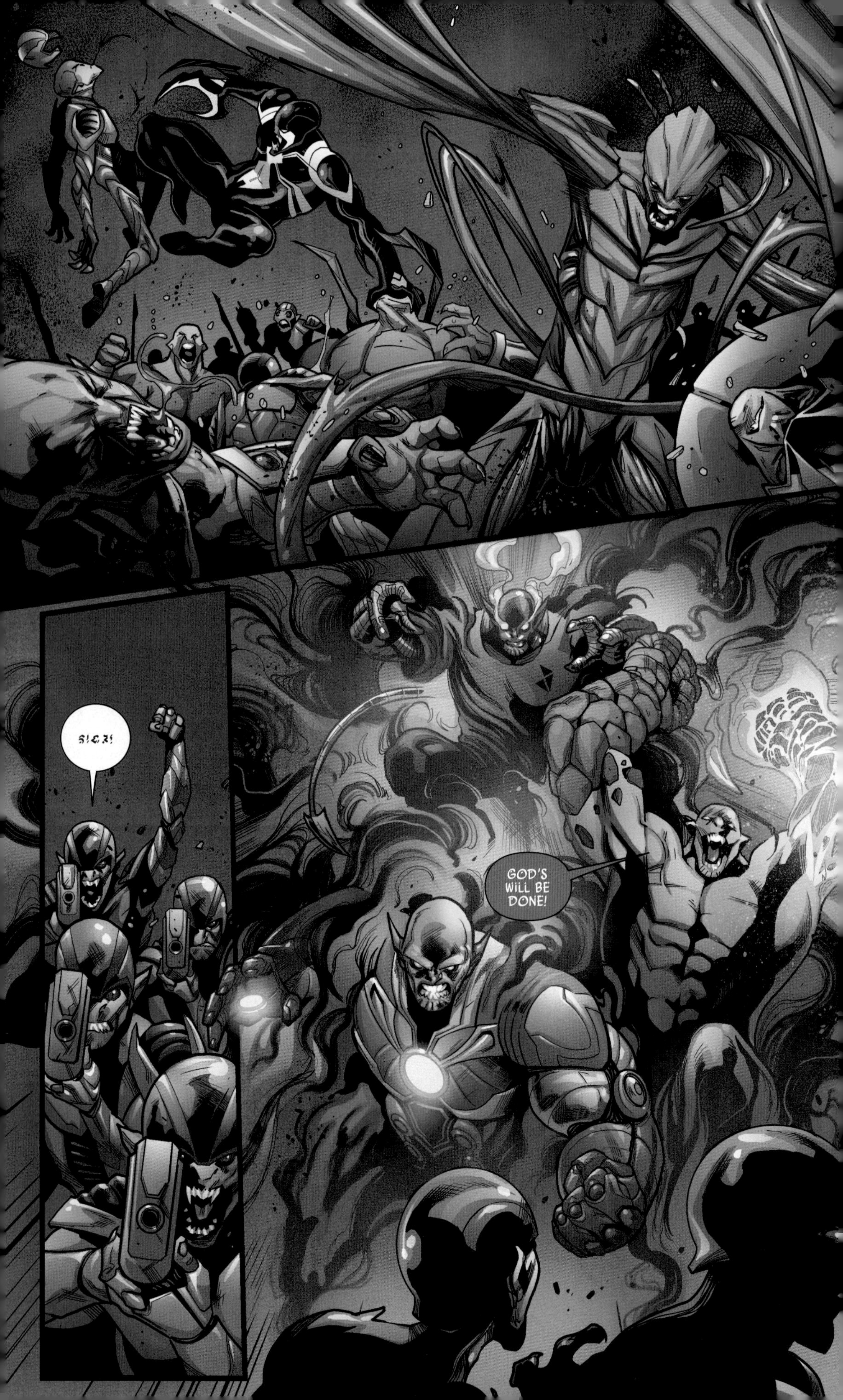
GOD'S WILL BE DONE!

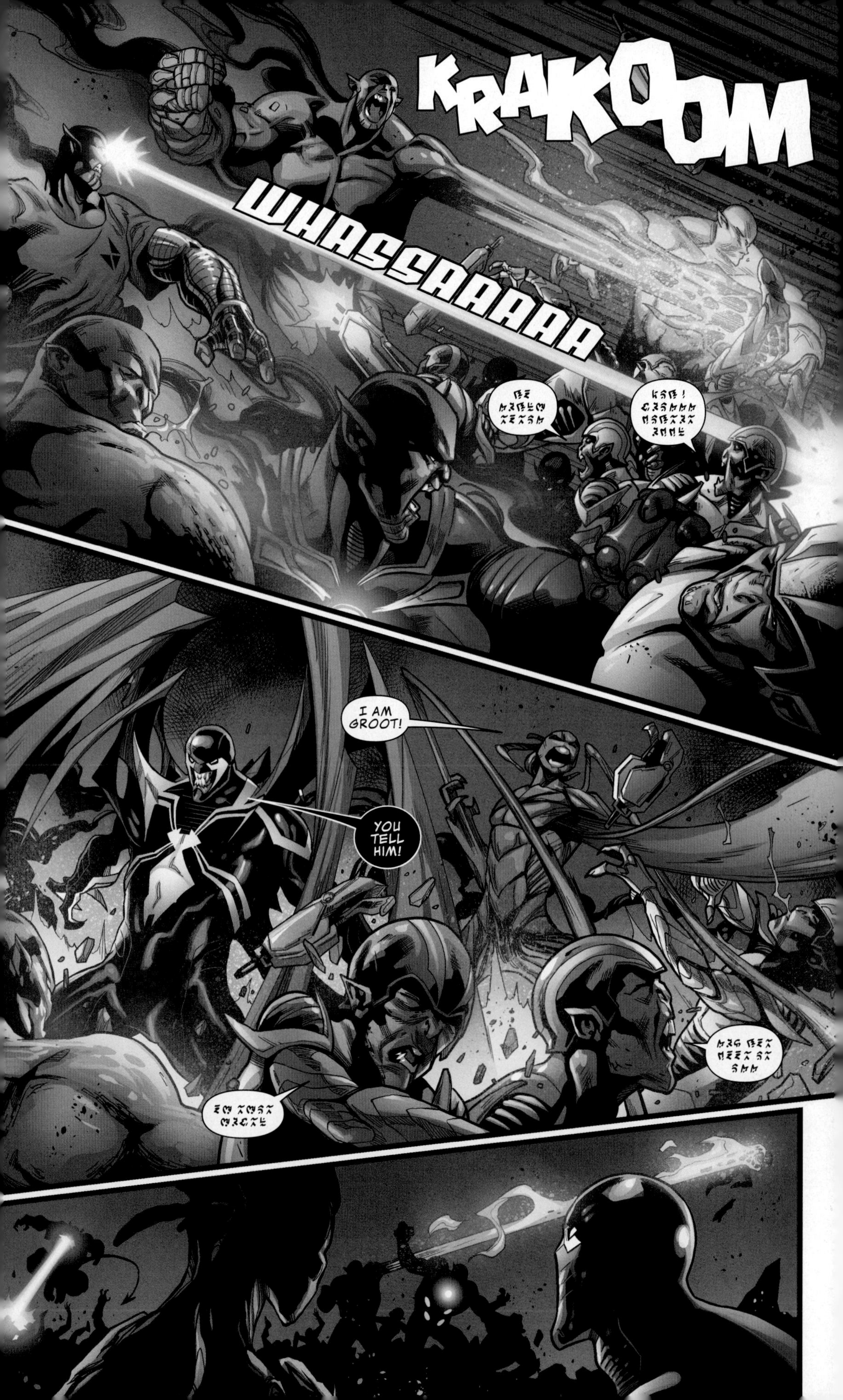
KRAKOOOM
WHASSAAAAAA
I AM GROOT!
YOU TELL HIM!

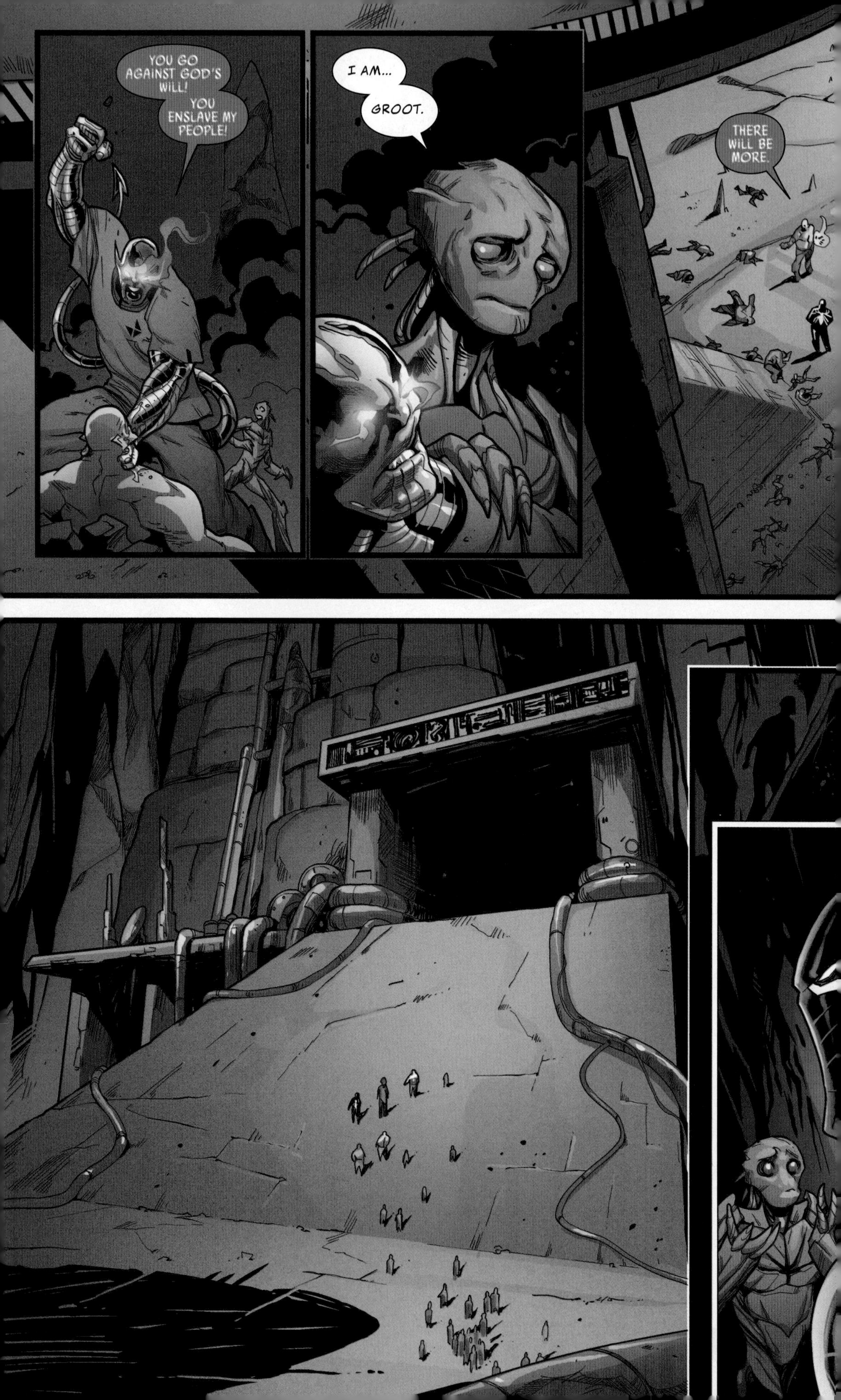
YOU GO AGAINST GOD'S WILL!
YOU ENSLAVE MY PEOPLE!
I AM...
GROOT.
THERE WILL BE MORE.

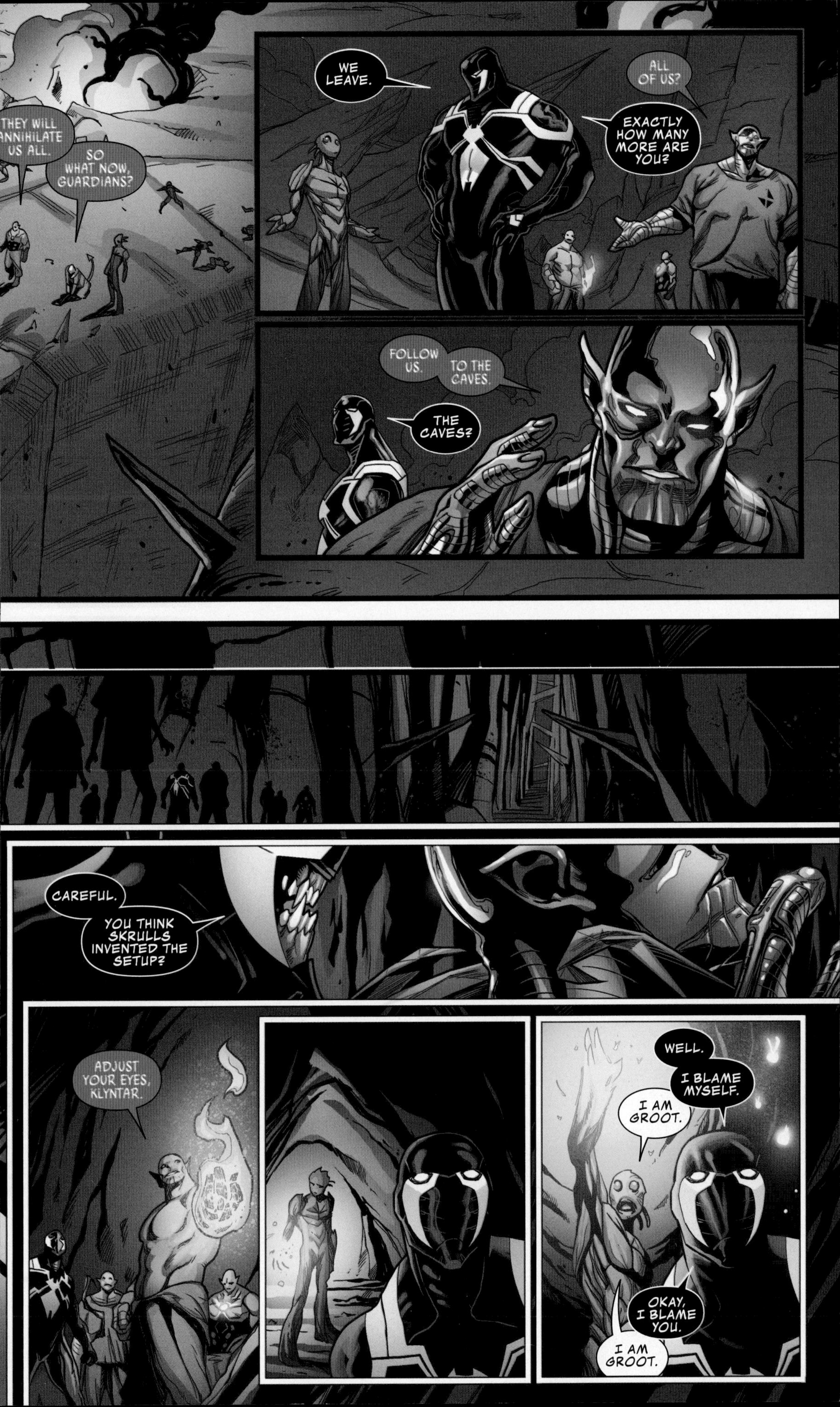
THEY WILL ANNIHILATE US ALL.
SO WHAT NOW, GUARDIANS?
WE LEAVE.
ALL OF US?
EXACTLY HOW MANY MORE ARE YOU?
FOLLOW US.
TO THE CAVES.
THE CAVES?
CAREFUL.
YOU THINK SKRULLS INVENTED THE SETUP?
ADJUST YOUR EYES, KLYNTAR.
WELL.
I BLAME MYSELF.
I AM GROOT.
OKAY, I BLAME YOU.
I AM GROOT.

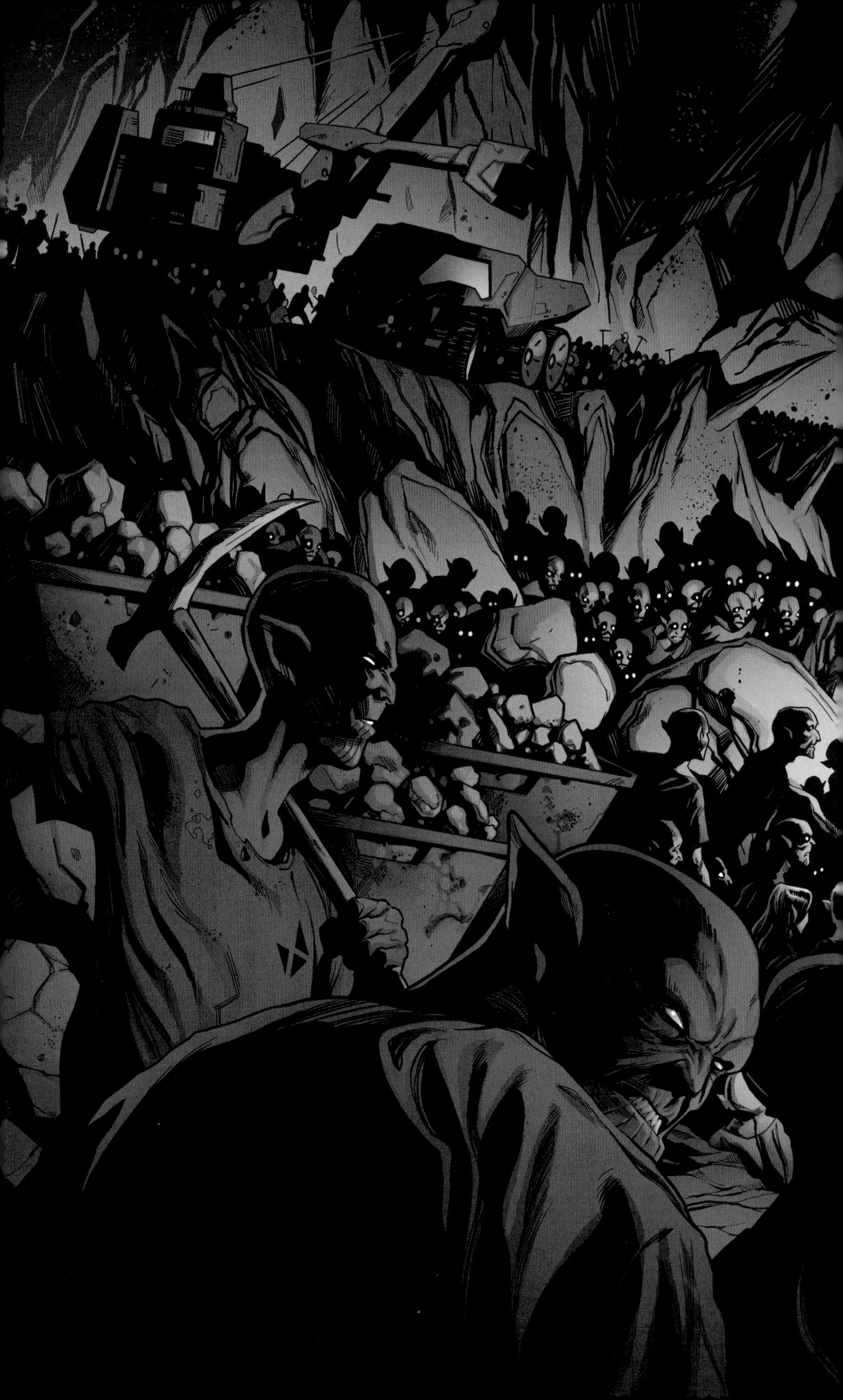

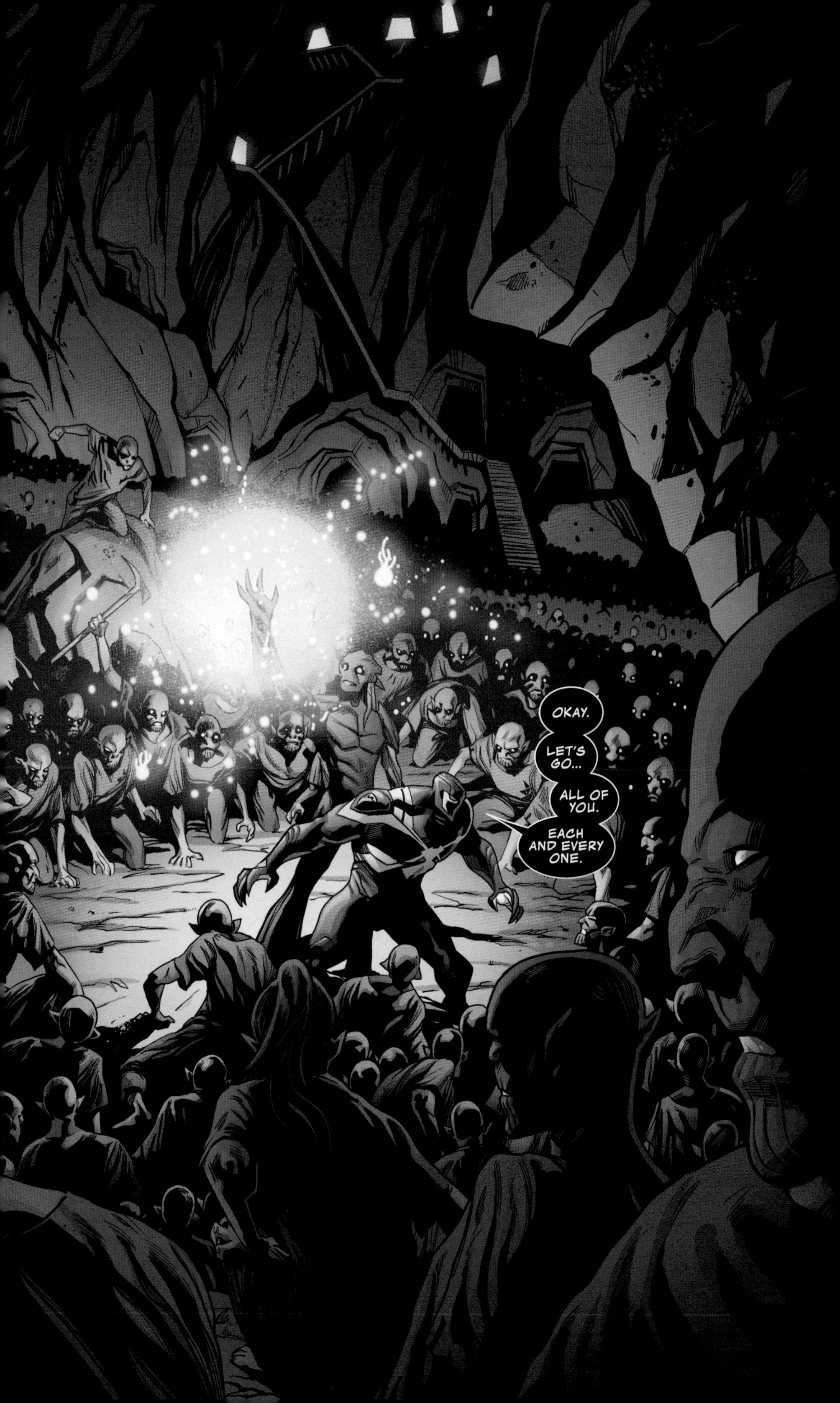
OKAY.
LET'S GO...
ALL OF YOU.
EACH AND EVERY ONE.

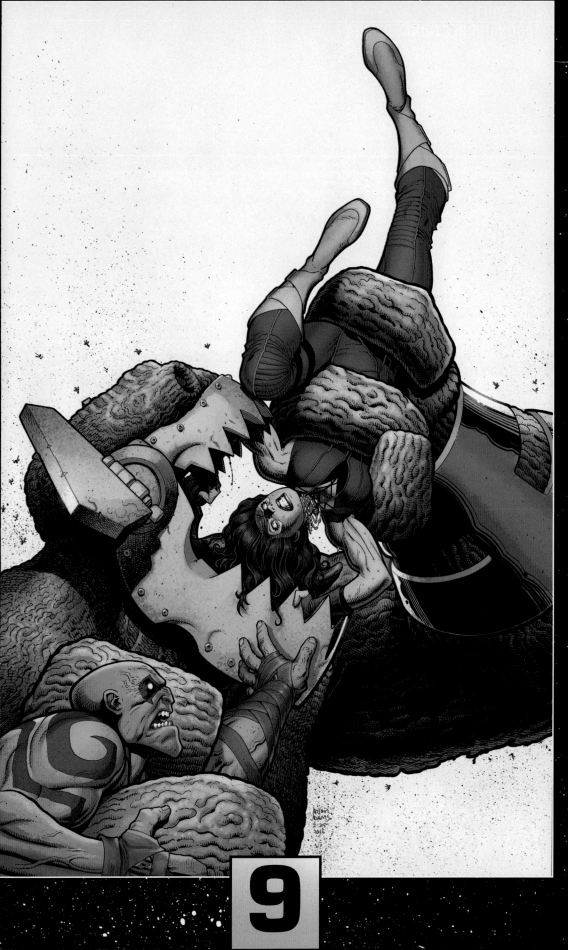

9

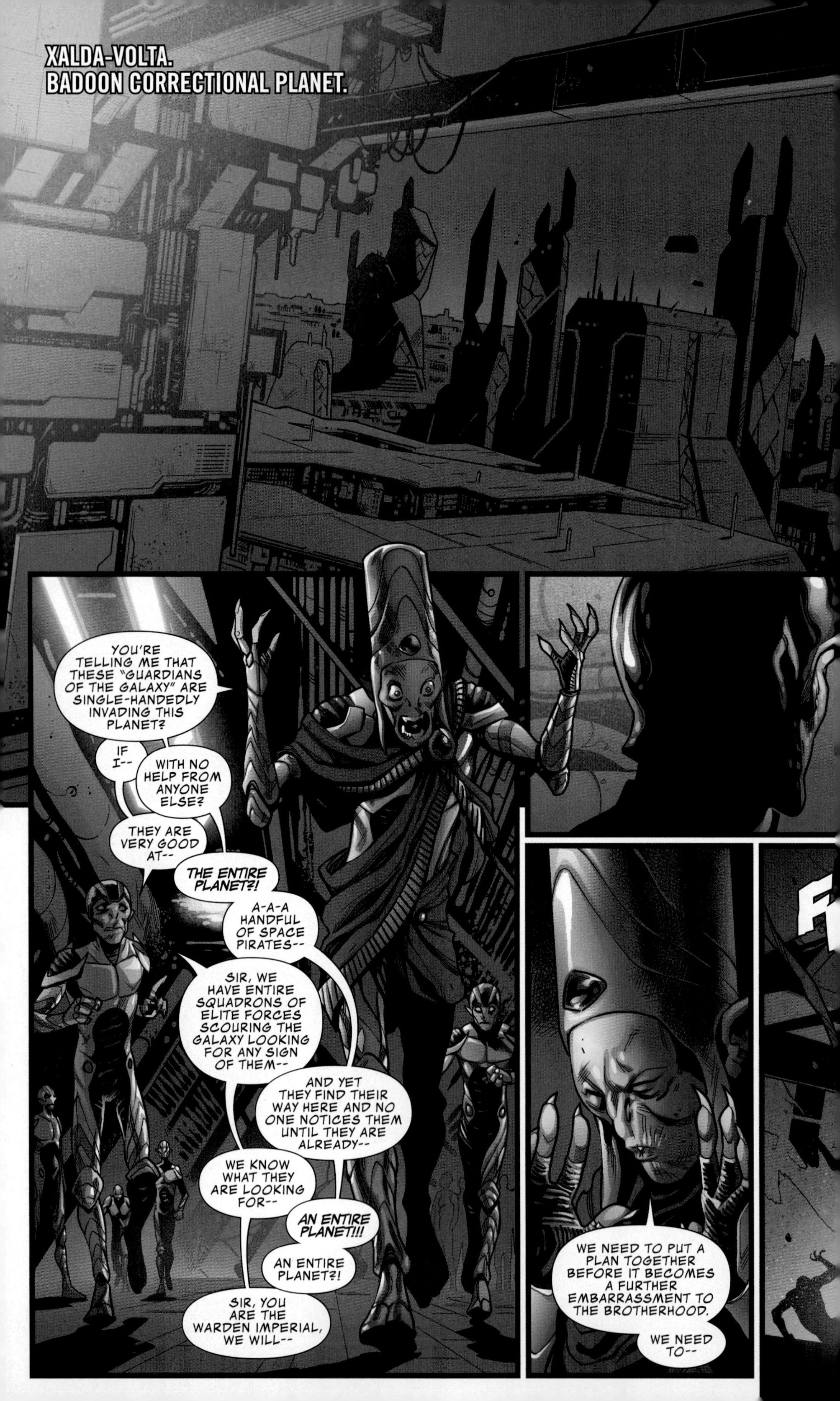
XALDA-VOLTA.
BADOON CORRECTIONAL PLANET.
YOU'RE TELLING ME THAT THESE "GUARDIANS OF THE GALAXY" ARE SINGLE-HANDEDLY INVADING THIS PLANET?
IF I--
WITH NO HELP FROM ANYONE ELSE?
THEY ARE VERY GOOD AT--
THE ENTIRE PLANET?!
A-A-A HANDFUL OF SPACE PIRATES--
SIR, WE HAVE ENTIRE SQUADRONS OF ELITE FORCES SCOURING THE GALAXY LOOKING FOR ANY SIGN OF THEM--
AND YET THEY FIND THEIR WAY HERE AND NO ONE NOTICES THEM UNTIL THEY ARE ALREADY--
WE KNOW WHAT THEY ARE LOOKING FOR--
AN ENTIRE PLANET!!!
AN ENTIRE PLANET?!
SIR, YOU ARE THE WARDEN IMPERIAL, WE WILL--
WE NEED TO PUT A PLAN TOGETHER BEFORE IT BECOMES A FURTHER EMBARRASSMENT TO THE BROTHERHOOD.
WE NEED TO--

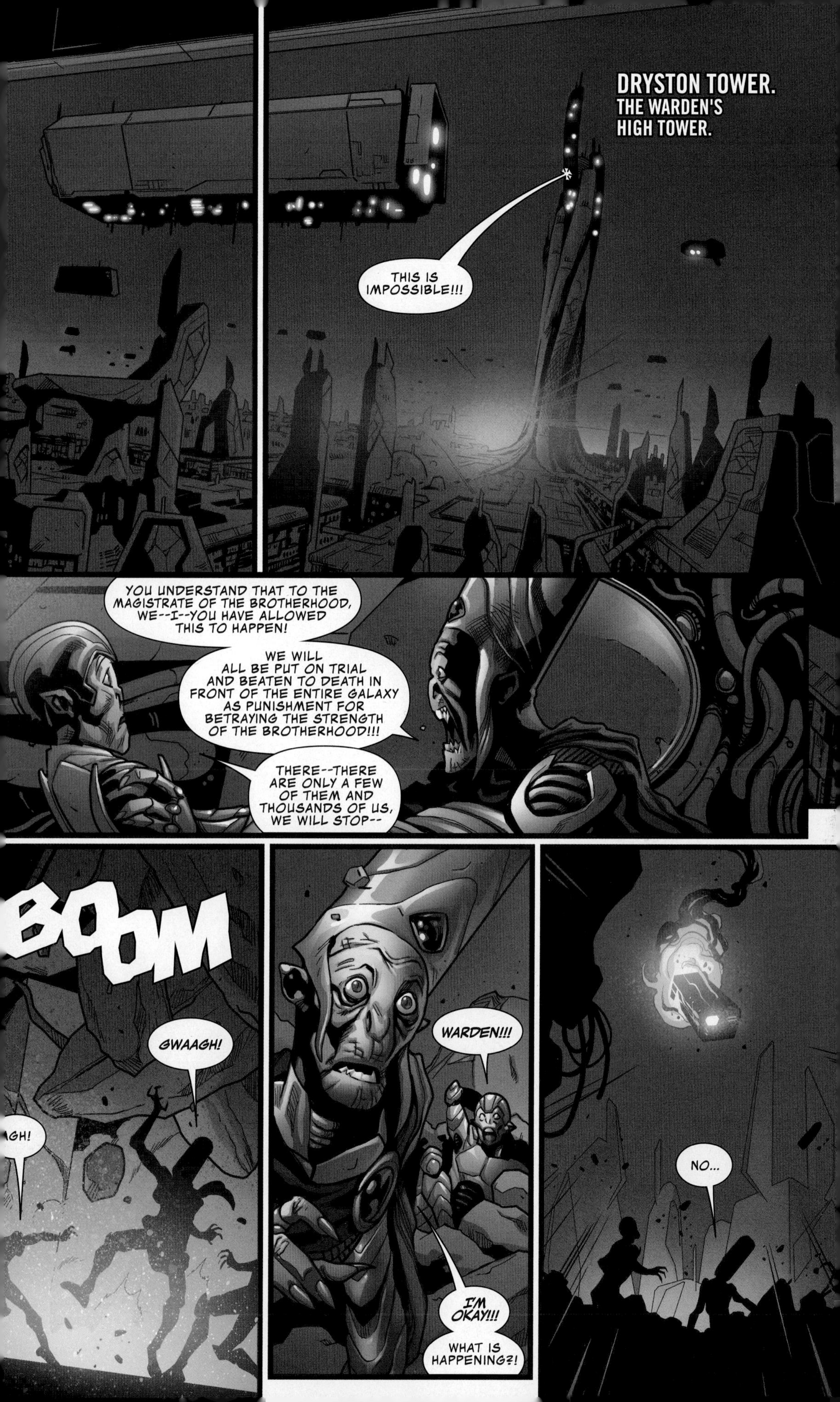

DRYSTON TOWER.
THE WARDEN'S HIGH TOWER.
THIS IS IMPOSSIBLE!!!
YOU UNDERSTAND THAT TO THE MAGISTRATE OF THE BROTHERHOOD, WE--I--YOU HAVE ALLOWED THIS TO HAPPEN!
WE WILL ALL BE PUT ON TRIAL AND BEATEN TO DEATH IN FRONT OF THE ENTIRE GALAXY AS PUNISHMENT FOR BETRAYING THE STRENGTH OF THE BROTHERHOOD!!!
THERE--THERE ARE ONLY A FEW OF THEM AND THOUSANDS OF US, WE WILL STOP--
BOOM
GWAAGH!
GH!
WARDEN!!!
I'M OKAY!!!
WHAT IS HAPPENING?!
NO...

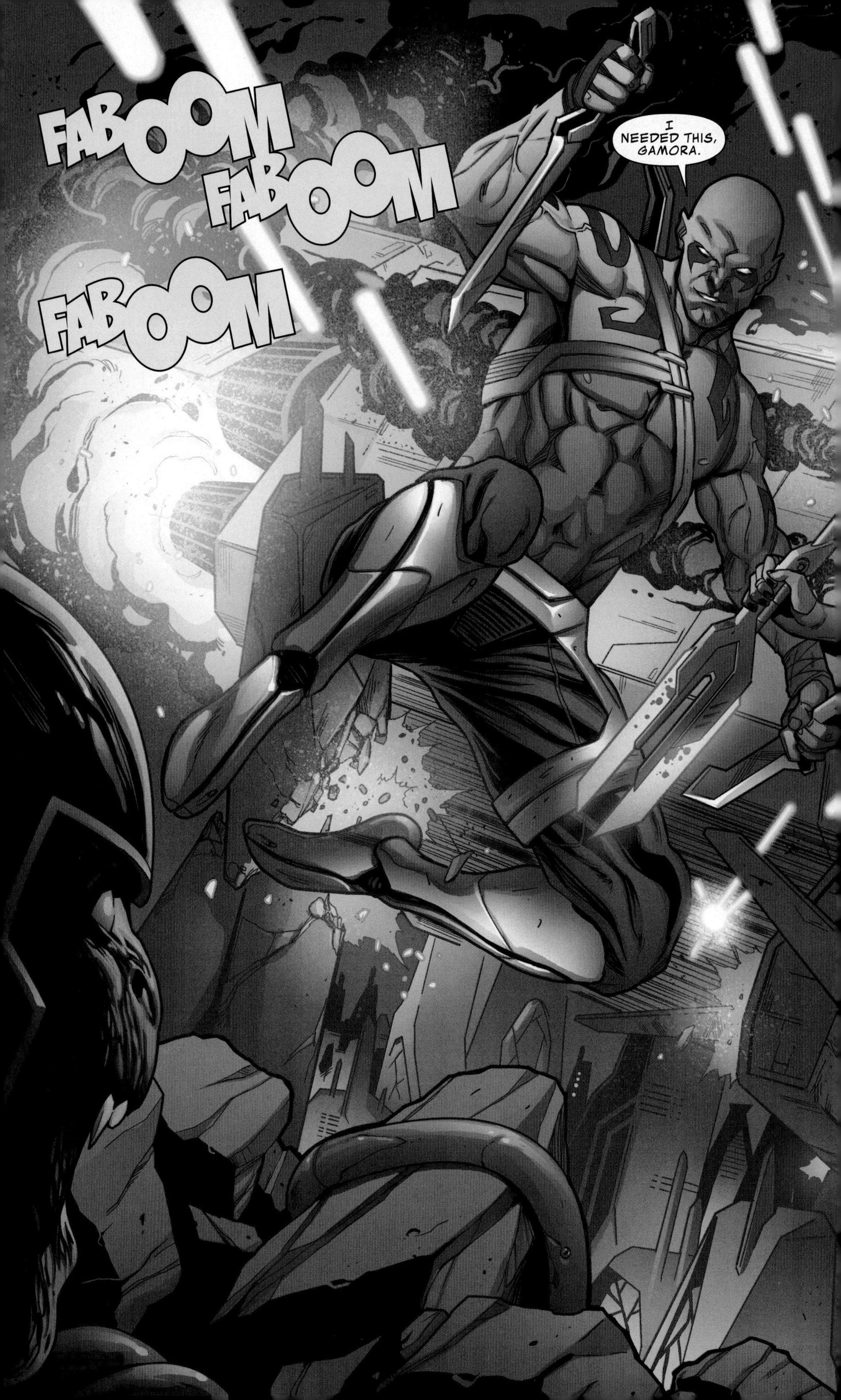
FABOOM
FABOOM
FABOOM
I NEEDED THIS, GAMORA.

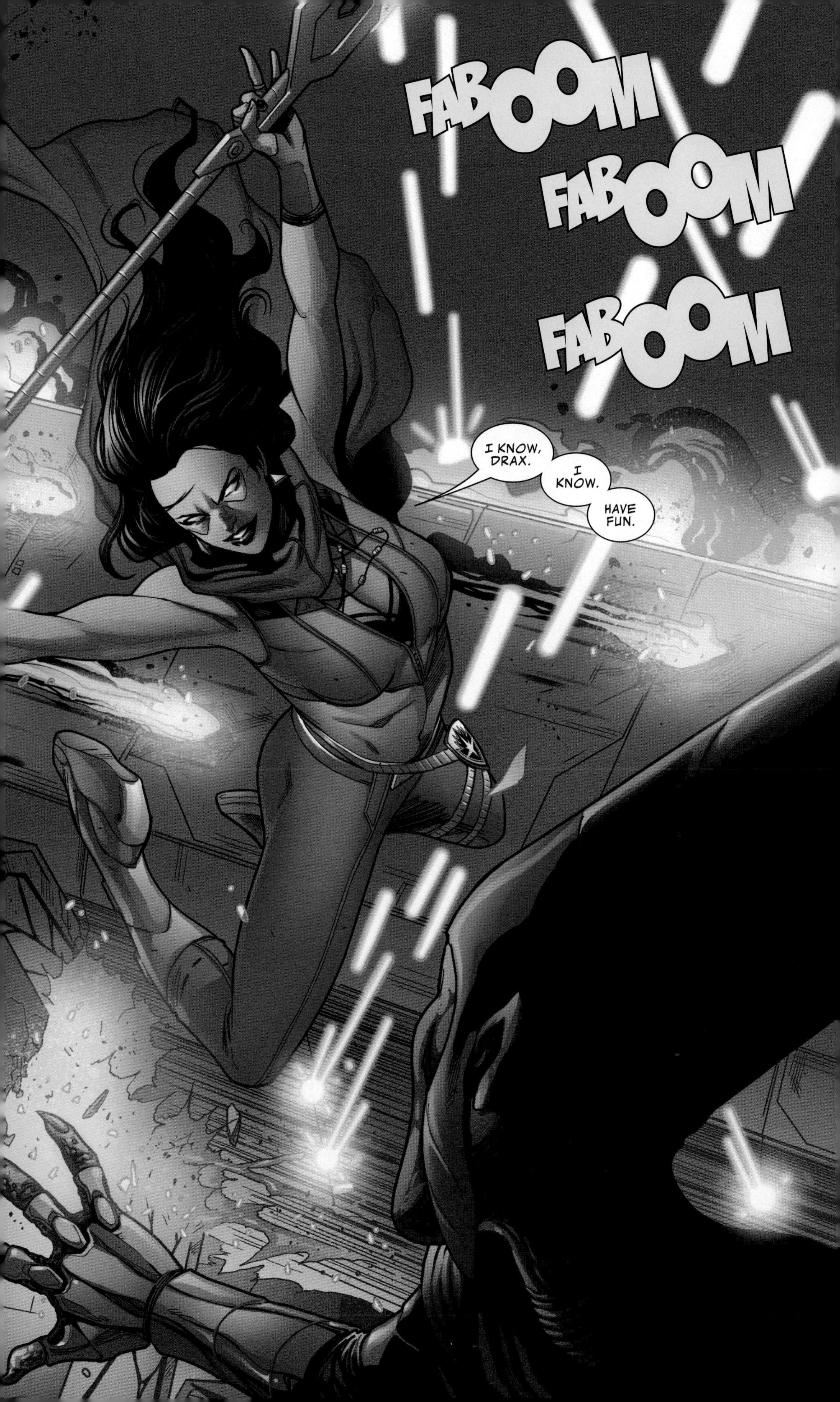
FABOOM
FABOOM
FABOOM
I KNOW, DRAX.
I KNOW.
HAVE FUN.

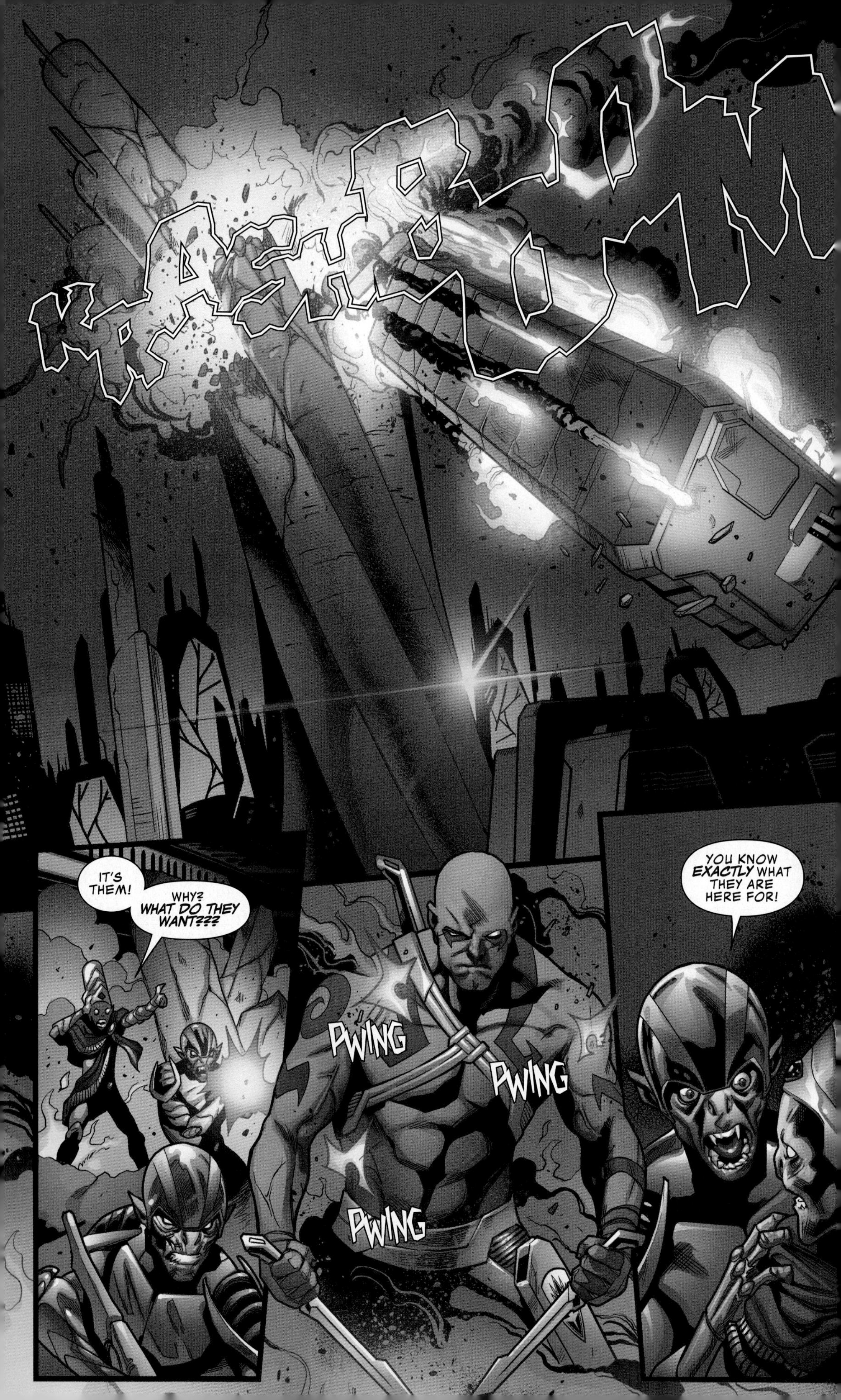
KRAKADOOOM
IT'S THEM!
WHY? WHAT DO THEY WANT???
PWING
PWING
PWING
YOU KNOW EXACTLY WHAT THEY ARE HERE FOR!

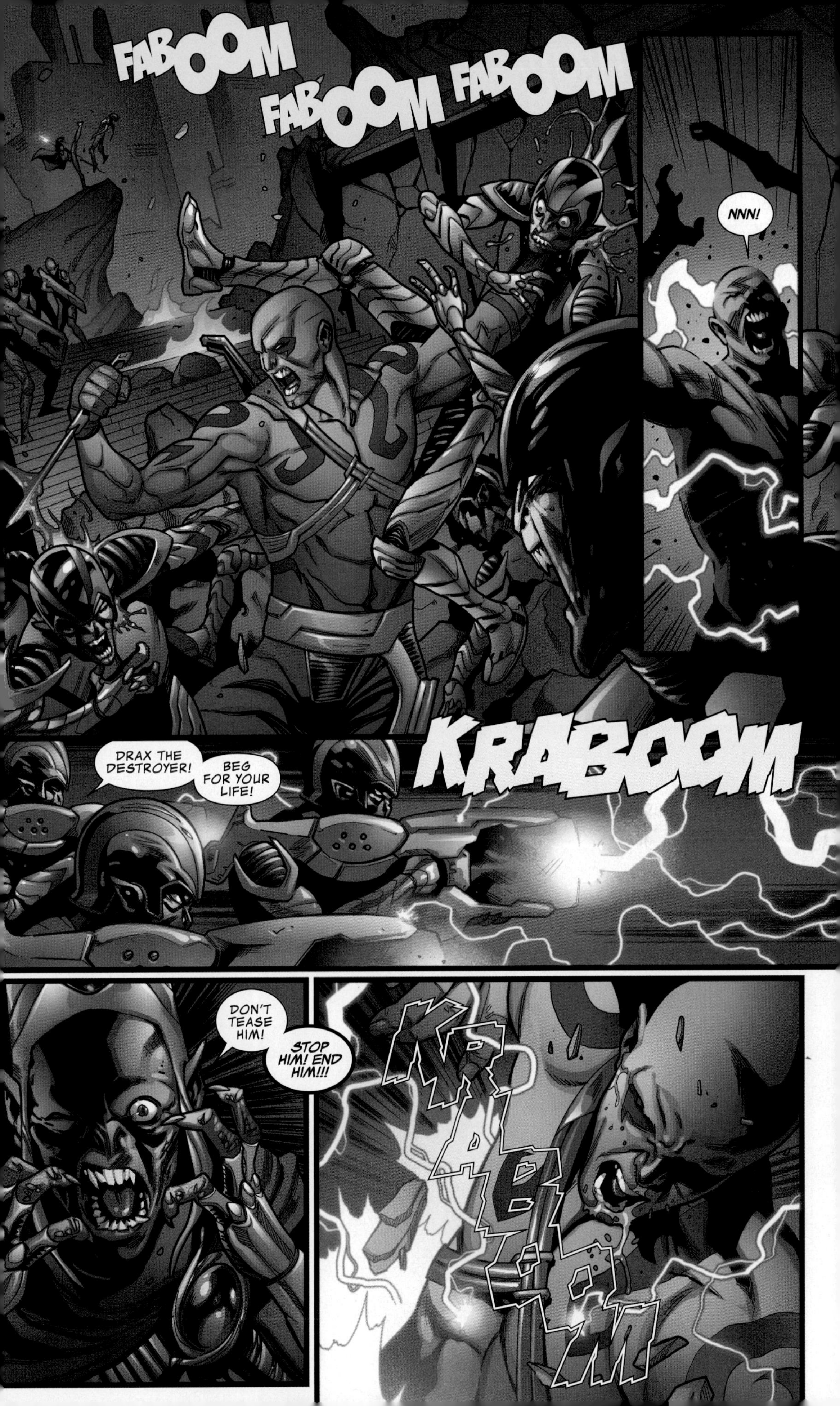

FABOOM
FABOOM FABOOM
NNN!
KRABOOM
DRAX THE DESTROYER!
BEG FOR YOUR LIFE!
DON'T TEASE HIM!
STOP HIM! END HIM!!!

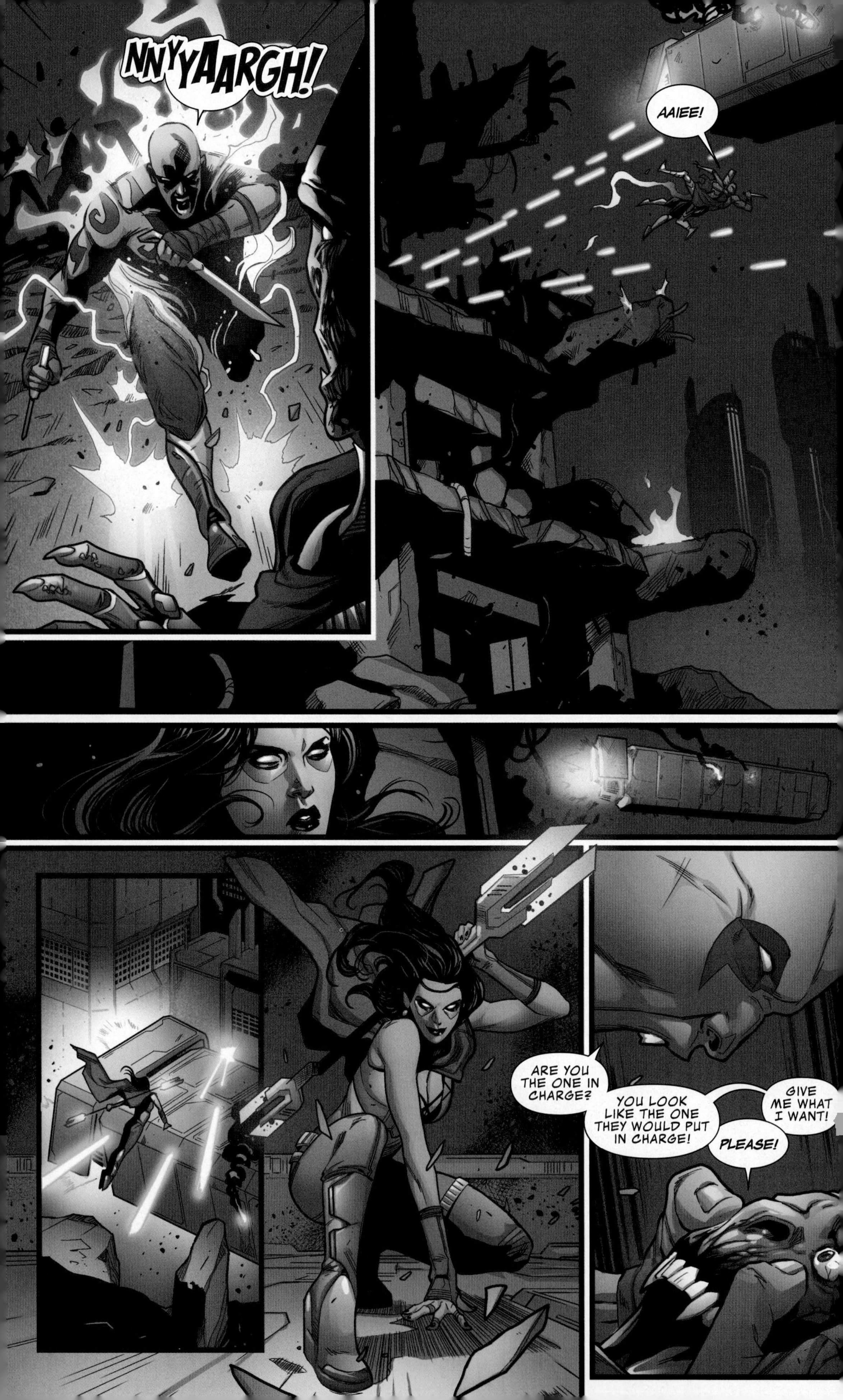
NNYYAARGH!
AAIEE!
ARE YOU THE ONE IN CHARGE?
YOU LOOK LIKE THE ONE THEY WOULD PUT IN CHARGE!
GIVE ME WHAT I WANT!
PLEASE!

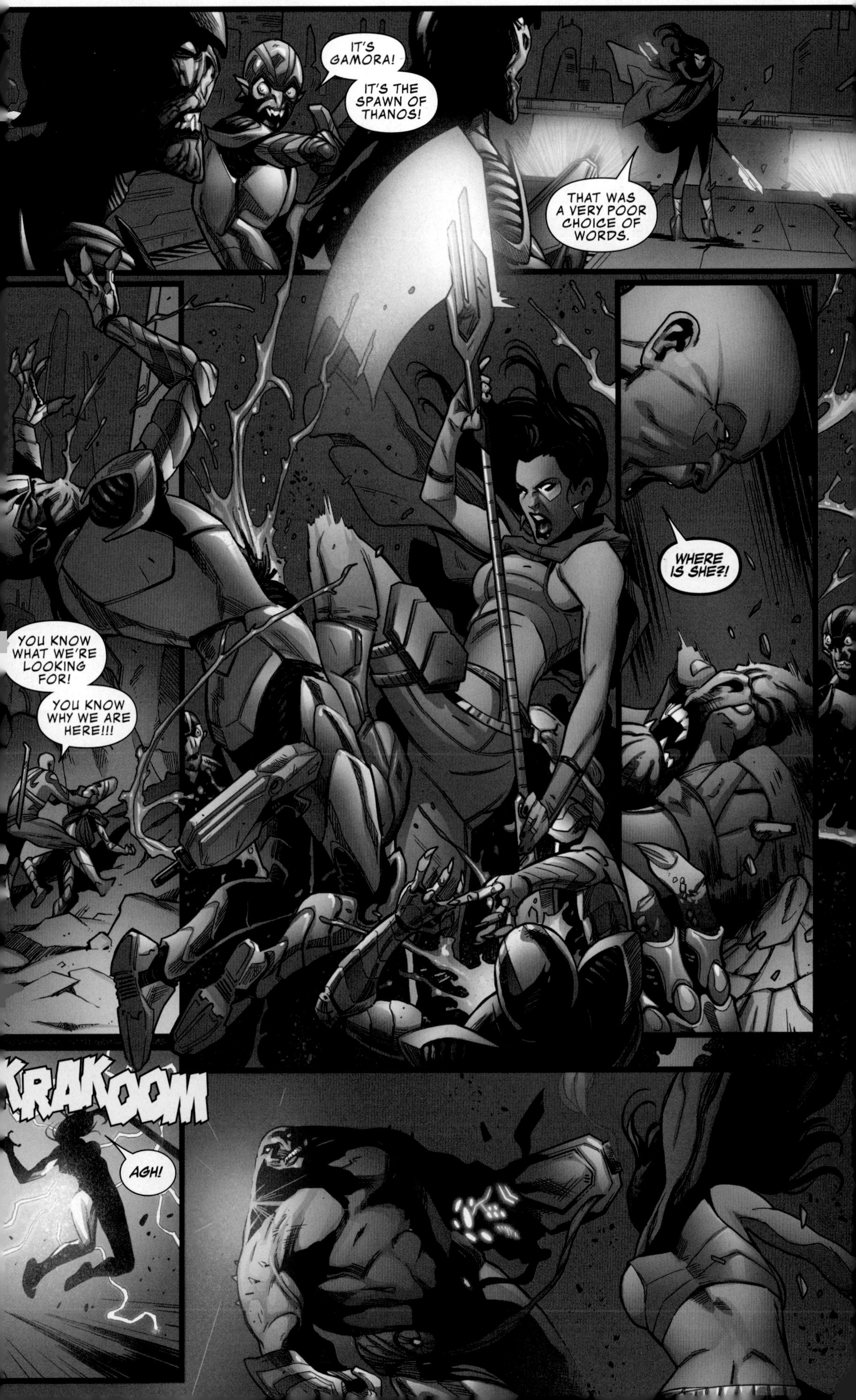

IT'S GAMORA!
IT'S THE SPAWN OF THANOS!
THAT WAS A VERY POOR CHOICE OF WORDS.
WHERE IS SHE?!
YOU KNOW WHAT WE'RE LOOKING FOR!
YOU KNOW WHY WE ARE HERE!!!
KRAKOOM
AGH!

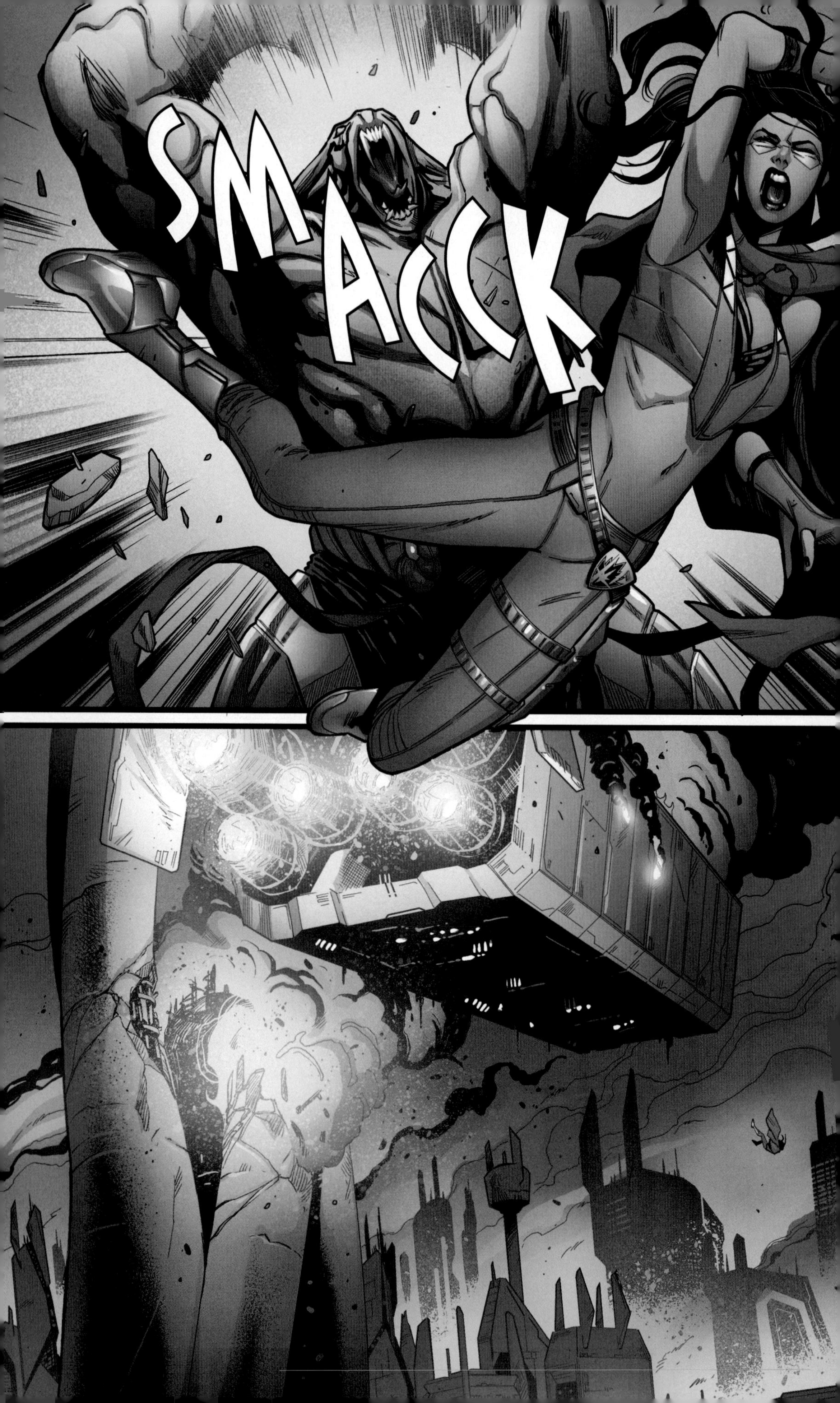
SMACCK

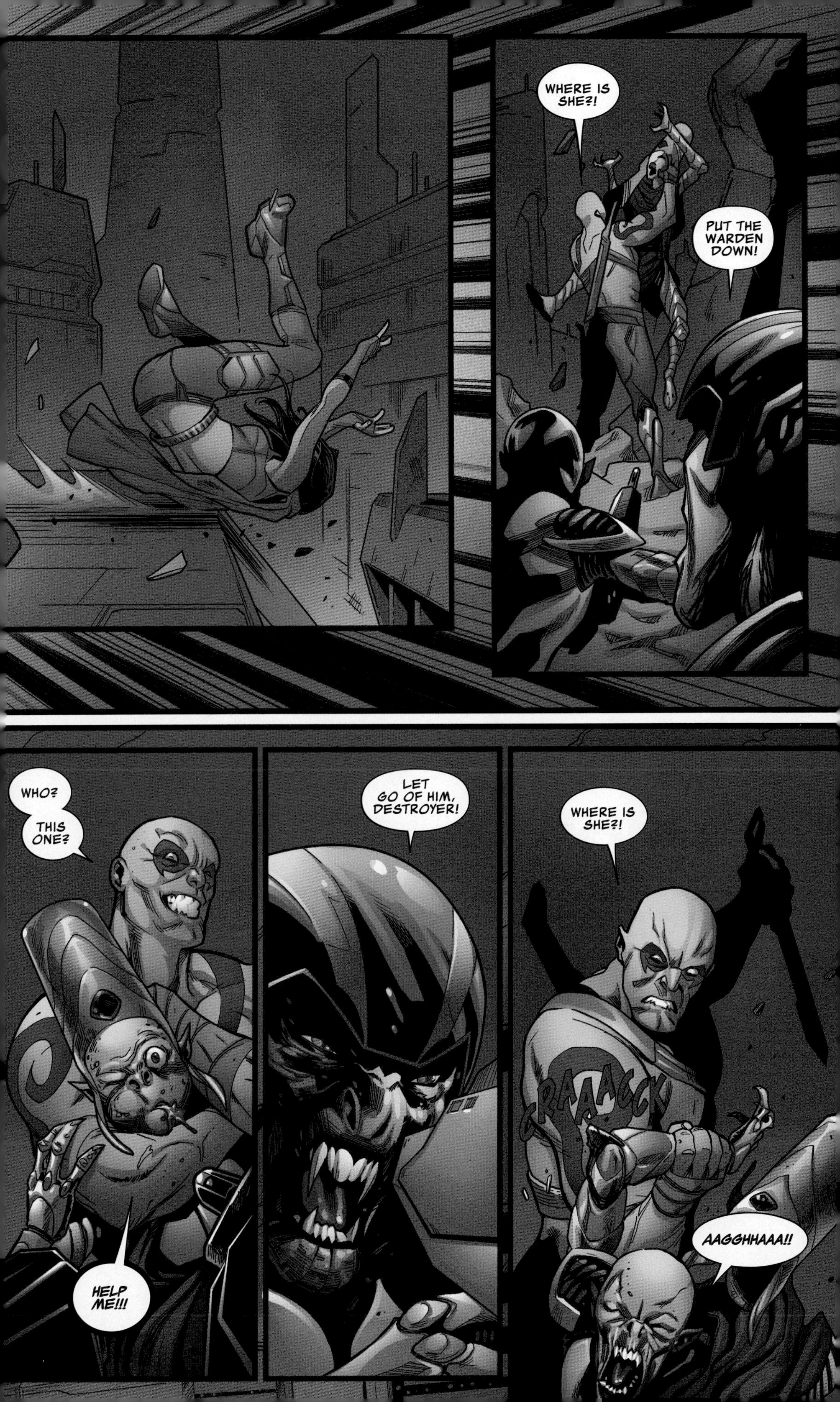
WHERE IS SHE?!
PUT THE WARDEN DOWN!
WHO?
THIS ONE?
HELP ME!!!
LET GO OF HIM, DESTROYER!
WHERE IS SHE?!
GRAAACK
AAGGHHAAA!!

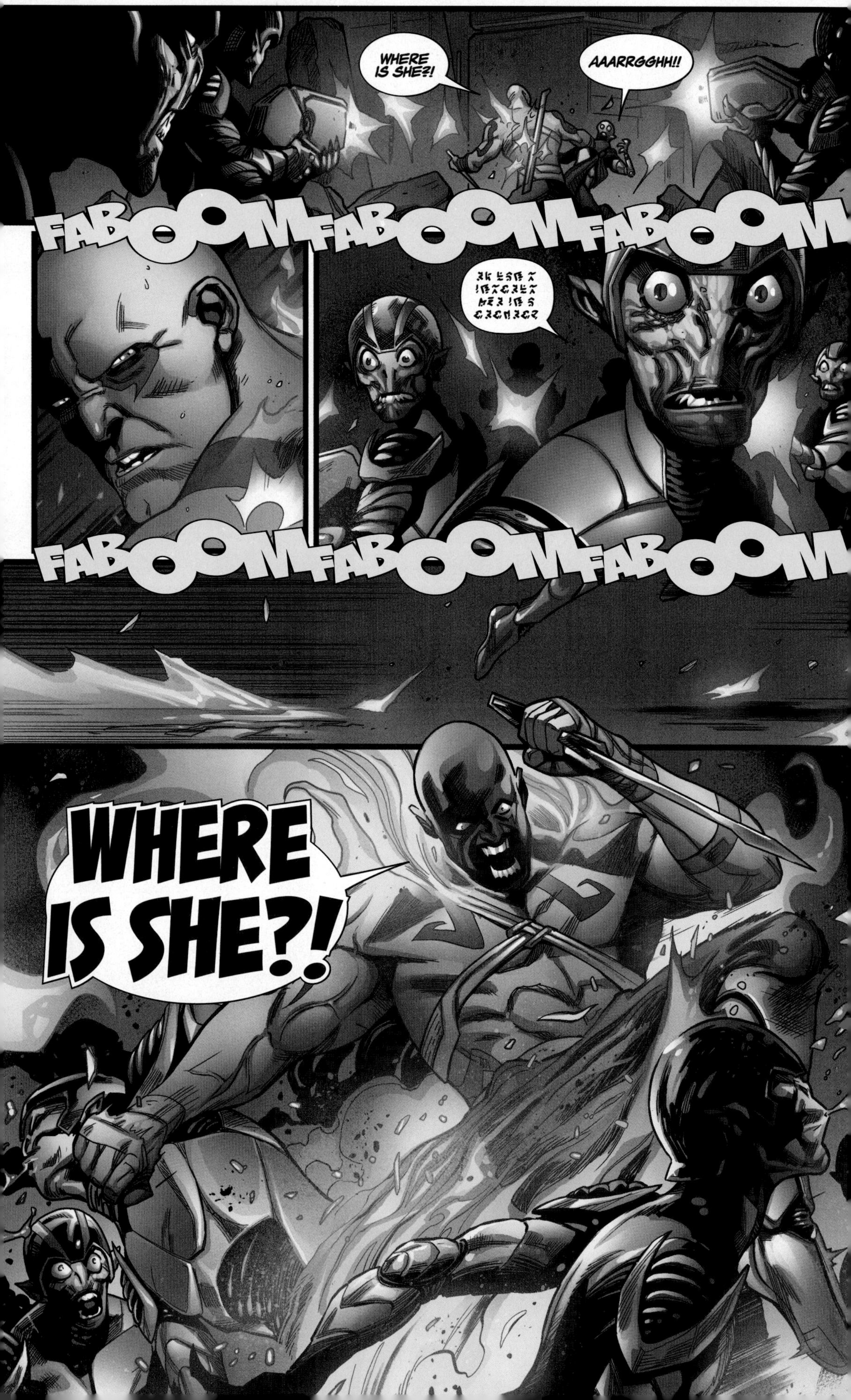
WHERE IS SHE?!
AAARRGGHH!!
FABOOM FABOOM FABOOM
FABOOM FABOOM FABOOM
WHERE IS SHE?!

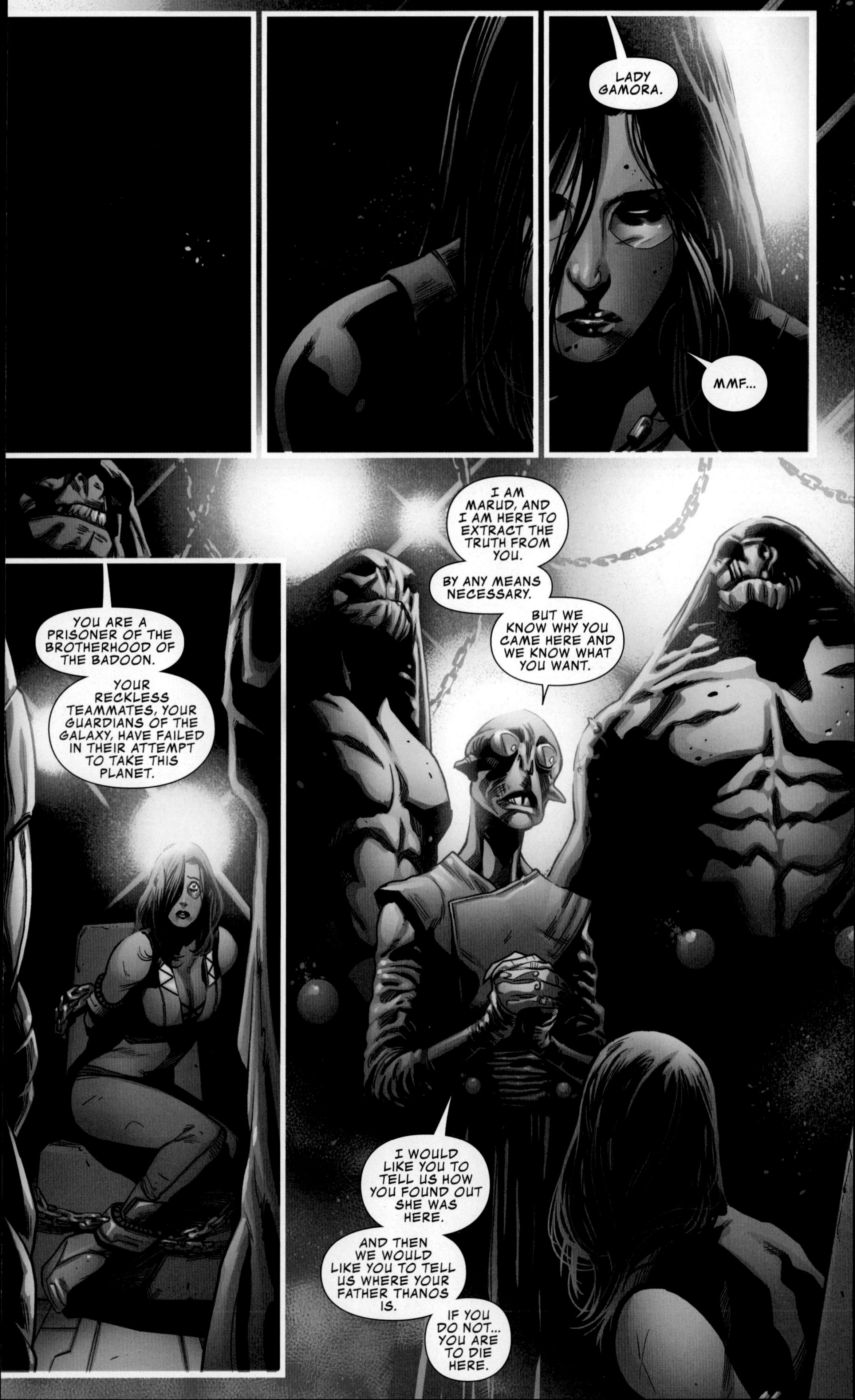
LADY GAMORA.
MMF...
YOU ARE A PRISONER OF THE BROTHERHOOD OF THE BADOON.
YOUR RECKLESS TEAMMATES, YOUR GUARDIANS OF THE GALAXY, HAVE FAILED IN THEIR ATTEMPT TO TAKE THIS PLANET.
I AM MARUD, AND I AM HERE TO EXTRACT THE TRUTH FROM YOU.
BY ANY MEANS NECESSARY.
BUT WE KNOW WHY YOU CAME HERE AND WE KNOW WHAT YOU WANT.
I WOULD LIKE YOU TO TELL US HOW YOU FOUND OUT SHE WAS HERE.
AND THEN WE WOULD LIKE YOU TO TELL US WHERE YOUR FATHER THANOS IS.
IF YOU DO NOT... YOU ARE TO DIE HERE.

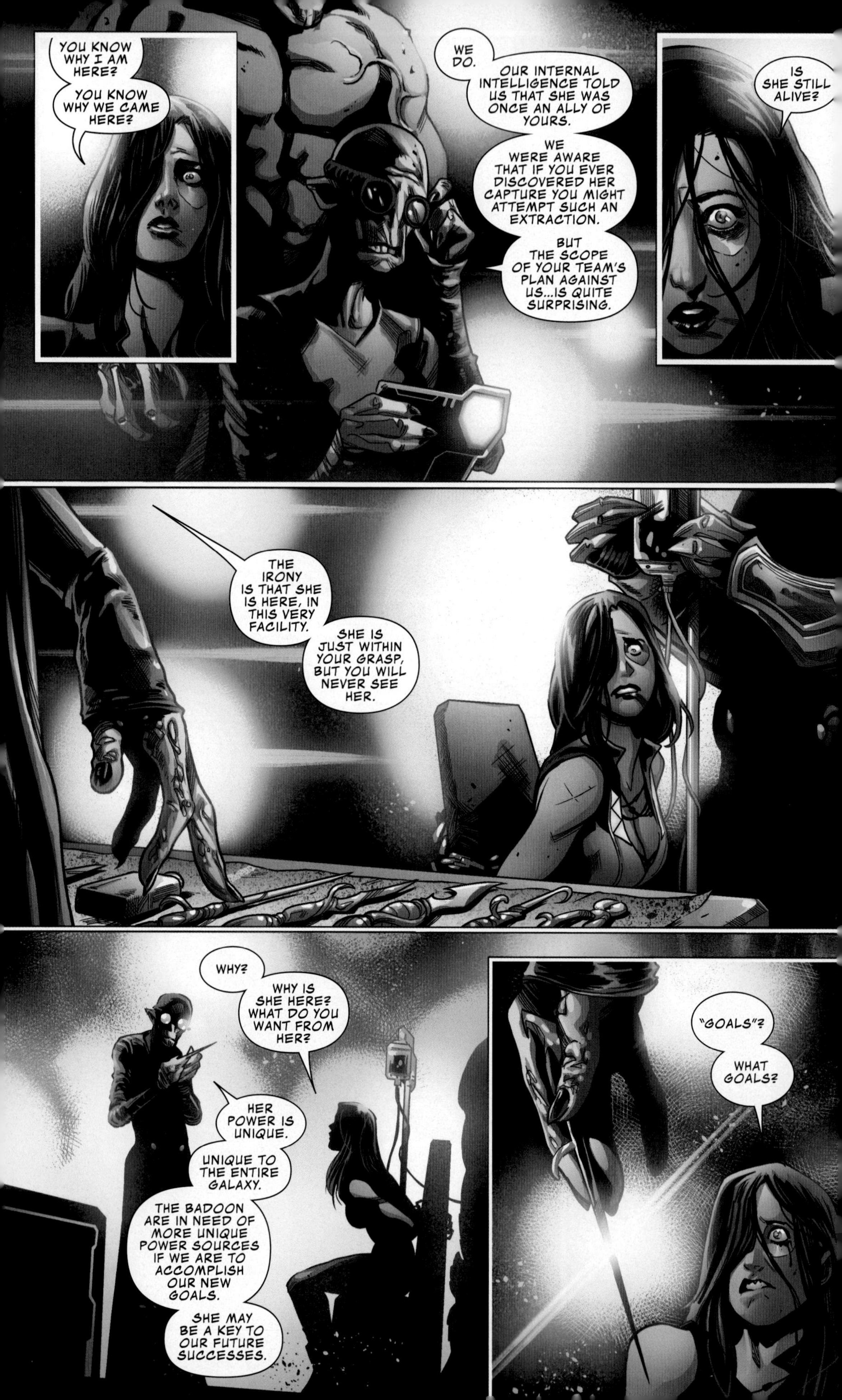
YOU KNOW WHY I AM HERE?
YOU KNOW WHY WE CAME HERE?
WE DO.
OUR INTERNAL INTELLIGENCE TOLD US THAT SHE WAS ONCE AN ALLY OF YOURS.
WE WERE AWARE THAT IF YOU EVER DISCOVERED HER CAPTURE YOU MIGHT ATTEMPT SUCH AN EXTRACTION.
BUT THE SCOPE OF YOUR TEAM'S PLAN AGAINST US...IS QUITE SURPRISING.
IS SHE STILL ALIVE?
THE IRONY IS THAT SHE IS HERE, IN THIS VERY FACILITY.
SHE IS JUST WITHIN YOUR GRASP, BUT YOU WILL NEVER SEE HER.
WHY?
WHY IS SHE HERE? WHAT DO YOU WANT FROM HER?
HER POWER IS UNIQUE.
UNIQUE TO THE ENTIRE GALAXY.
THE BADOON ARE IN NEED OF MORE UNIQUE POWER SOURCES IF WE ARE TO ACCOMPLISH OUR NEW GOALS.
SHE MAY BE A KEY TO OUR FUTURE SUCCESSES.
"GOALS"?
WHAT GOALS?

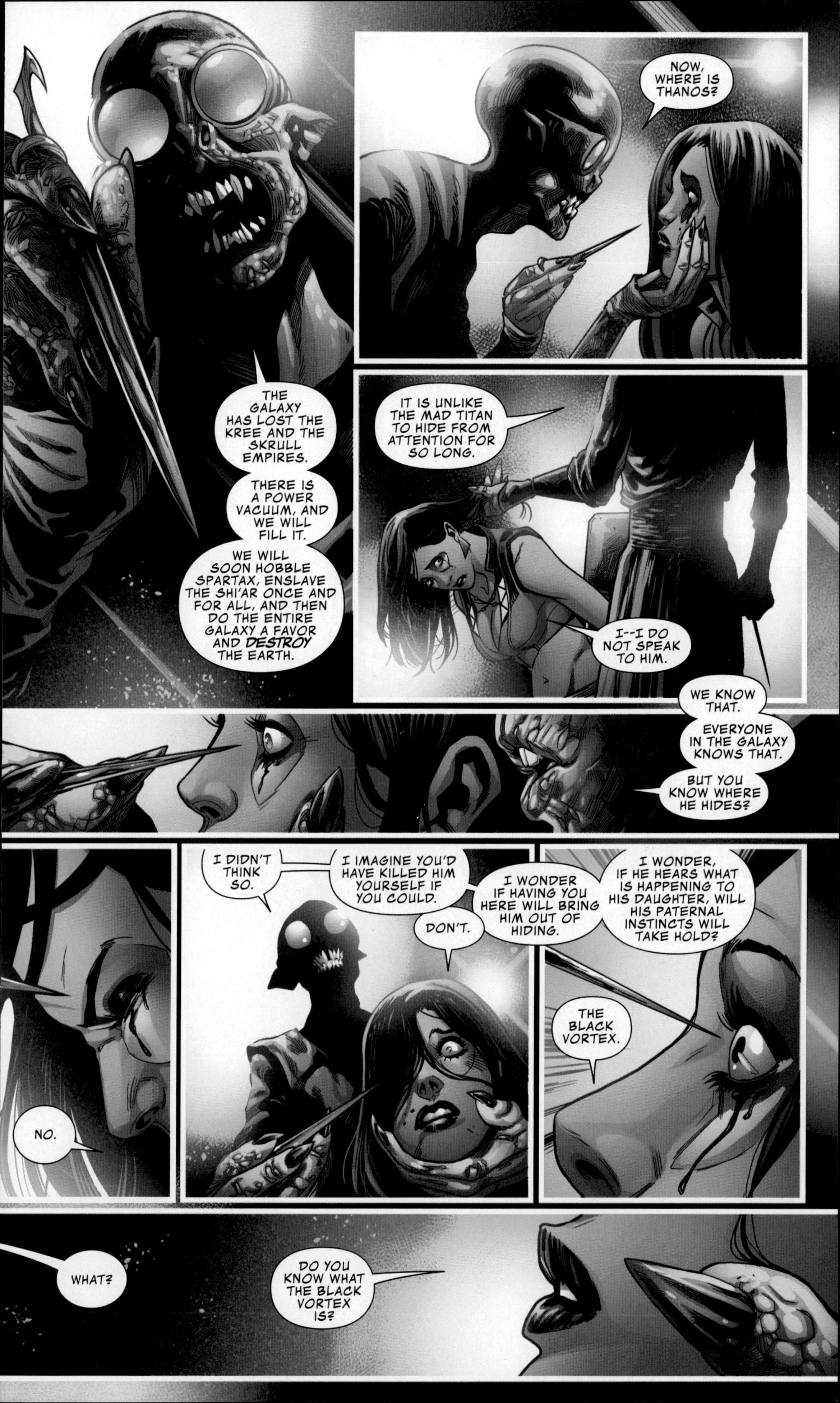

NOW, WHERE IS THANOS?
THE GALAXY HAS LOST THE KREE AND THE SKRULL EMPIRES.
THERE IS A POWER VACUUM, AND WE WILL FILL IT.
WE WILL SOON HOBBLE SPARTAX, ENSLAVE THE SHI'AR ONCE AND FOR ALL, AND THEN DO THE ENTIRE GALAXY A FAVOR AND *DESTROY* THE EARTH.
IT IS UNLIKE THE MAD TITAN TO HIDE FROM ATTENTION FOR SO LONG.
I--I DO NOT SPEAK TO HIM.
WE KNOW THAT.
EVERYONE IN THE GALAXY KNOWS THAT.
BUT YOU KNOW WHERE HE HIDES?
NO.
I DIDN'T THINK SO.
I IMAGINE YOU'D HAVE KILLED HIM YOURSELF IF YOU COULD.
DON'T.
I WONDER IF HAVING YOU HERE WILL BRING HIM OUT OF HIDING.
I WONDER, IF HE HEARS WHAT IS HAPPENING TO HIS DAUGHTER, WILL HIS PATERNAL INSTINCTS WILL TAKE HOLD?
THE BLACK VORTEX.
WHAT?
DO YOU KNOW WHAT THE BLACK VORTEX IS?

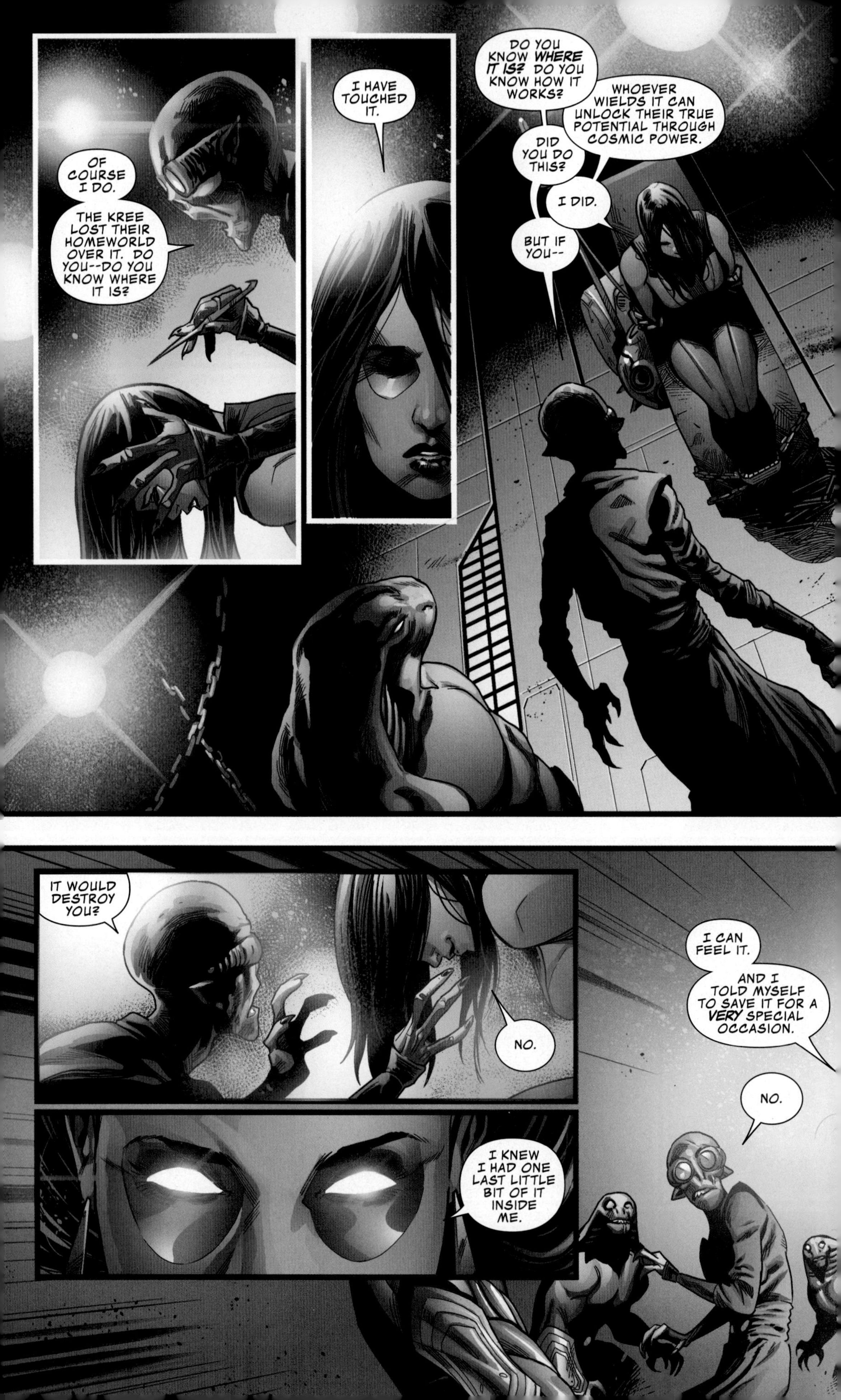

OF COURSE I DO.
THE KREE LOST THEIR HOMEWORLD OVER IT. DO YOU--DO YOU KNOW WHERE IT IS?
I HAVE TOUCHED IT.
DO YOU KNOW WHERE IT IS? DO YOU KNOW HOW IT WORKS?
WHOEVER WIELDS IT CAN UNLOCK THEIR TRUE POTENTIAL THROUGH COSMIC POWER.
DID YOU DO THIS?
I DID.
BUT IF YOU--
IT WOULD DESTROY YOU?
NO.
I CAN FEEL IT.
AND I TOLD MYSELF TO SAVE IT FOR A VERY SPECIAL OCCASION.
NO.
I KNEW I HAD ONE LAST LITTLE BIT OF IT INSIDE ME.

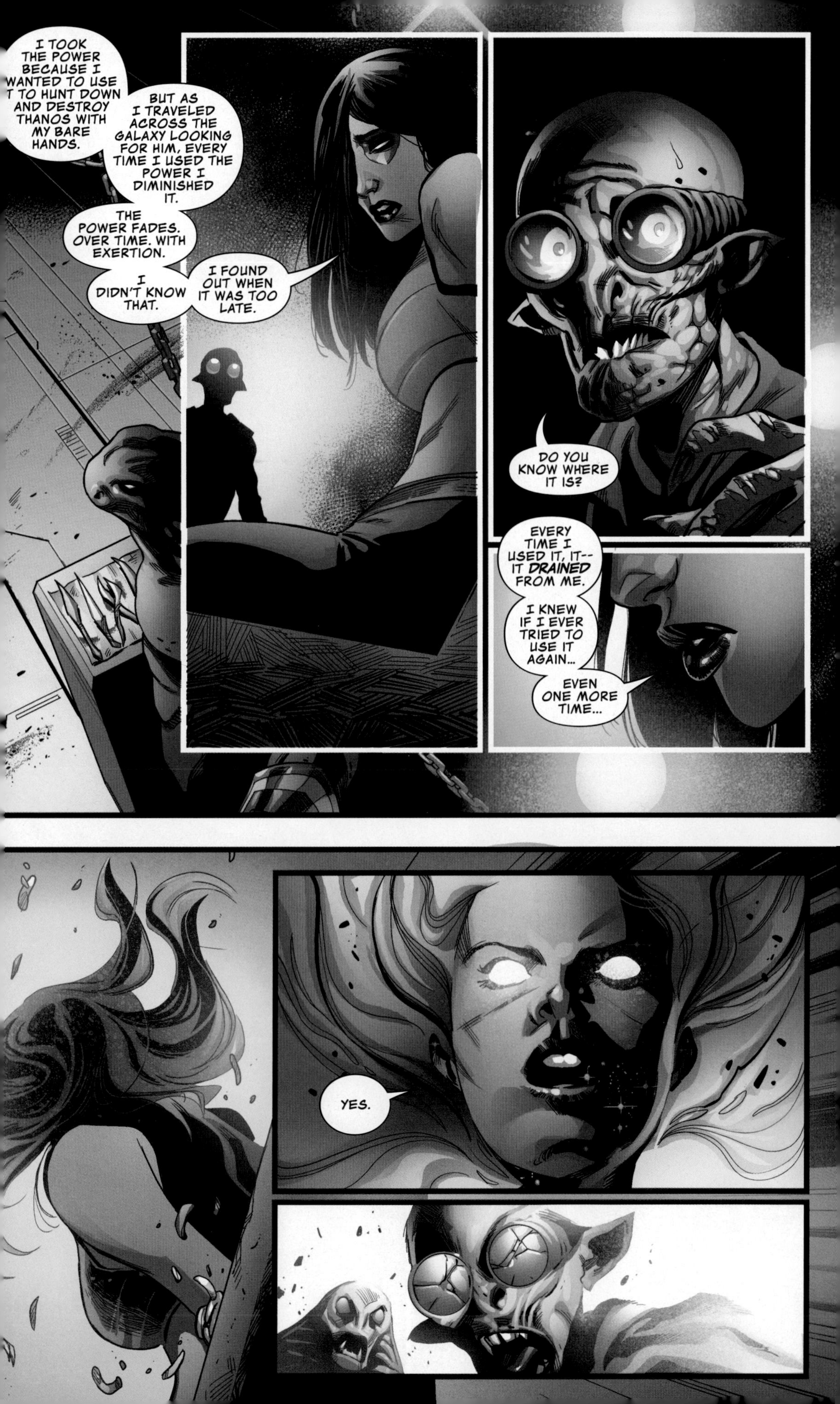

I TOOK THE POWER BECAUSE I WANTED TO USE IT TO HUNT DOWN AND DESTROY THANOS WITH MY BARE HANDS.
BUT AS I TRAVELED ACROSS THE GALAXY LOOKING FOR HIM, EVERY TIME I USED THE POWER I DIMINISHED IT.
THE POWER FADES. OVER TIME. WITH EXERTION.
I DIDN'T KNOW THAT.
I FOUND OUT WHEN IT WAS TOO LATE.
DO YOU KNOW WHERE IT IS?
EVERY TIME I USED IT, IT-- IT DRAINED FROM ME.
I KNEW IF I EVER TRIED TO USE IT AGAIN...
EVEN ONE MORE TIME...
YES.

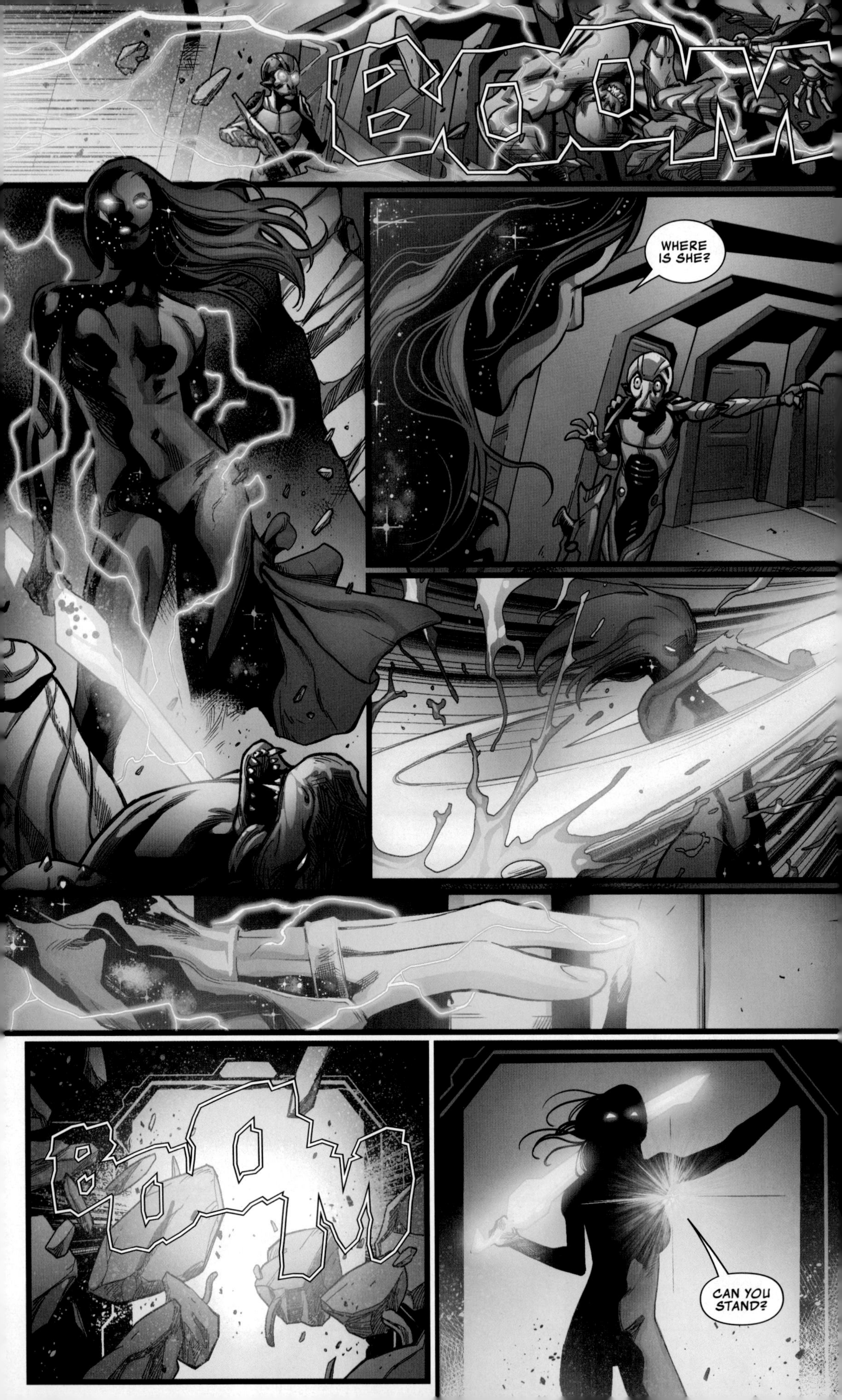
BOOOM
WHERE IS SHE?
BOOM
CAN YOU STAND?

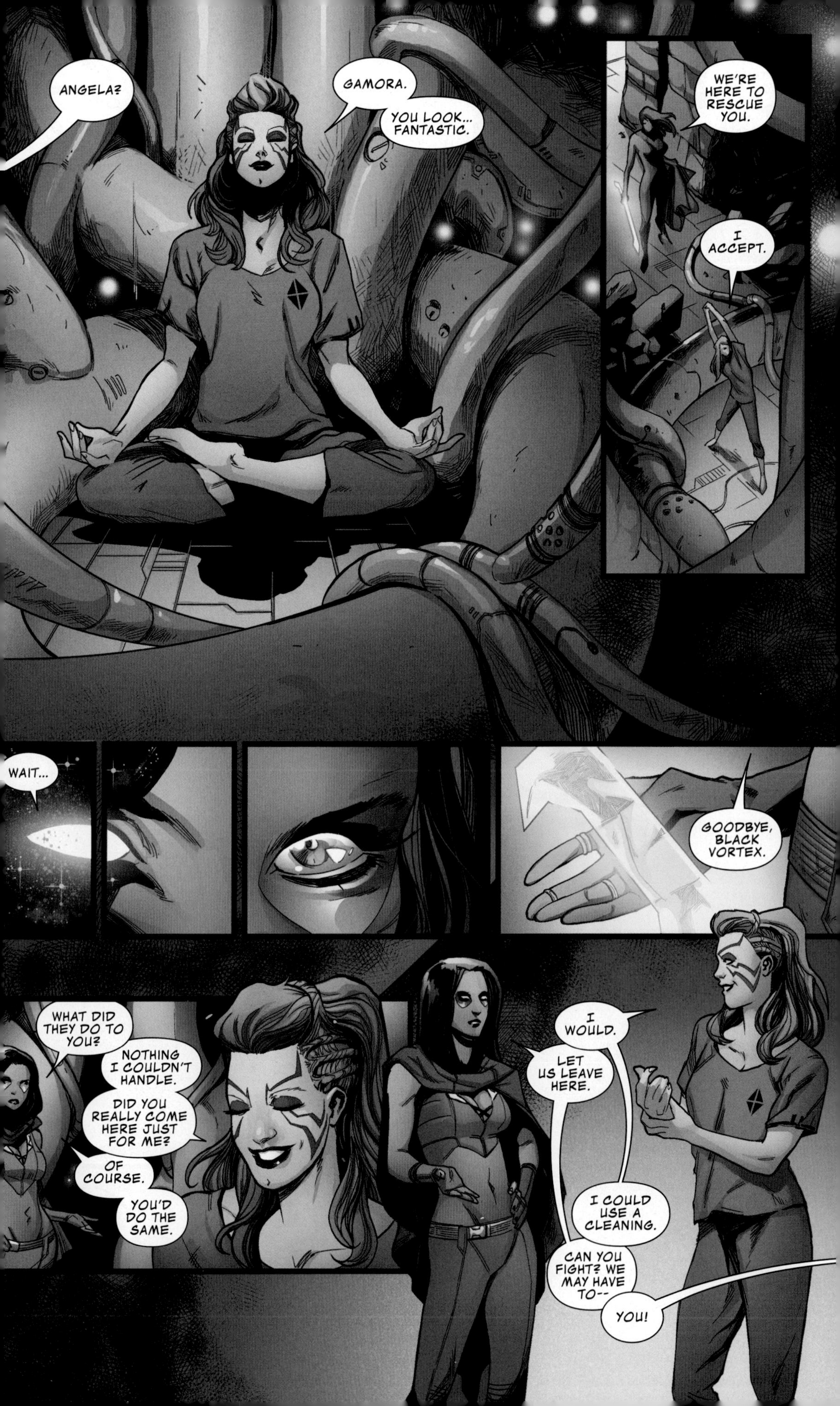
ANGELA?
GAMORA.
YOU LOOK... FANTASTIC.
WE'RE HERE TO RESCUE YOU.
I ACCEPT.
WAIT...
GOODBYE, BLACK VORTEX.
WHAT DID THEY DO TO YOU?
NOTHING I COULDN'T HANDLE.
DID YOU REALLY COME HERE JUST FOR ME?
OF COURSE.
YOU'D DO THE SAME.
I WOULD.
LET US LEAVE HERE.
I COULD USE A CLEANING.
CAN YOU FIGHT? WE MAY HAVE TO--
YOU!

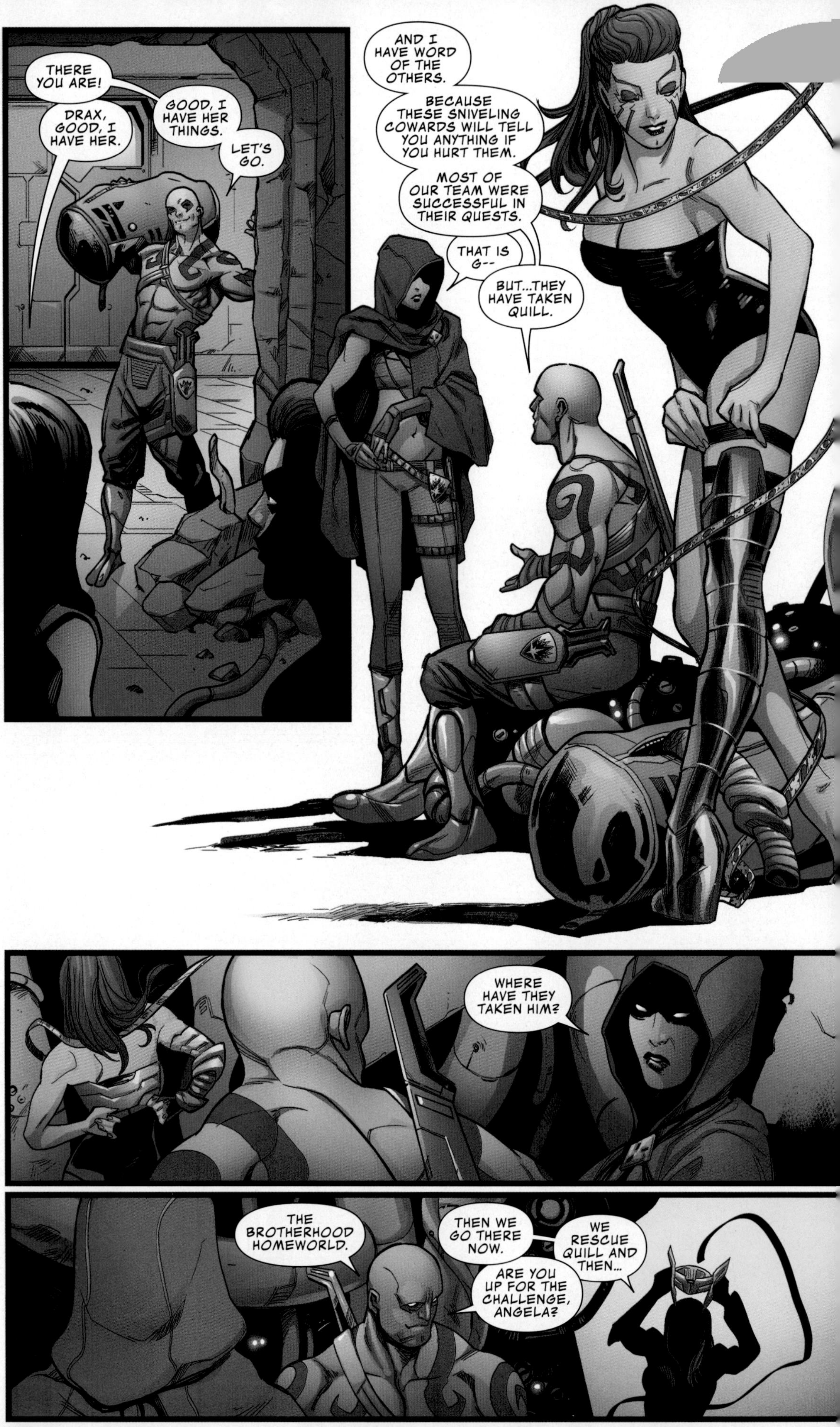
THERE YOU ARE!
DRAX, GOOD, I HAVE HER.
GOOD, I HAVE HER THINGS.
LET'S GO.
AND I HAVE WORD OF THE OTHERS.
BECAUSE THESE SNIVELING COWARDS WILL TELL YOU ANYTHING IF YOU HURT THEM.
MOST OF OUR TEAM WERE SUCCESSFUL IN THEIR QUESTS.
THAT IS G--
BUT...THEY HAVE TAKEN QUILL.
WHERE HAVE THEY TAKEN HIM?
THE BROTHERHOOD HOMEWORLD.
THEN WE GO THERE NOW.
WE RESCUE QUILL AND THEN...
ARE YOU UP FOR THE CHALLENGE, ANGELA?

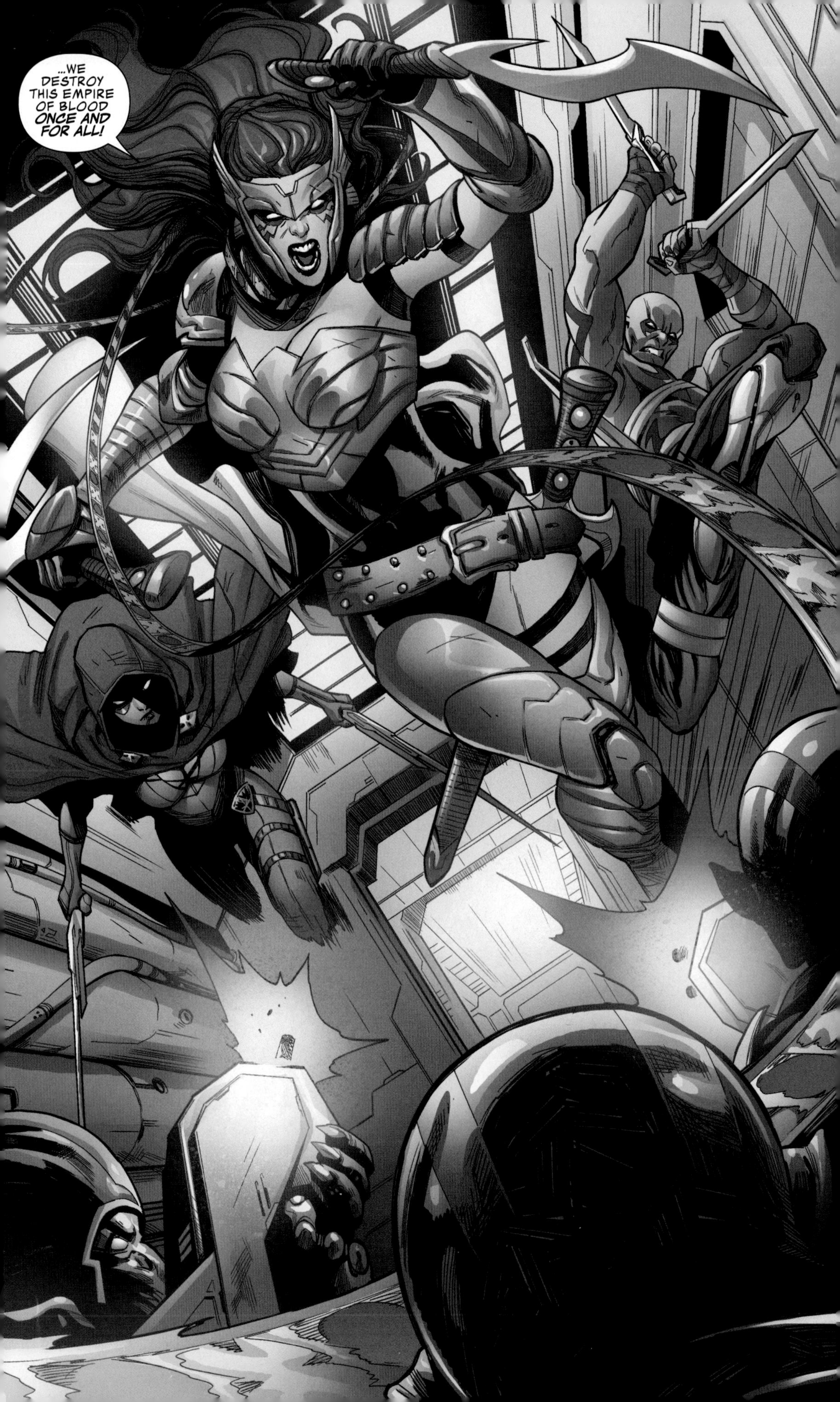
...WE DESTROY THIS EMPIRE OF BLOOD ONCE AND FOR ALL!

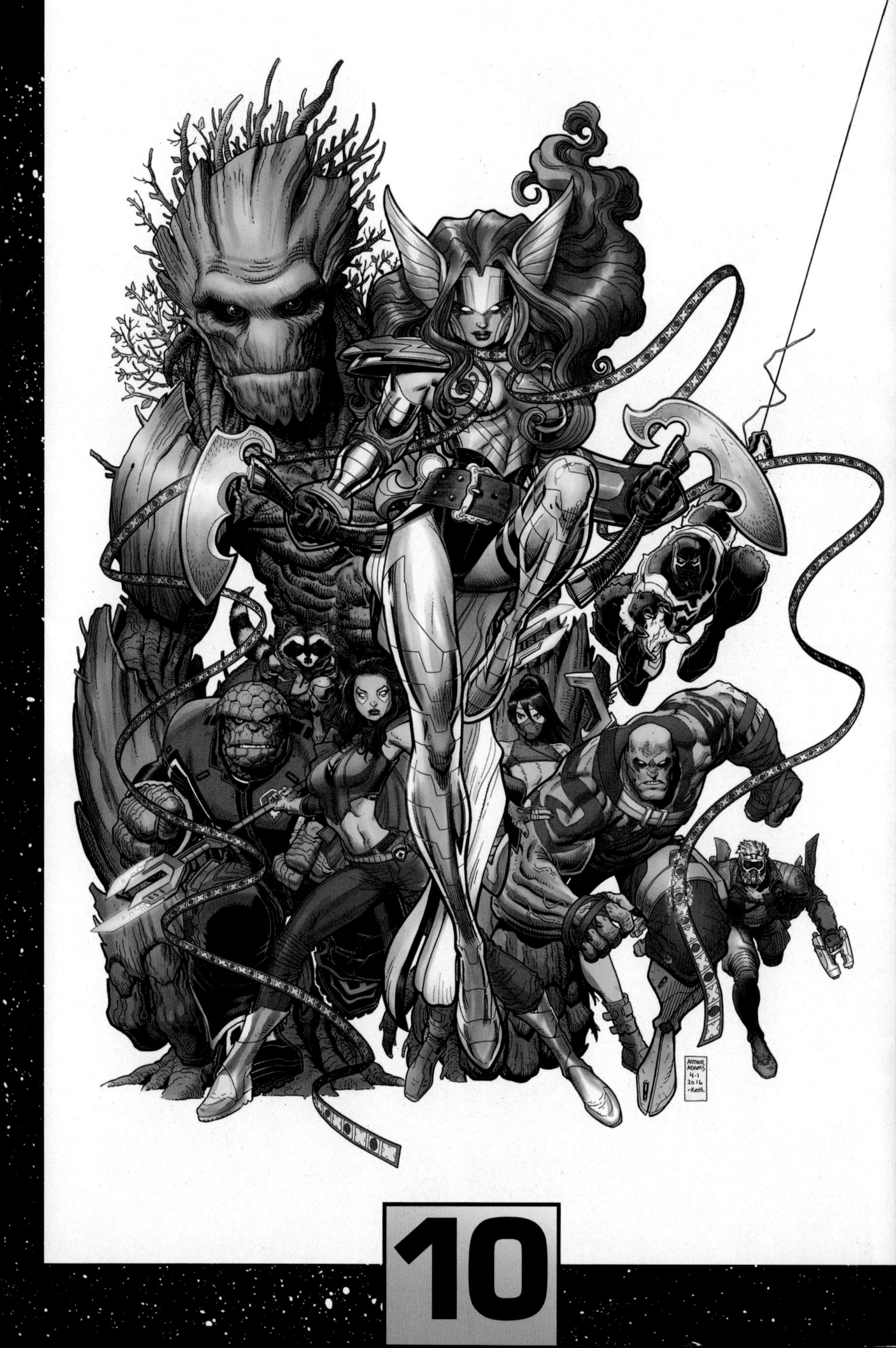
ARTHUR ADAMS 4-1 2016 +Keith

10

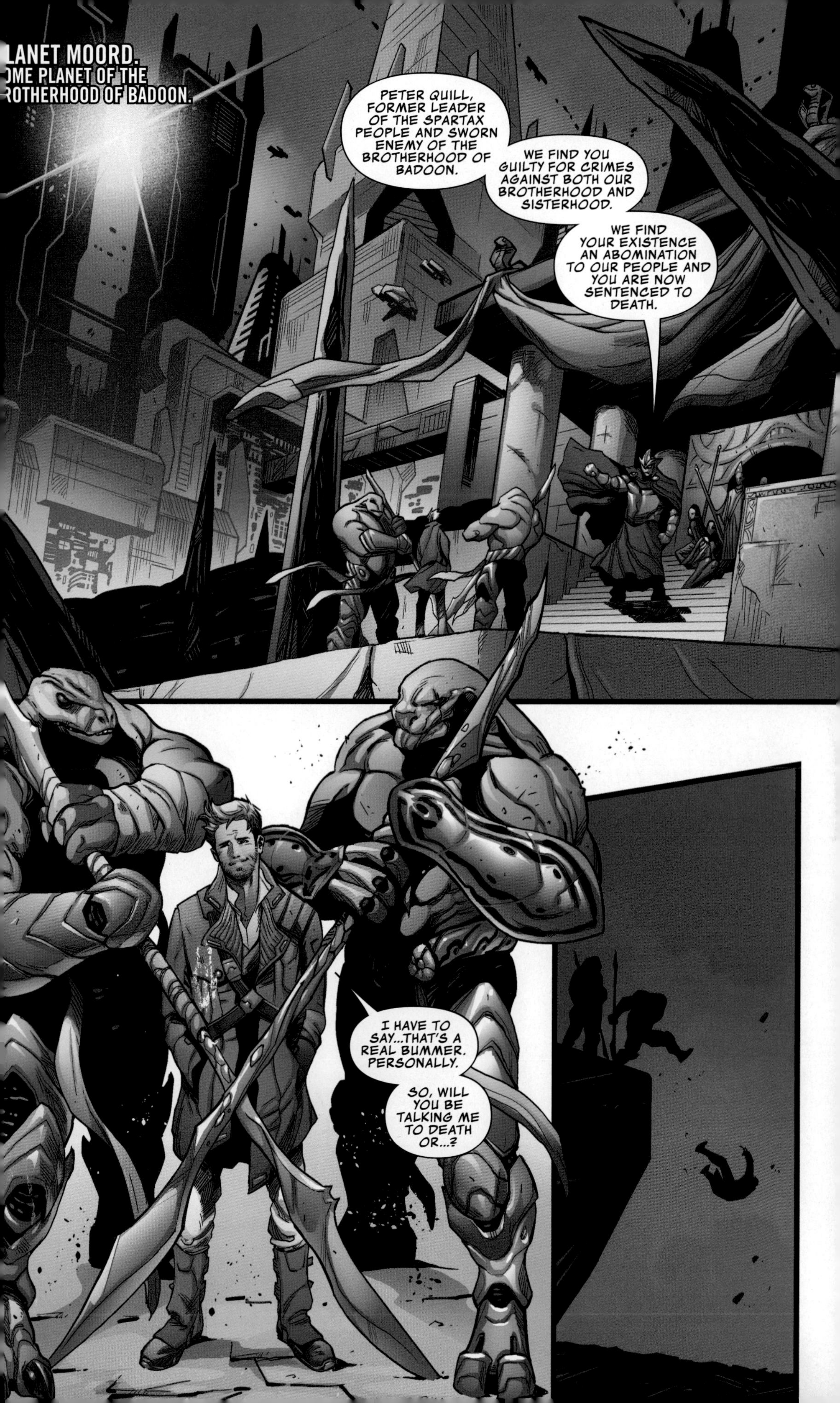
LANET MOORD.
OME PLANET OF THE
ROTHERHOOD OF BADOON.
PETER QUILL, FORMER LEADER OF THE SPARTAX PEOPLE AND SWORN ENEMY OF THE BROTHERHOOD OF BADOON.
WE FIND YOU GUILTY FOR CRIMES AGAINST BOTH OUR BROTHERHOOD AND SISTERHOOD.
WE FIND YOUR EXISTENCE AN ABOMINATION TO OUR PEOPLE AND YOU ARE NOW SENTENCED TO DEATH.
I HAVE TO SAY...THAT'S A REAL BUMMER. PERSONALLY.
SO, WILL YOU BE TALKING ME TO DEATH OR...?

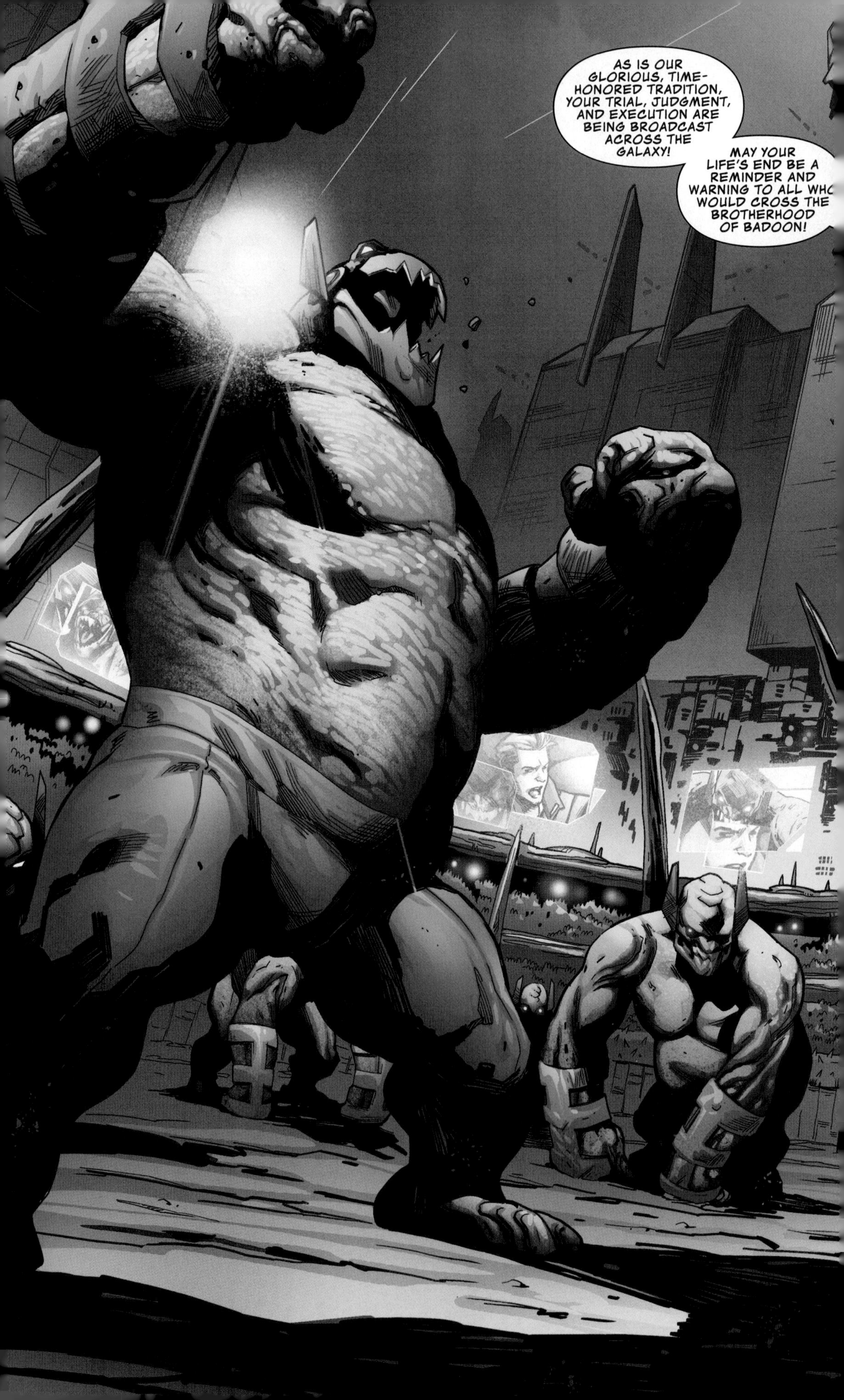
AS IS OUR GLORIOUS, TIME-HONORED TRADITION, YOUR TRIAL, JUDGMENT, AND EXECUTION ARE BEING BROADCAST ACROSS THE GALAXY!
MAY YOUR LIFE'S END BE A REMINDER AND WARNING TO ALL WHO WOULD CROSS THE BROTHERHOOD OF BADOON!

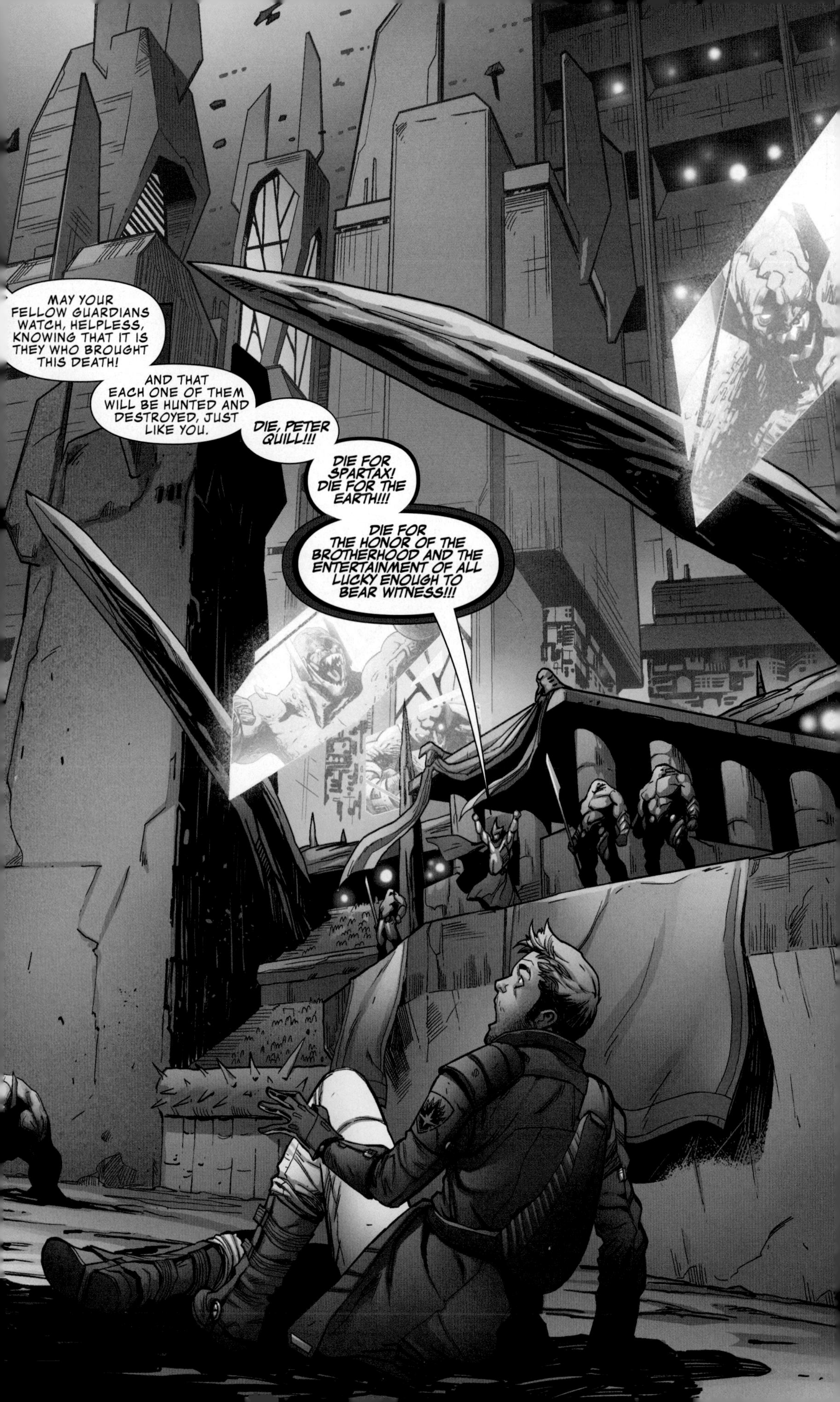
MAY YOUR FELLOW GUARDIANS WATCH, HELPLESS, KNOWING THAT IT IS THEY WHO BROUGHT THIS DEATH!
AND THAT EACH ONE OF THEM WILL BE HUNTED AND DESTROYED, JUST LIKE YOU.
DIE, PETER QUILL!!!
DIE FOR SPARTAX! DIE FOR THE EARTH!!!
DIE FOR THE HONOR OF THE BROTHERHOOD AND THE ENTERTAINMENT OF ALL LUCKY ENOUGH TO BEAR WITNESS!!!

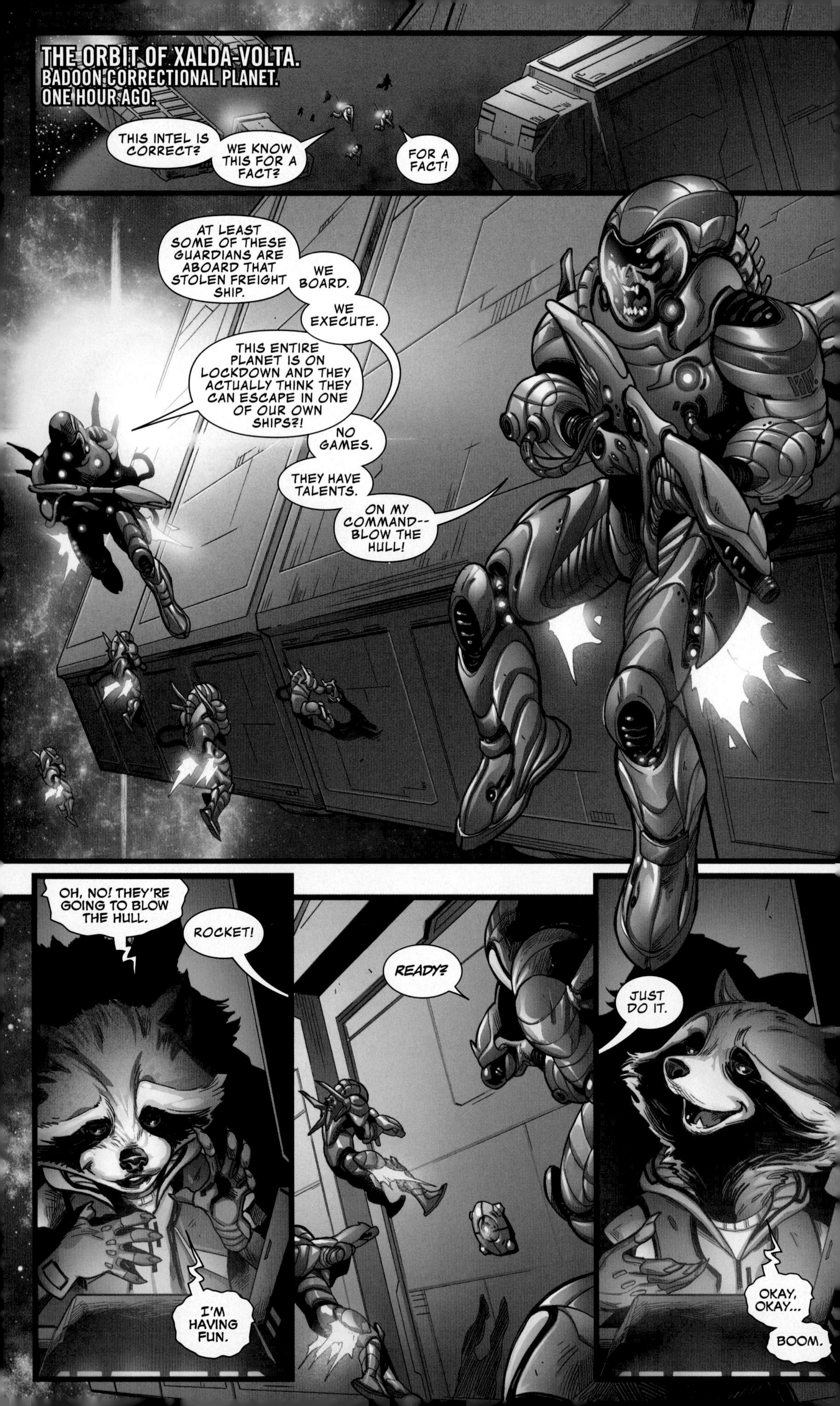
THE ORBIT OF XALDA-VOLTA.
BADOON CORRECTIONAL PLANET.
ONE HOUR AGO.
THIS INTEL IS CORRECT?
WE KNOW THIS FOR A FACT?
FOR A FACT!
AT LEAST SOME OF THESE GUARDIANS ARE ABOARD THAT STOLEN FREIGHT SHIP.
WE BOARD.
WE EXECUTE.
THIS ENTIRE PLANET IS ON LOCKDOWN AND THEY ACTUALLY THINK THEY CAN ESCAPE IN ONE OF OUR OWN SHIPS?!
NO GAMES.
THEY HAVE TALENTS.
ON MY COMMAND-- BLOW THE HULL!
OH, NO! THEY'RE GOING TO BLOW THE HULL.
ROCKET!
I'M HAVING FUN.
READY?
JUST DO IT.
OKAY, OKAY...
BOOM.

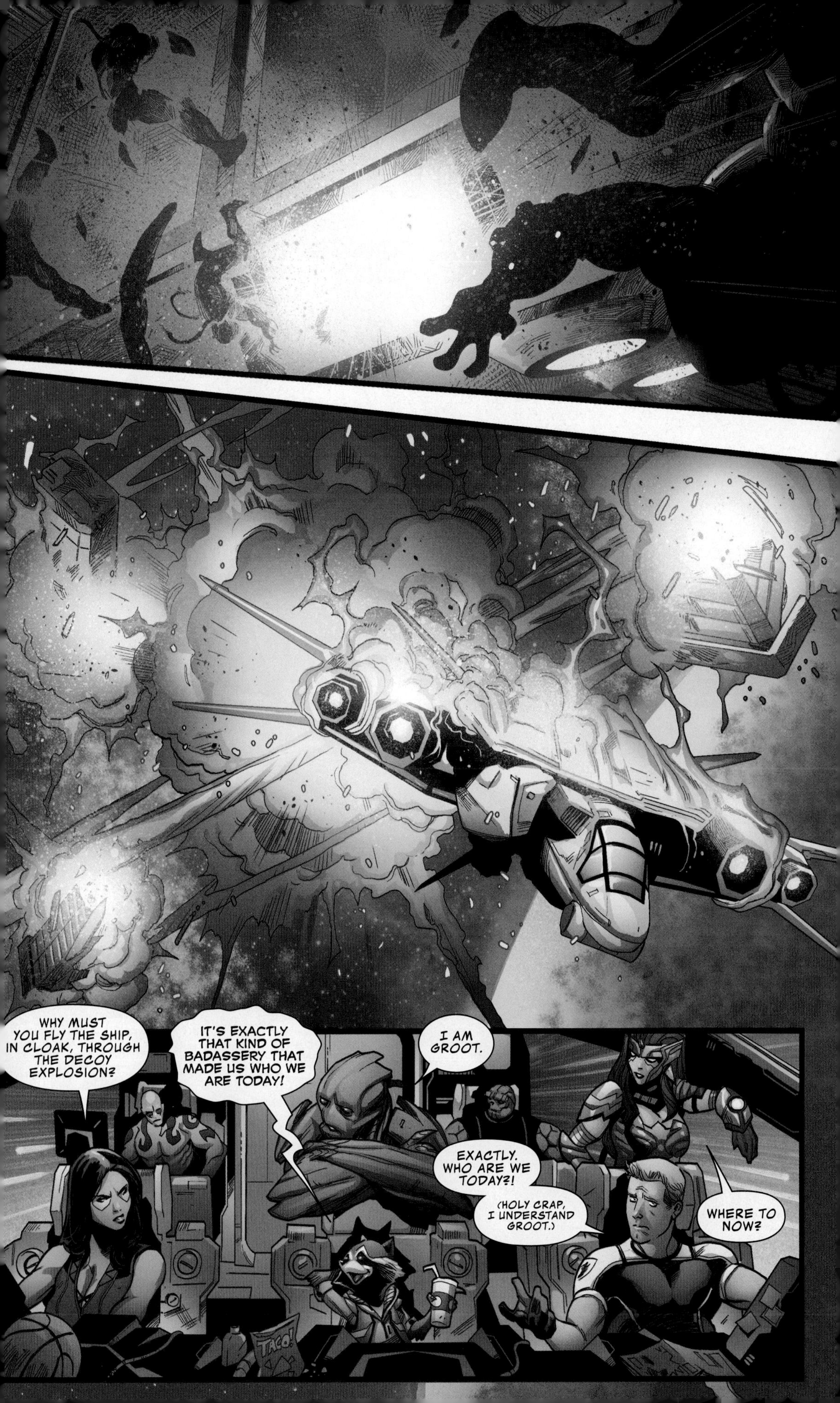
WHY MUST YOU FLY THE SHIP, IN CLOAK, THROUGH THE DECOY EXPLOSION?
IT'S EXACTLY THAT KIND OF BADASSERY THAT MADE US WHO WE ARE TODAY!
I AM GROOT.
EXACTLY. WHO ARE WE TODAY?!
(HOLY CRAP, I UNDERSTAND GROOT.)
WHERE TO NOW?
TACO!

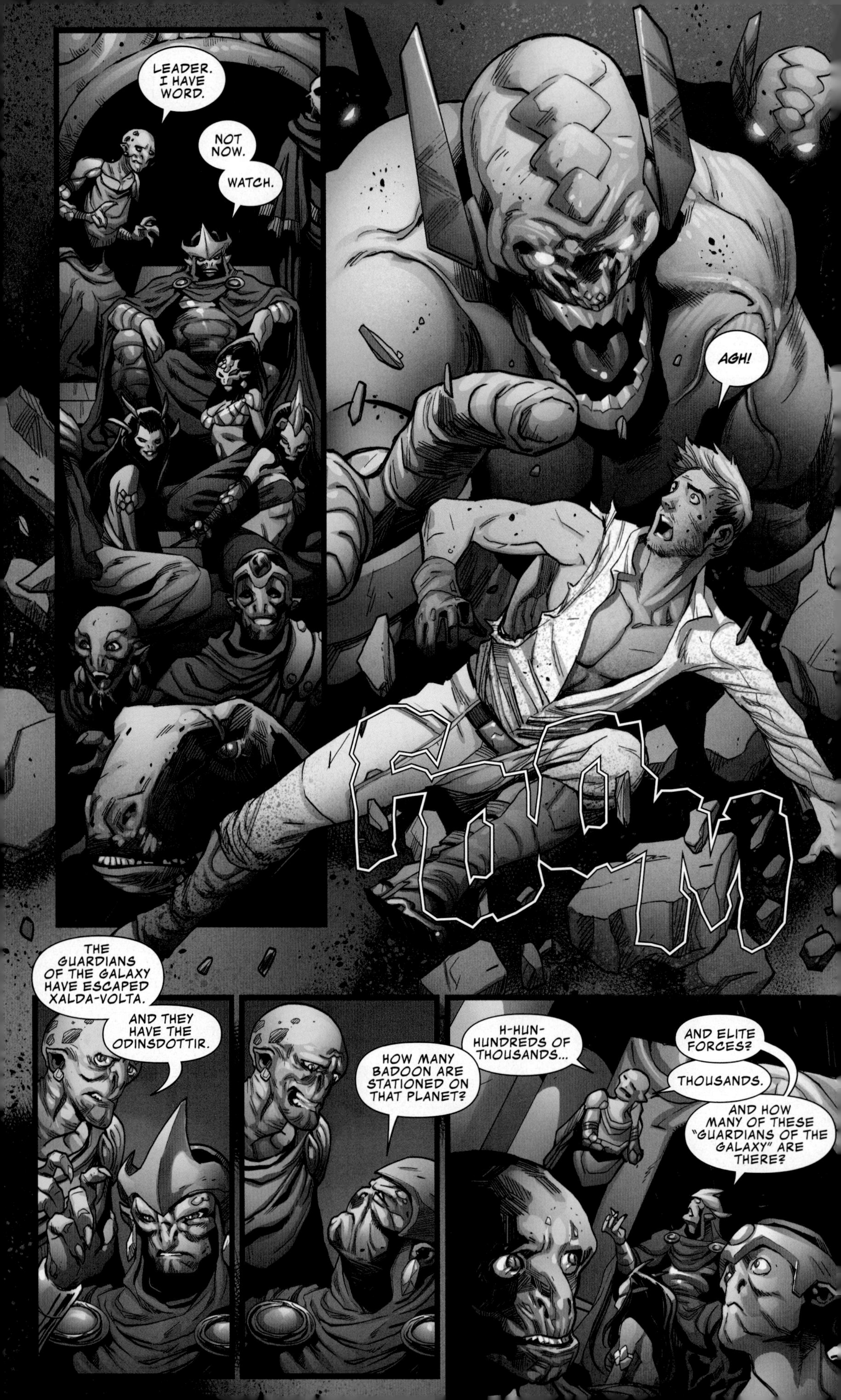
LEADER. I HAVE WORD.
NOT NOW.
WATCH.
AGH!
THE GUARDIANS OF THE GALAXY HAVE ESCAPED XALDA-VOLTA.
AND THEY HAVE THE ODINSDOTTIR.
HOW MANY BADOON ARE STATIONED ON THAT PLANET?
H-HUN-HUNDREDS OF THOUSANDS...
AND ELITE FORCES?
THOUSANDS.
AND HOW MANY OF THESE "GUARDIANS OF THE GALAXY" ARE THERE?

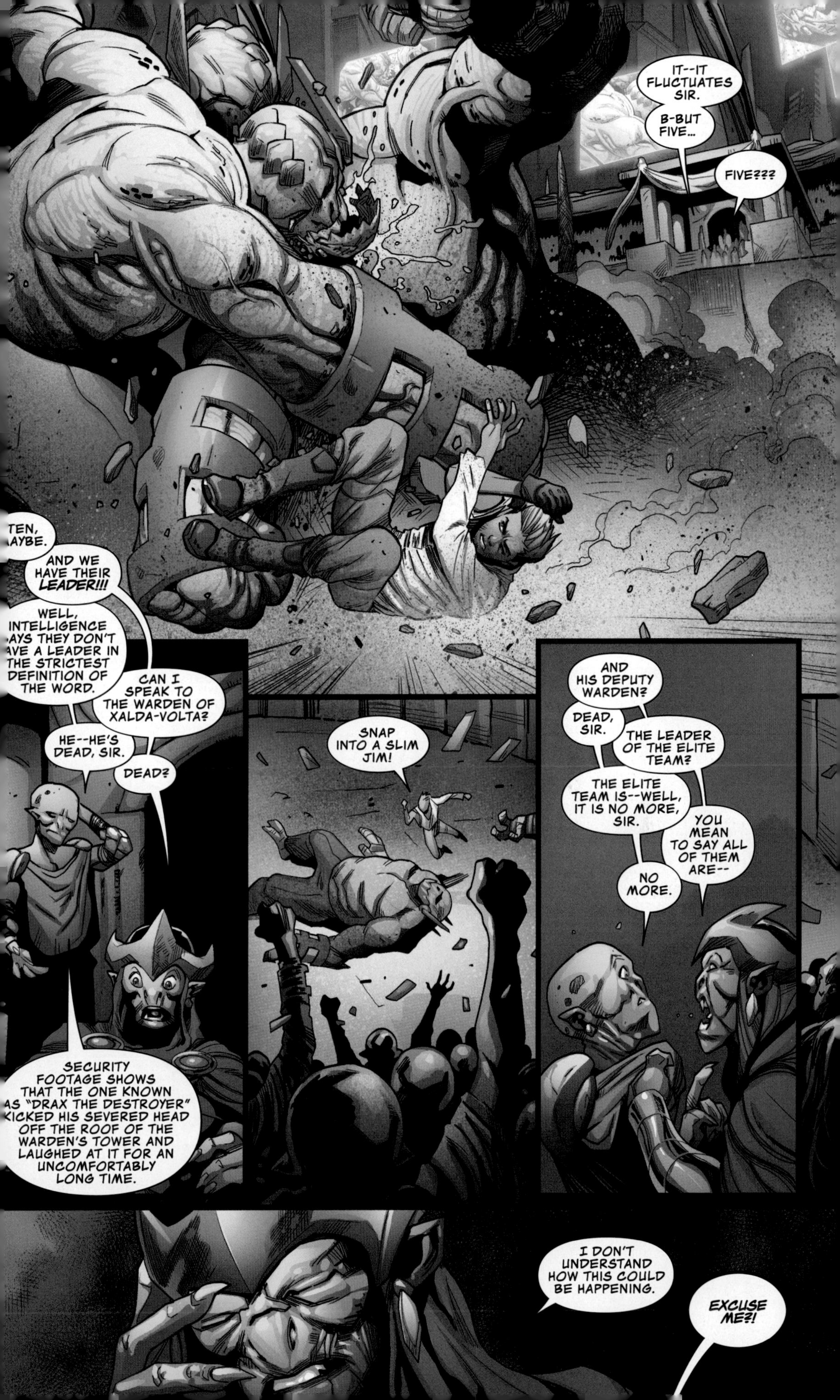
IT--IT FLUCTUATES SIR.
B-BUT FIVE...
FIVE???
TEN, MAYBE.
AND WE HAVE THEIR LEADER!!!
WELL, INTELLIGENCE SAYS THEY DON'T HAVE A LEADER IN THE STRICTEST DEFINITION OF THE WORD.
CAN I SPEAK TO THE WARDEN OF XALDA-VOLTA?
HE--HE'S DEAD, SIR.
DEAD?
SECURITY FOOTAGE SHOWS THAT THE ONE KNOWN AS "DRAX THE DESTROYER" KICKED HIS SEVERED HEAD OFF THE ROOF OF THE WARDEN'S TOWER AND LAUGHED AT IT FOR AN UNCOMFORTABLY LONG TIME.
SNAP INTO A SLIM JIM!
AND HIS DEPUTY WARDEN?
DEAD, SIR.
THE LEADER OF THE ELITE TEAM?
THE ELITE TEAM IS--WELL, IT IS NO MORE, SIR.
YOU MEAN TO SAY ALL OF THEM ARE--
NO MORE.
I DON'T UNDERSTAND HOW THIS COULD BE HAPPENING.
EXCUSE ME?!

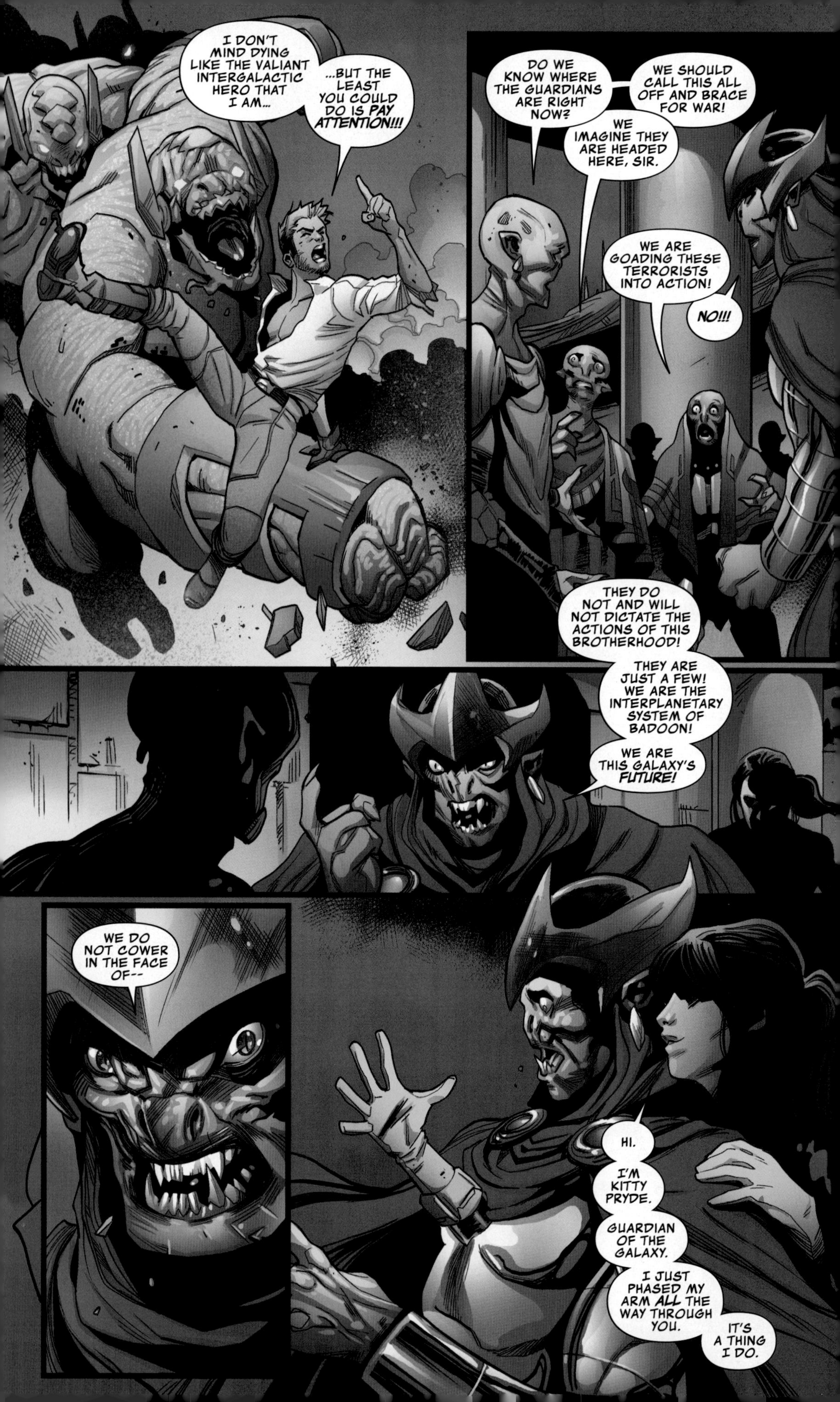

I DON'T MIND DYING LIKE THE VALIANT INTERGALACTIC HERO THAT I AM...
...BUT THE LEAST YOU COULD DO IS PAY ATTENTION!!!
DO WE KNOW WHERE THE GUARDIANS ARE RIGHT NOW?
WE SHOULD CALL THIS ALL OFF AND BRACE FOR WAR!
WE IMAGINE THEY ARE HEADED HERE, SIR.
WE ARE GOADING THESE TERRORISTS INTO ACTION!
NO!!!
THEY DO NOT AND WILL NOT DICTATE THE ACTIONS OF THIS BROTHERHOOD!
THEY ARE JUST A FEW! WE ARE THE INTERPLANETARY SYSTEM OF BADOON!
WE ARE THIS GALAXY'S FUTURE!
WE DO NOT COWER IN THE FACE OF--
HI.
I'M KITTY PRYDE.
GUARDIAN OF THE GALAXY.
I JUST PHASED MY ARM ALL THE WAY THROUGH YOU.
IT'S A THING I DO.

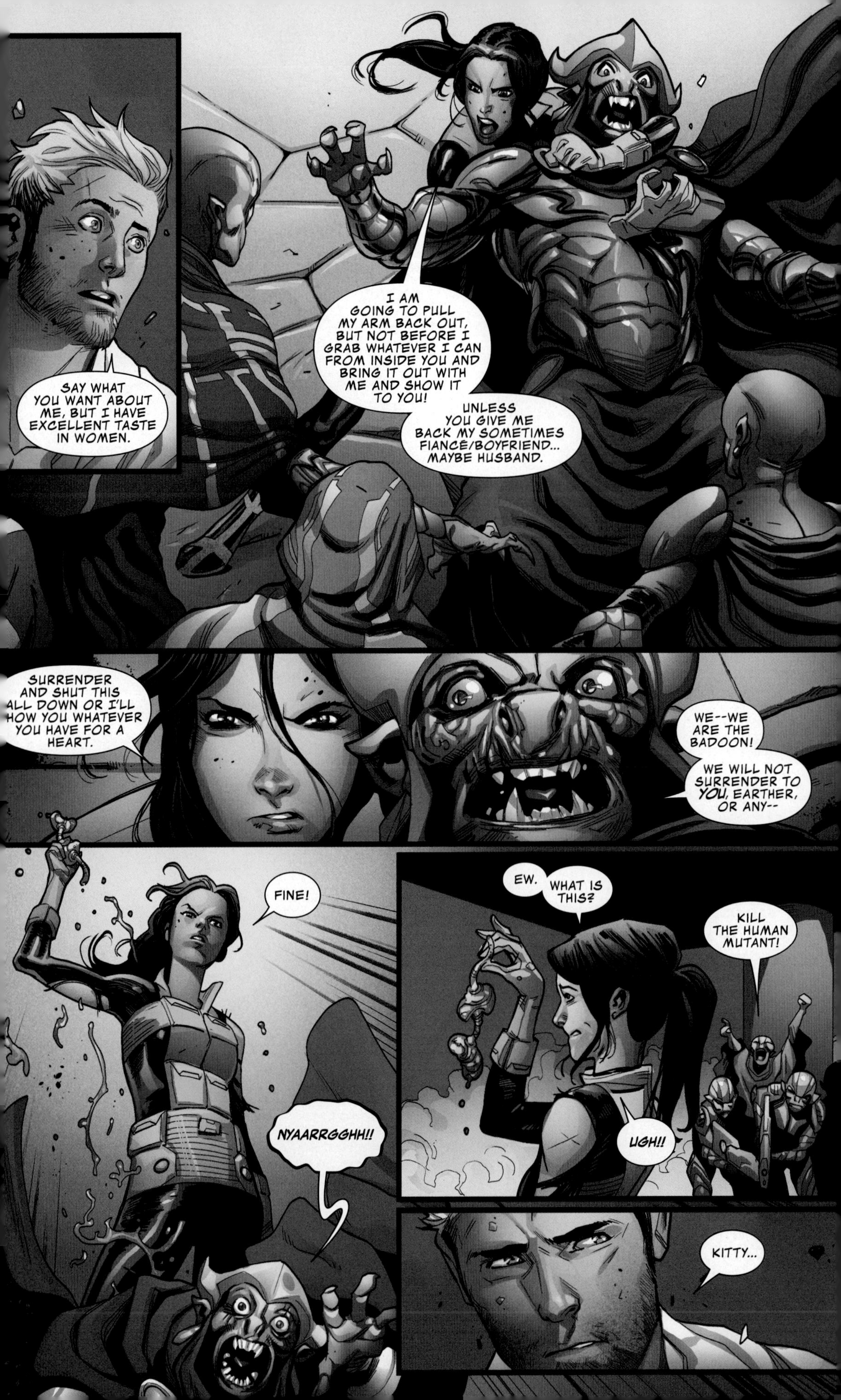
SAY WHAT YOU WANT ABOUT ME, BUT I HAVE EXCELLENT TASTE IN WOMEN.
I AM GOING TO PULL MY ARM BACK OUT, BUT NOT BEFORE I GRAB WHATEVER I CAN FROM INSIDE YOU AND BRING IT OUT WITH ME AND SHOW IT TO YOU!
UNLESS YOU GIVE ME BACK MY SOMETIMES FIANCÉ/BOYFRIEND... MAYBE HUSBAND.
SURRENDER AND SHUT THIS ALL DOWN OR I'LL HOW YOU WHATEVER YOU HAVE FOR A HEART.
WE--WE ARE THE BADOON!
WE WILL NOT SURRENDER TO *YOU*, EARTHER, OR ANY--
FINE!
NYAARRGGHH!!
EW.
WHAT IS THIS?
KILL THE HUMAN MUTANT!
UGH!!
KITTY...

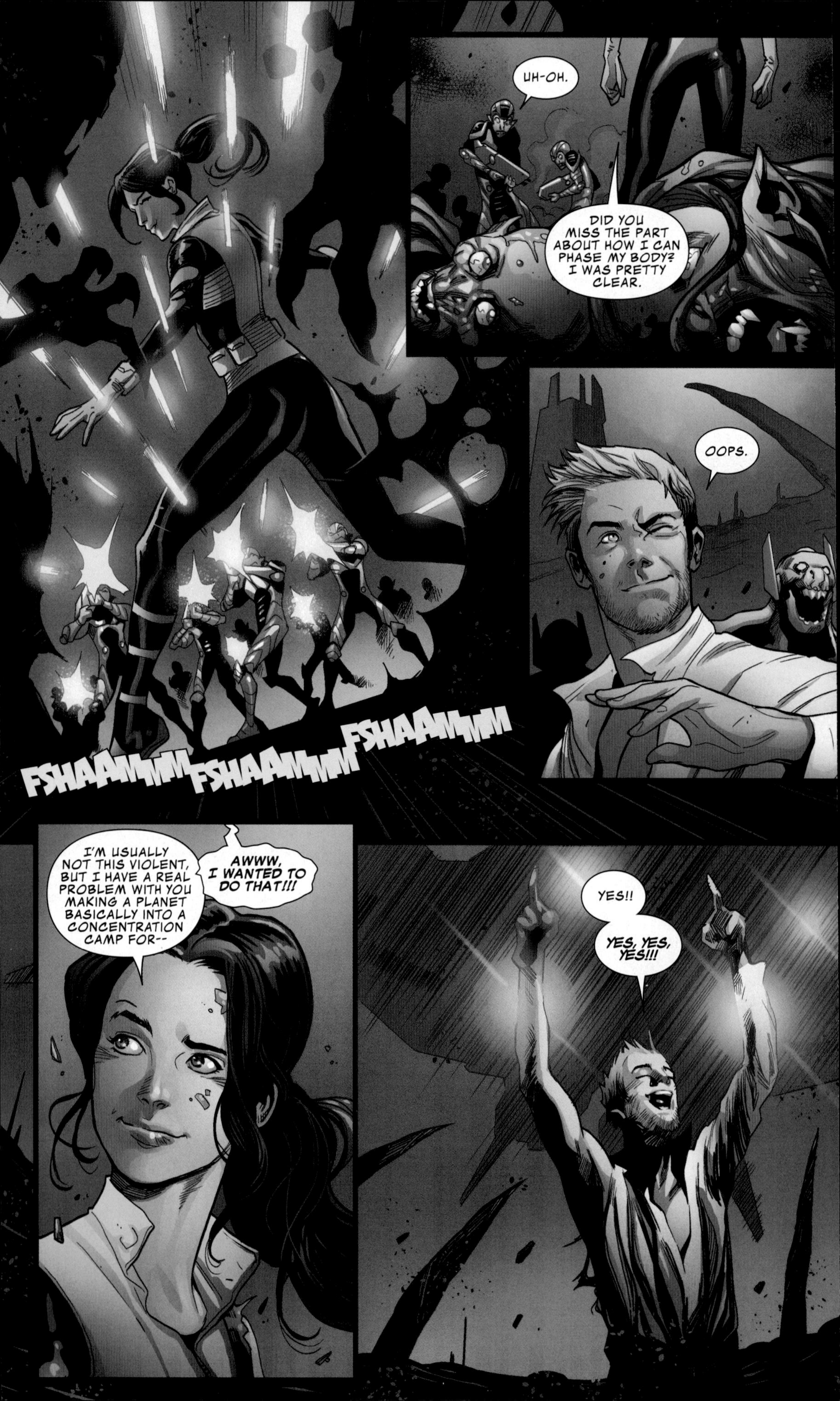
UH-OH.
DID YOU MISS THE PART ABOUT HOW I CAN PHASE MY BODY? I WAS PRETTY CLEAR.
OOPS.
FSHAAMMM FSHAAMMM FSHAAMMM
I'M USUALLY NOT THIS VIOLENT, BUT I HAVE A REAL PROBLEM WITH YOU MAKING A PLANET BASICALLY INTO A CONCENTRATION CAMP FOR--
AWWW, I WANTED TO DO THAT!!!
YES!!
YES, YES, YES!!!

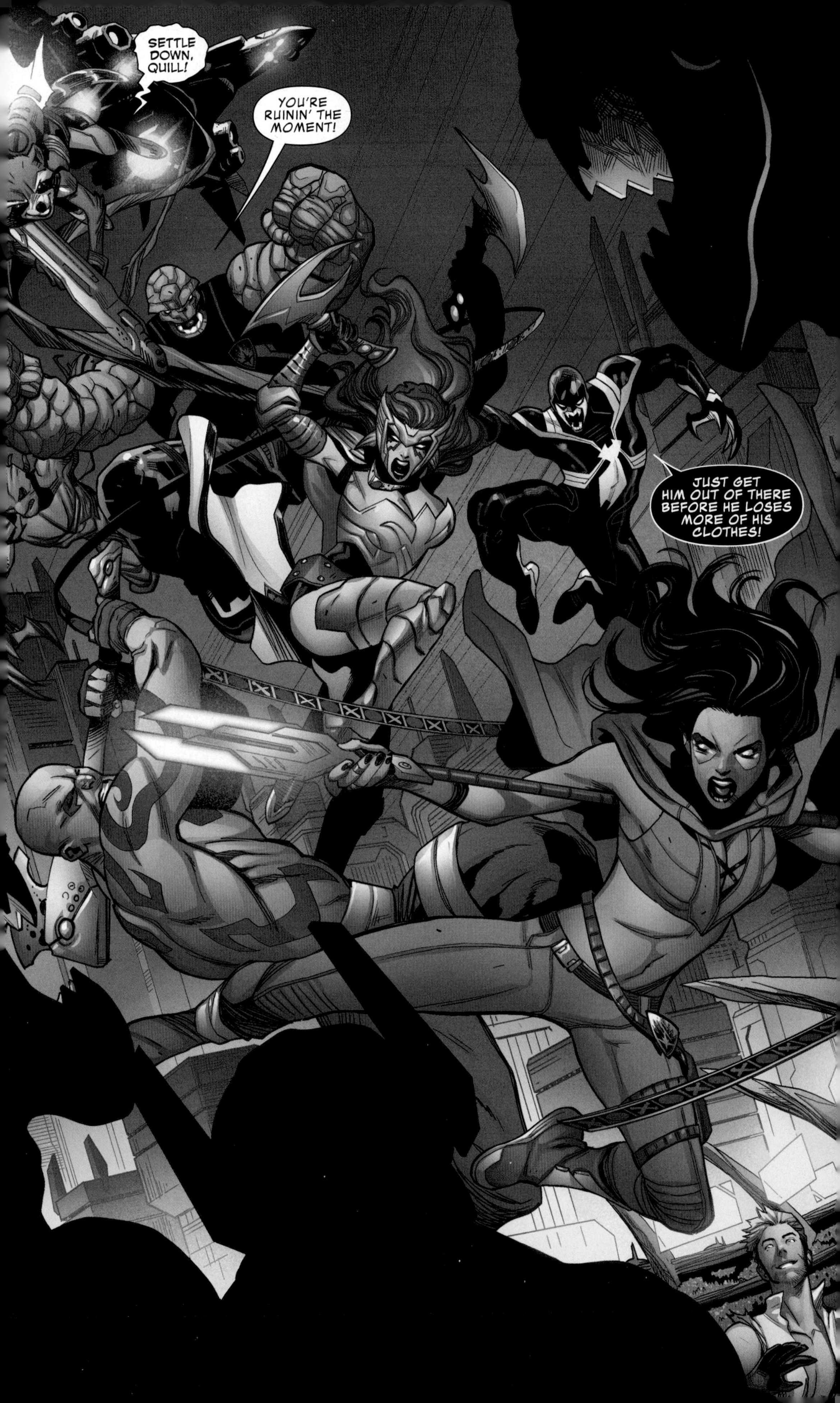
SETTLE DOWN, QUILL!
YOU'RE RUININ' THE MOMENT!
JUST GET HIM OUT OF THERE BEFORE HE LOSES MORE OF HIS CLOTHES!

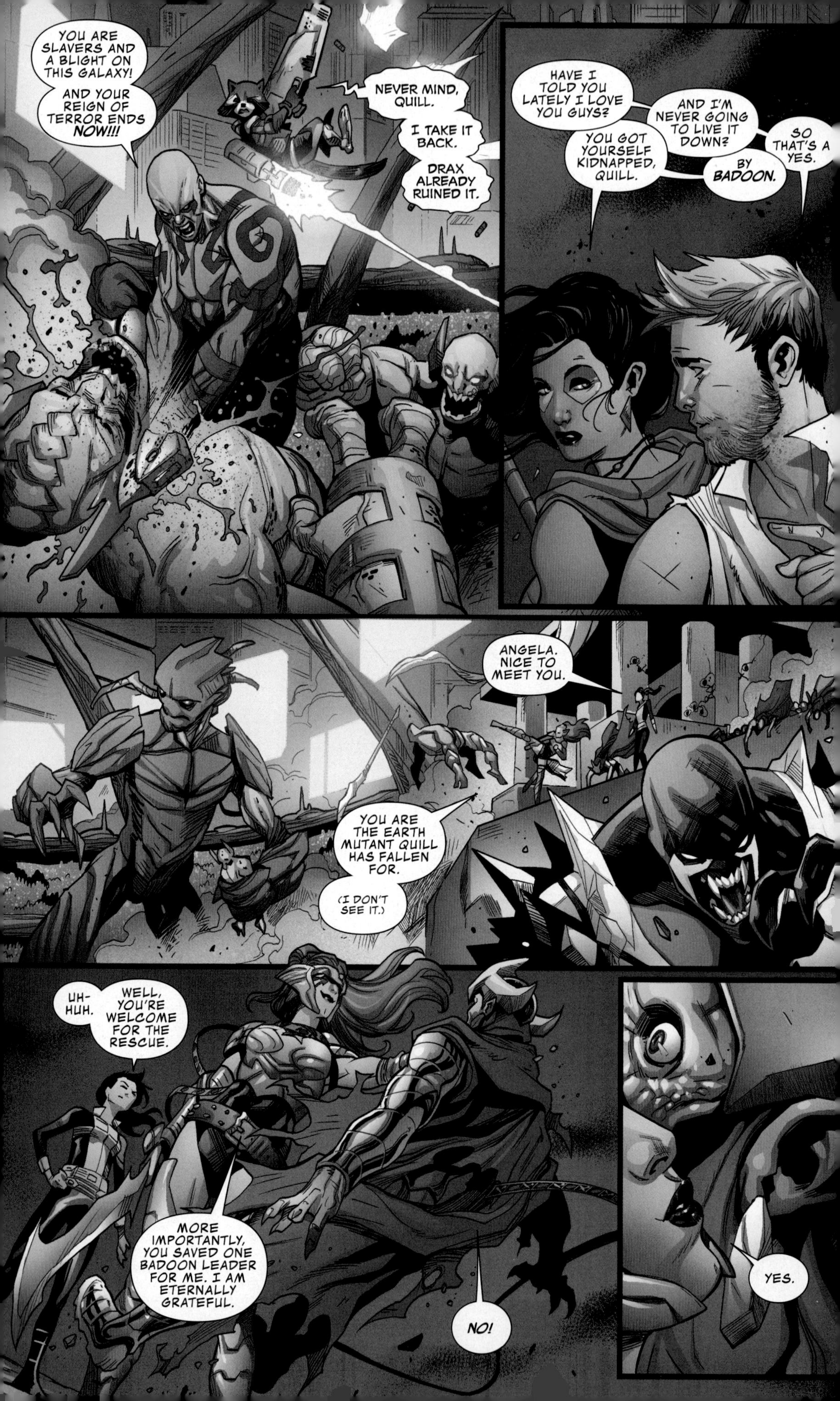

YOU ARE SLAVERS AND A BLIGHT ON THIS GALAXY!
AND YOUR REIGN OF TERROR ENDS NOW!!!
NEVER MIND, QUILL.
I TAKE IT BACK.
DRAX ALREADY RUINED IT.
HAVE I TOLD YOU LATELY I LOVE YOU GUYS?
AND I'M NEVER GOING TO LIVE IT DOWN?
YOU GOT YOURSELF KIDNAPPED, QUILL.
BY BADOON.
SO THAT'S A YES.
ANGELA. NICE TO MEET YOU.
YOU ARE THE EARTH MUTANT QUILL HAS FALLEN FOR.
(I DON'T SEE IT.)
UH-HUH.
WELL, YOU'RE WELCOME FOR THE RESCUE.
MORE IMPORTANTLY, YOU SAVED ONE BADOON LEADER FOR ME. I AM ETERNALLY GRATEFUL.
NO!
YES.

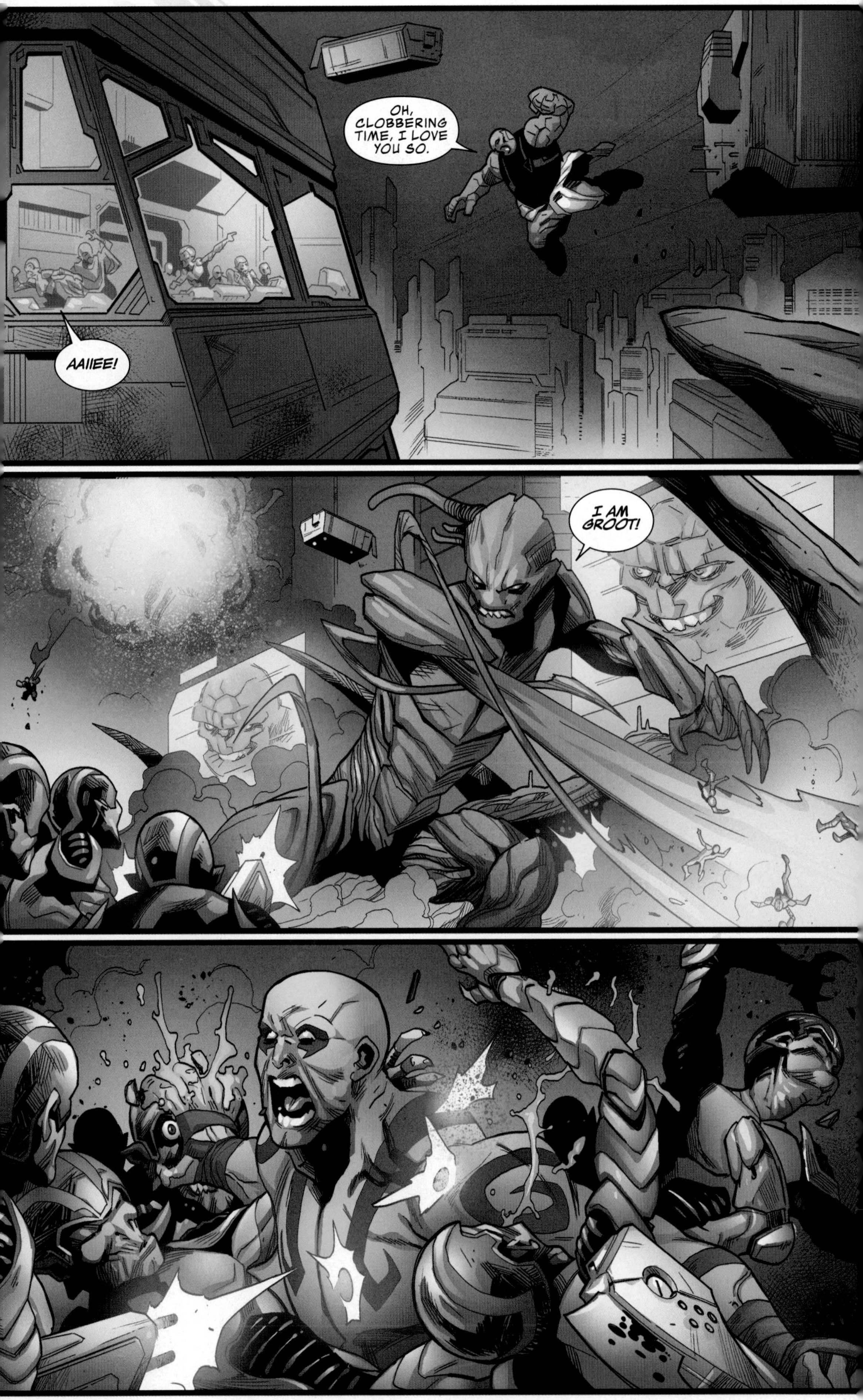
OH, CLOBBERING TIME, I LOVE YOU SO.
AAIIEE!
I AM GROOT!

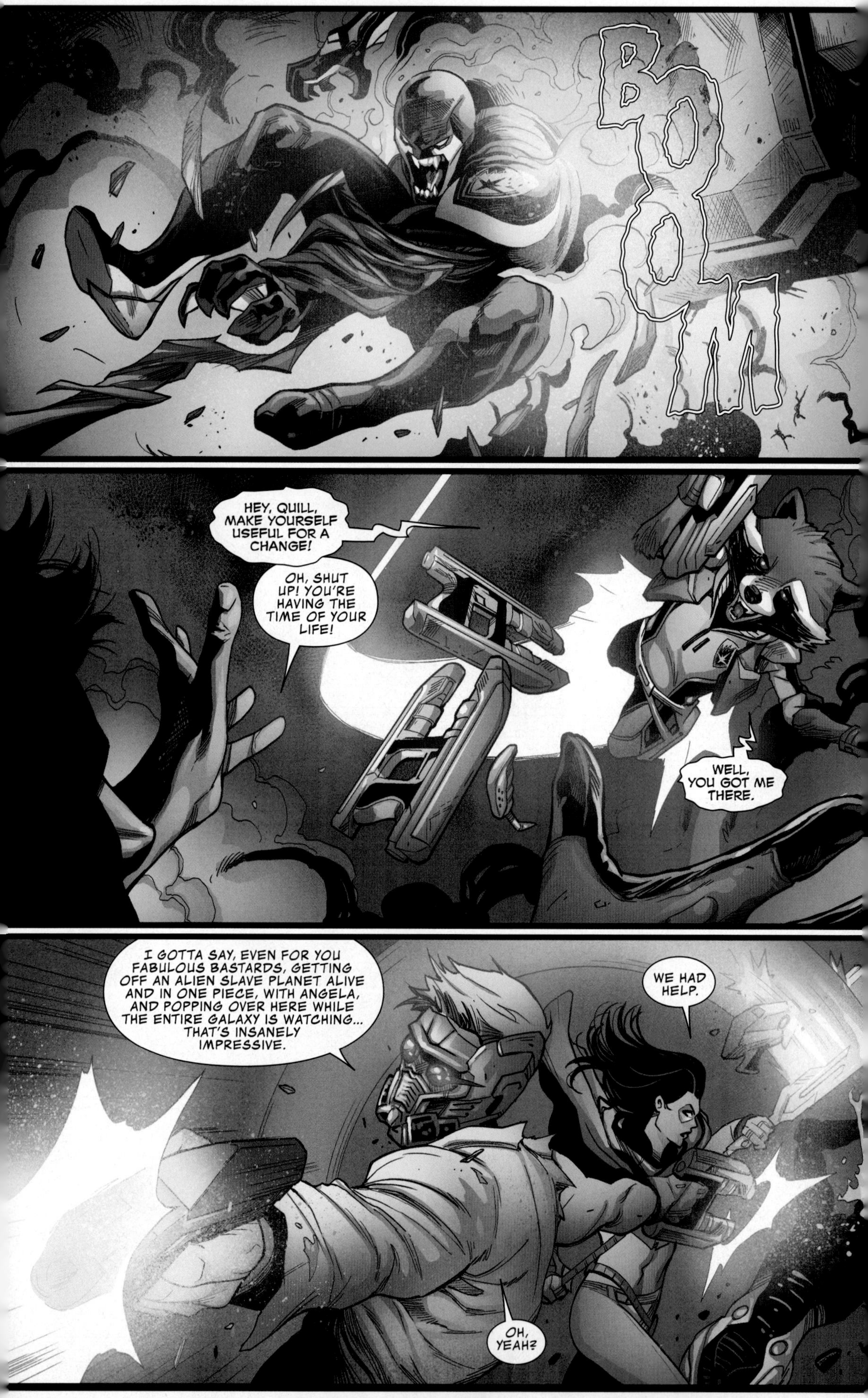
BOOM
HEY, QUILL, MAKE YOURSELF USEFUL FOR A CHANGE!
OH, SHUT UP! YOU'RE HAVING THE TIME OF YOUR LIFE!
WELL, YOU GOT ME THERE.
I GOTTA SAY, EVEN FOR YOU FABULOUS BASTARDS, GETTING OFF AN ALIEN SLAVE PLANET ALIVE AND IN ONE PIECE, WITH ANGELA, AND POPPING OVER HERE WHILE THE ENTIRE GALAXY IS WATCHING... THAT'S INSANELY IMPRESSIVE.
WE HAD HELP.
OH, YEAH?

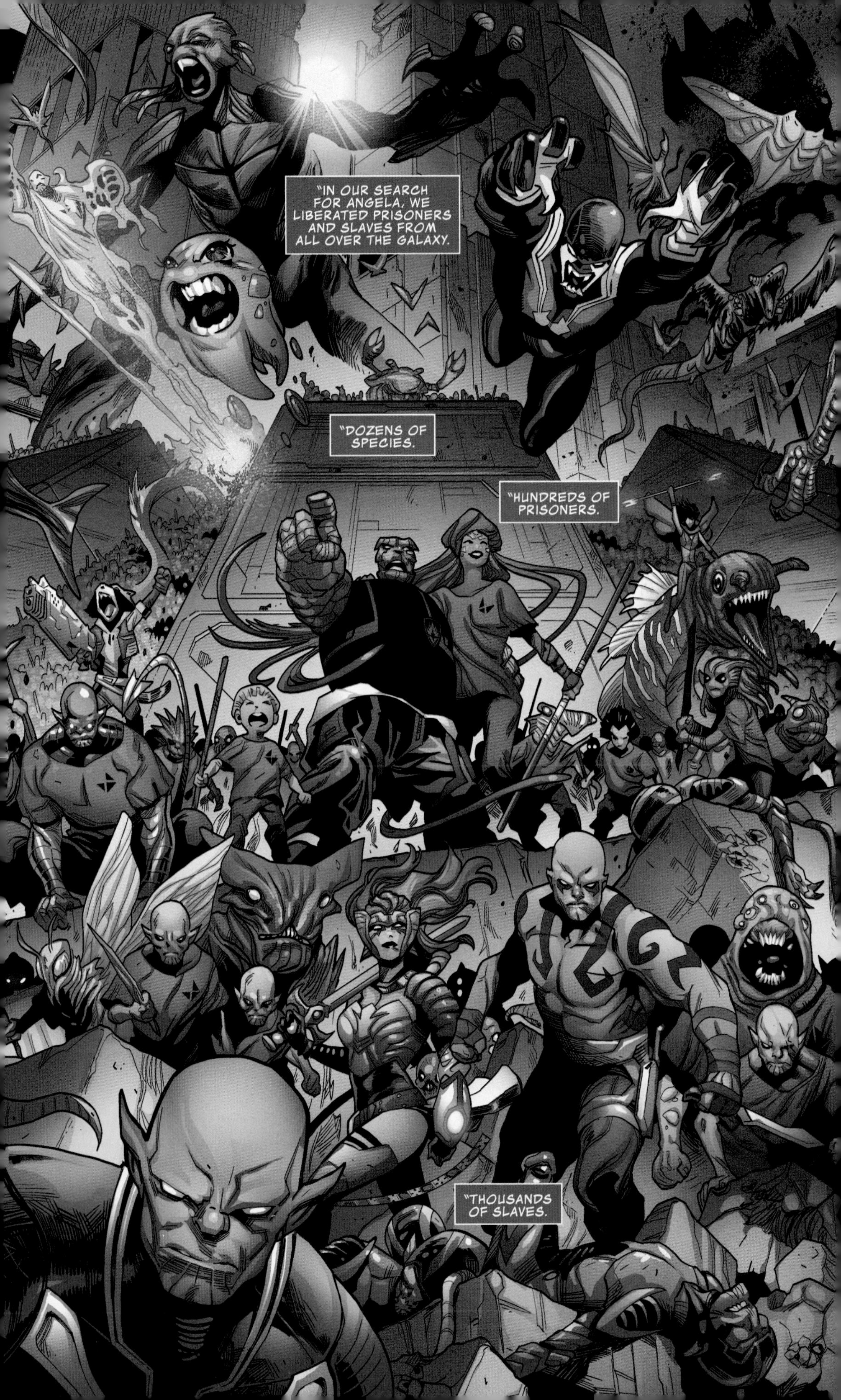
"IN OUR SEARCH FOR ANGELA, WE LIBERATED PRISONERS AND SLAVES FROM ALL OVER THE GALAXY.
"DOZENS OF SPECIES.
"HUNDREDS OF PRISONERS.
"THOUSANDS OF SLAVES.

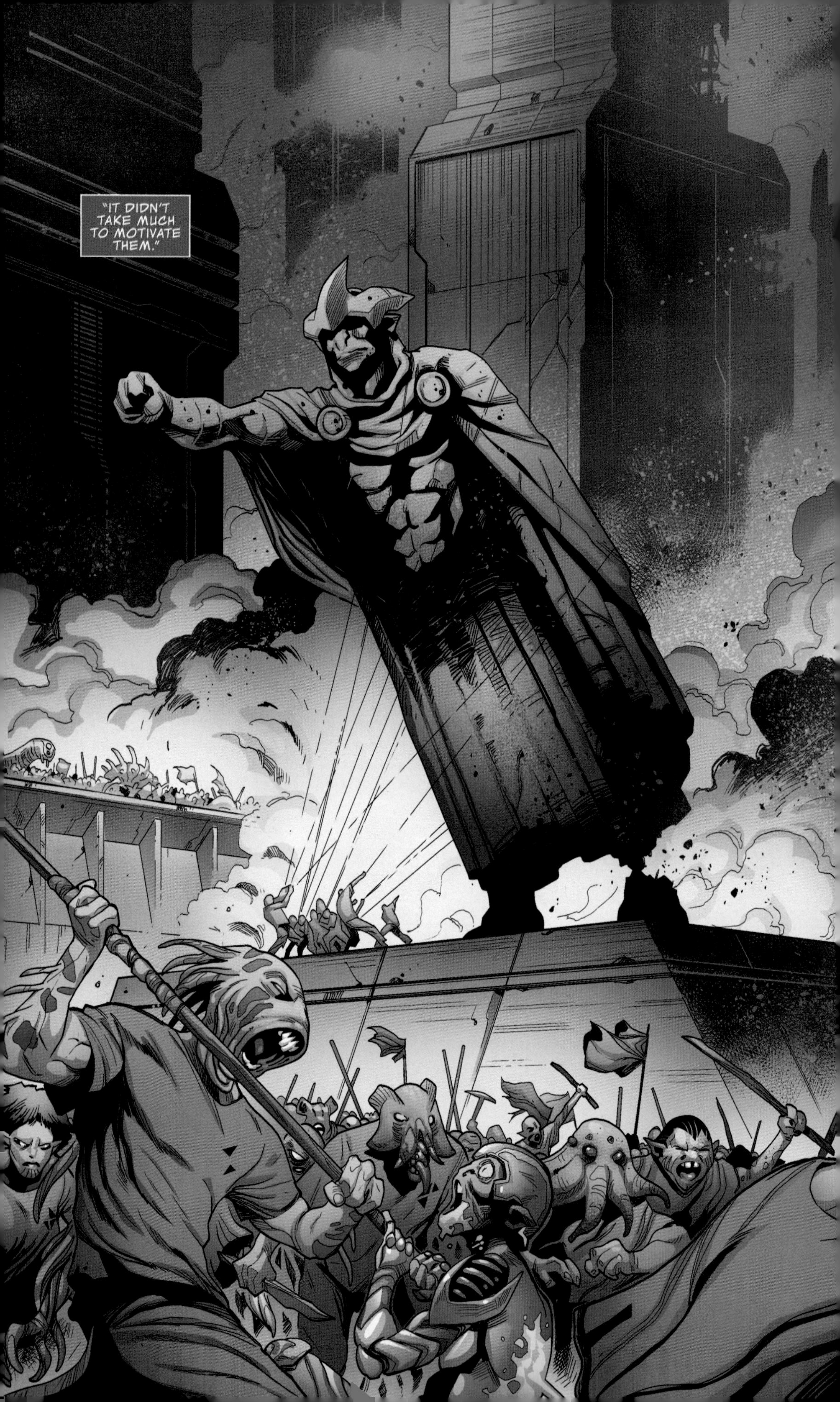
"IT DIDN'T TAKE MUCH TO MOTIVATE THEM."

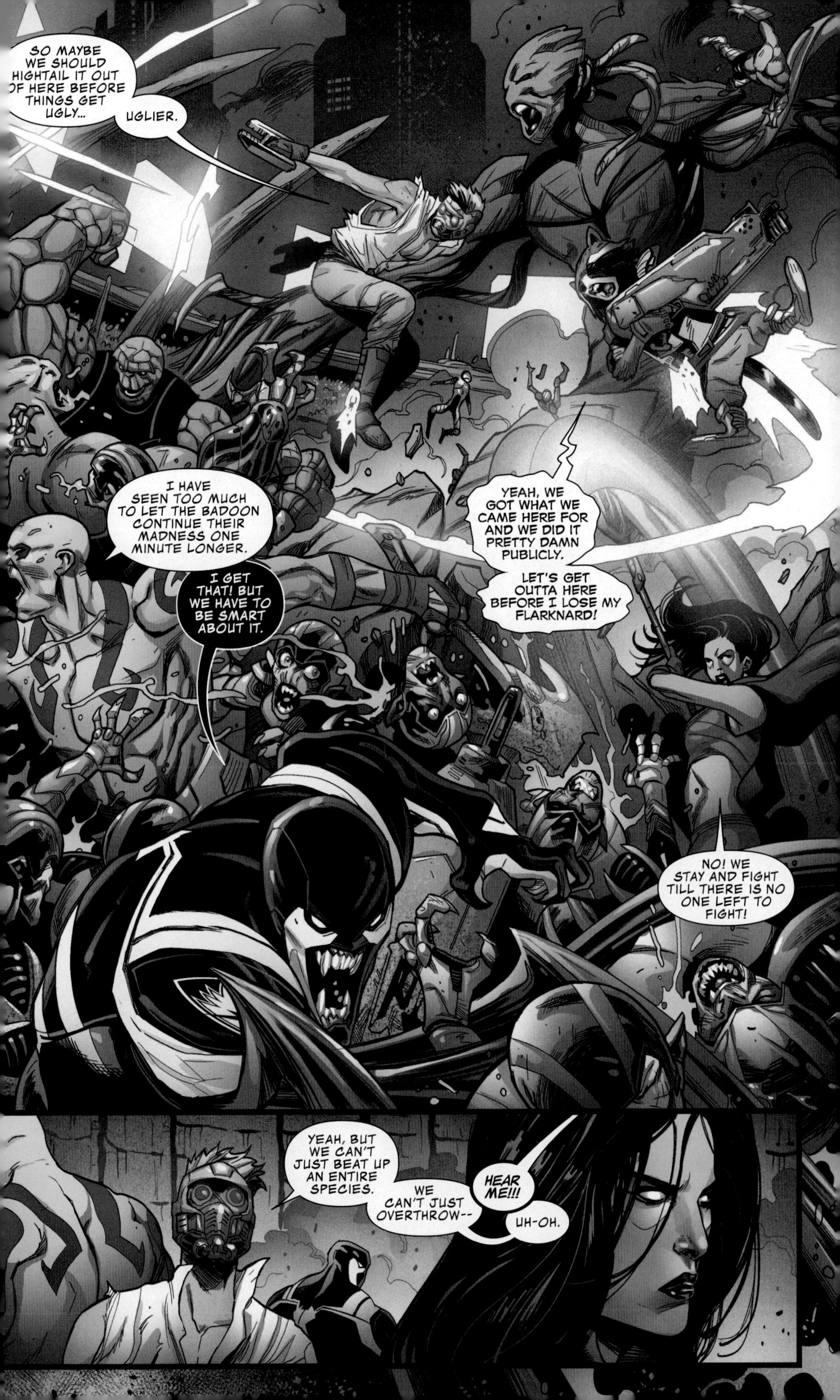

SO MAYBE WE SHOULD HIGHTAIL IT OUT OF HERE BEFORE THINGS GET UGLY...
UGLIER.
I HAVE SEEN TOO MUCH TO LET THE BADOON CONTINUE THEIR MADNESS ONE MINUTE LONGER.
I GET THAT! BUT WE HAVE TO BE SMART ABOUT IT.
YEAH, WE GOT WHAT WE CAME HERE FOR AND WE DID IT PRETTY DAMN PUBLICLY.
LET'S GET OUTTA HERE BEFORE I LOSE MY FLARKNARD!
NO! WE STAY AND FIGHT TILL THERE IS NO ONE LEFT TO FIGHT!
YEAH, BUT WE CAN'T JUST BEAT UP AN ENTIRE SPECIES.
WE CAN'T JUST OVERTHROW--
HEAR ME!!!
UH-OH.

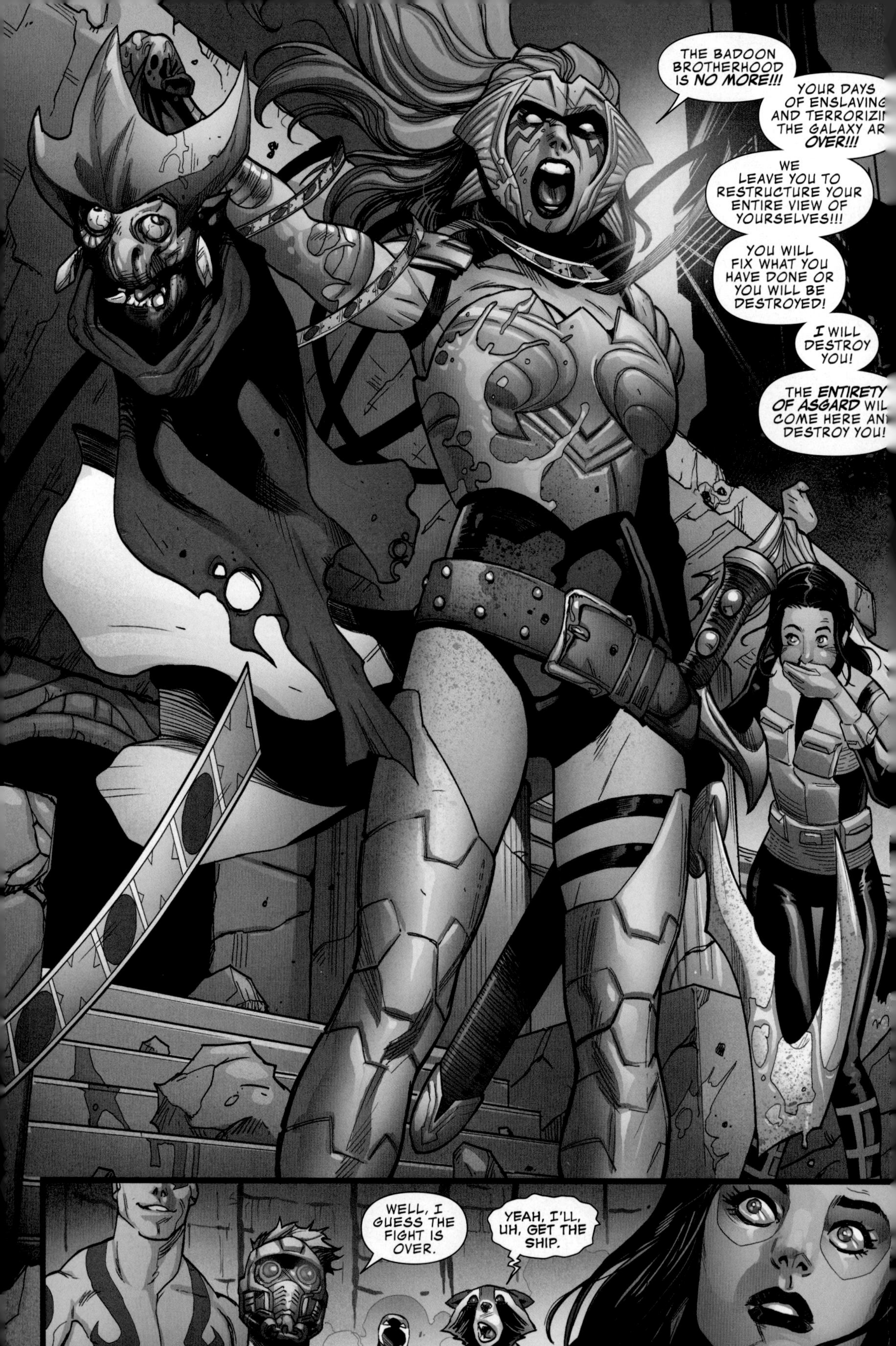
THE BADOON BROTHERHOOD IS *NO MORE!!!*
YOUR DAYS OF ENSLAVING AND TERRORIZI THE GALAXY AR *OVER!!!*
WE LEAVE YOU TO RESTRUCTURE YOUR ENTIRE VIEW OF YOURSELVES!!!
YOU WILL FIX WHAT YOU HAVE DONE OR YOU WILL BE DESTROYED!
I WILL DESTROY YOU!
THE *ENTIRETY OF ASGARD* WIL COME HERE AN DESTROY YOU!

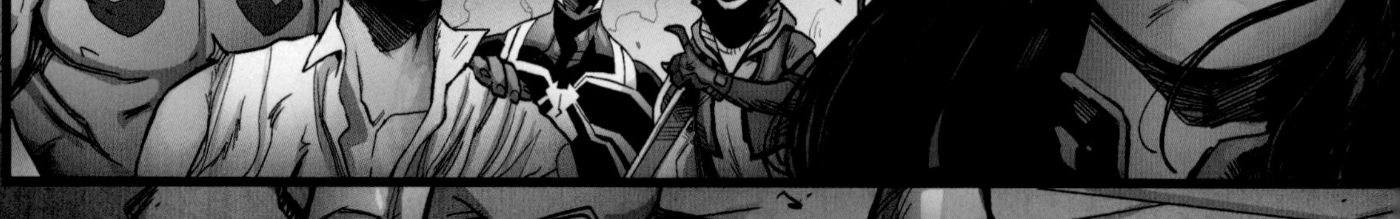
WELL, I GUESS THE FIGHT IS OVER.
YEAH, I'LL, UH, GET THE SHIP.

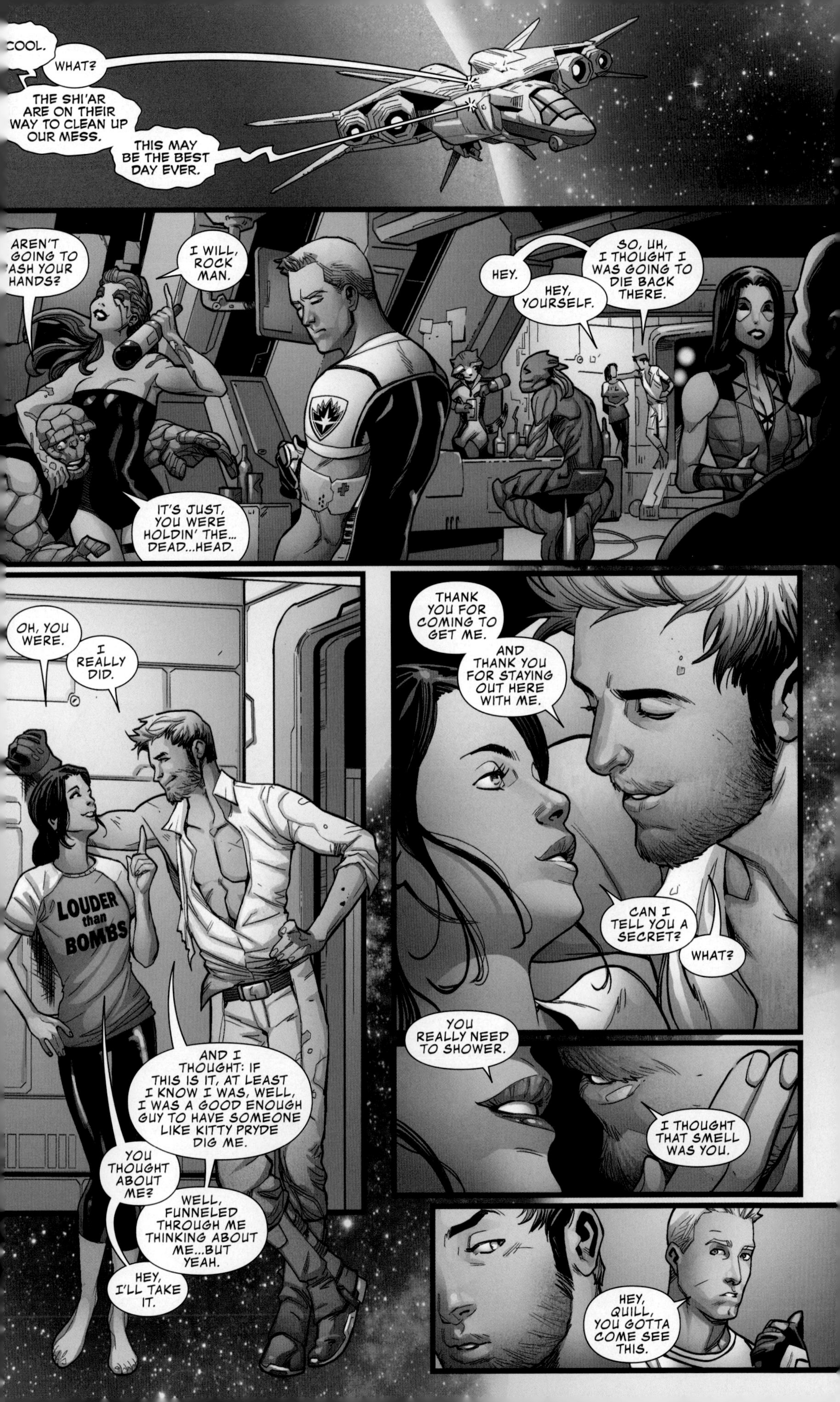

COOL.
WHAT?
THE SHI'AR ARE ON THEIR WAY TO CLEAN UP OUR MESS.
THIS MAY BE THE BEST DAY EVER.
AREN'T GOING TO ASH YOUR HANDS?
I WILL, ROCK MAN.
IT'S JUST, YOU WERE HOLDIN' THE... DEAD...HEAD.
HEY.
HEY, YOURSELF.
SO, UH, I THOUGHT I WAS GOING TO DIE BACK THERE.
OH, YOU WERE.
I REALLY DID.
LOUDER than BOMBS
AND I THOUGHT: IF THIS IS IT, AT LEAST I KNOW I WAS, WELL, I WAS A GOOD ENOUGH GUY TO HAVE SOMEONE LIKE KITTY PRYDE DIG ME.
YOU THOUGHT ABOUT ME?
WELL, FUNNELED THROUGH ME THINKING ABOUT ME...BUT YEAH.
HEY, I'LL TAKE IT.
THANK YOU FOR COMING TO GET ME.
AND THANK YOU FOR STAYING OUT HERE WITH ME.
CAN I TELL YOU A SECRET?
WHAT?
YOU REALLY NEED TO SHOWER.
I THOUGHT THAT SMELL WAS YOU.
HEY, QUILL, YOU GOTTA COME SEE THIS.

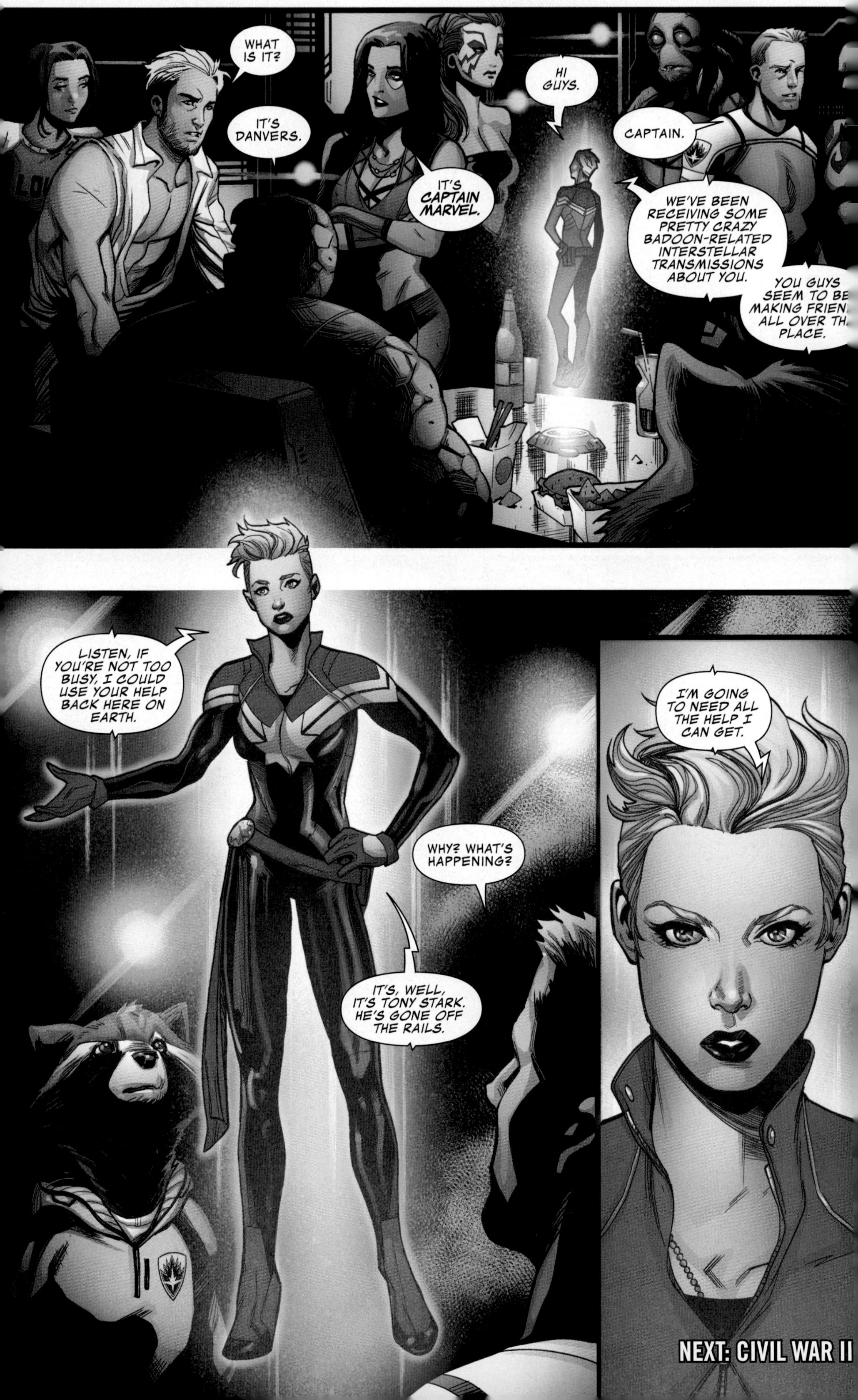
WHAT IS IT?
IT'S DANVERS.
IT'S CAPTAIN MARVEL.
HI GUYS.
CAPTAIN.
WE'VE BEEN RECEIVING SOME PRETTY CRAZY BADOON-RELATED INTERSTELLAR TRANSMISSIONS ABOUT YOU.
LISTEN, IF YOU'RE NOT TOO BUSY, I COULD USE YOUR HELP BACK HERE ON EARTH.
WHY? WHAT'S HAPPENING?
IT'S, WELL, IT'S TONY STARK. HE'S GONE OFF THE RAILS.
I'M GOING TO NEED ALL THE HELP I CAN GET.
NEXT: CIVIL WAR II

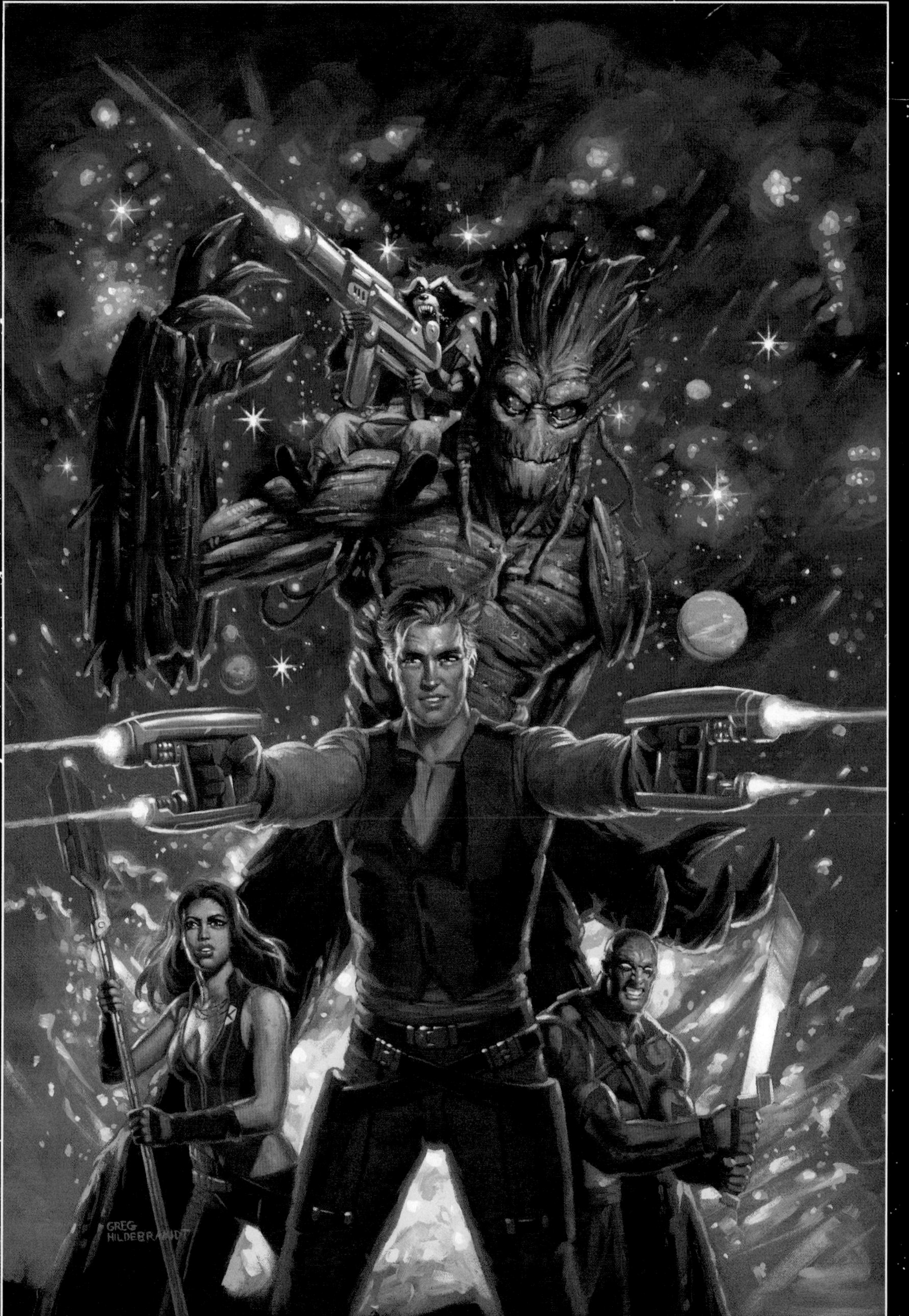
GREG
HILDEBRANDT

#6 VARIANT BY
GREG HILDEBRANT

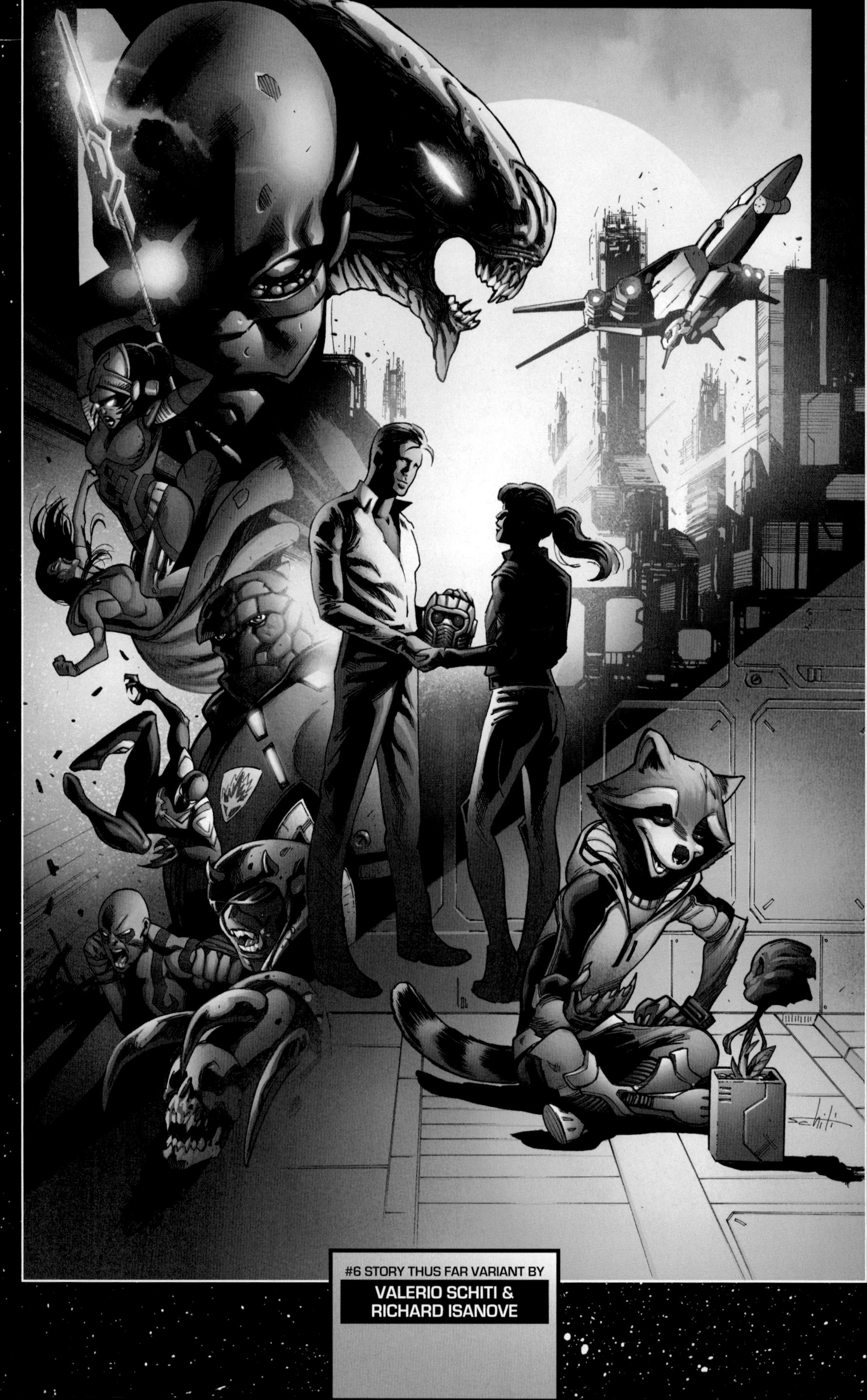
schiti

#6 STORY THUS FAR VARIANT BY

VALERIO SCHITI & RICHARD ISANOVE

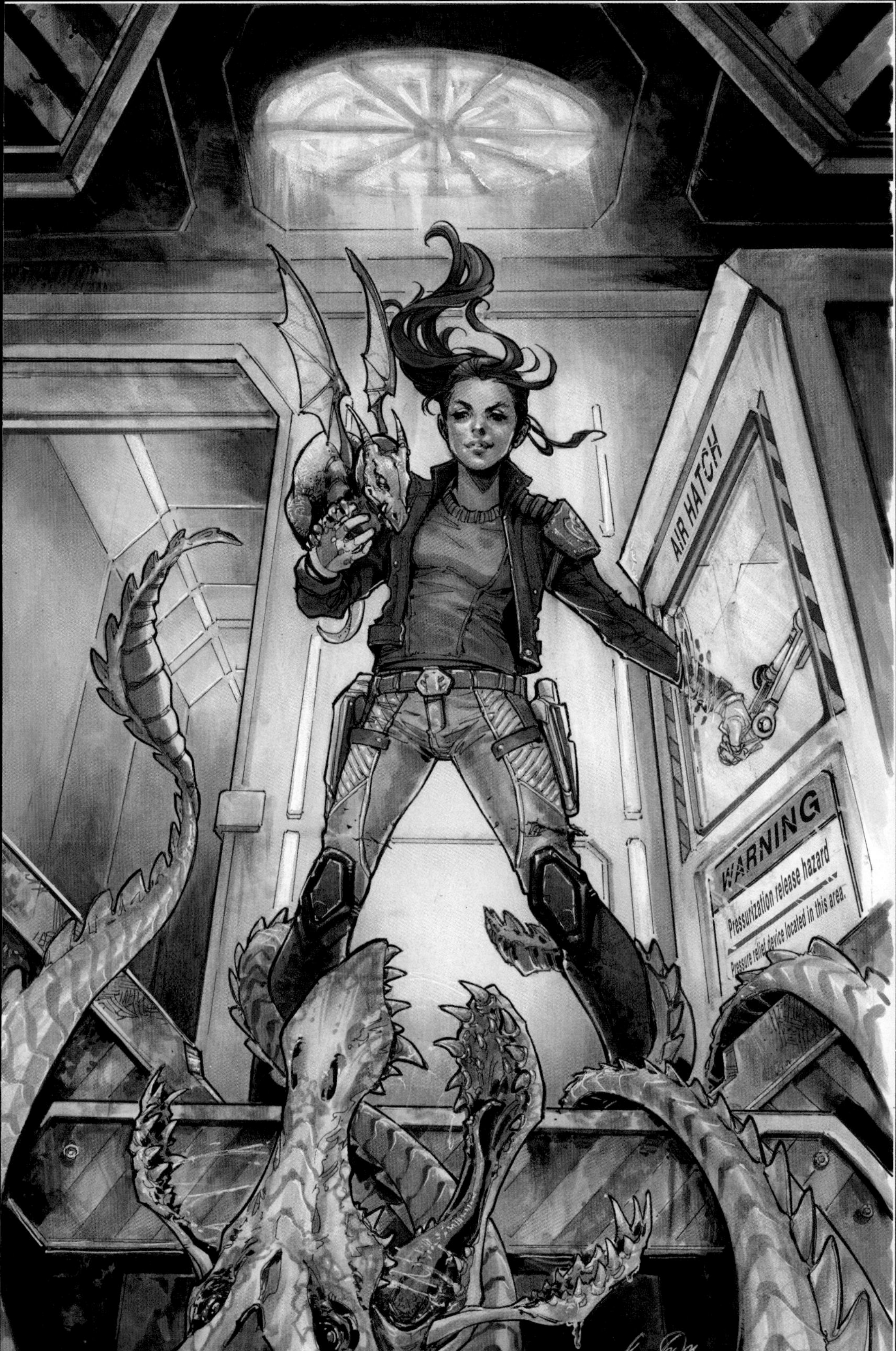
AIR HATCH
WARNING
Pressurization release hazard
Pressure relief device located in this area.

#6 WOMAN OF POWER
VARIANT BY
SIYA OUM

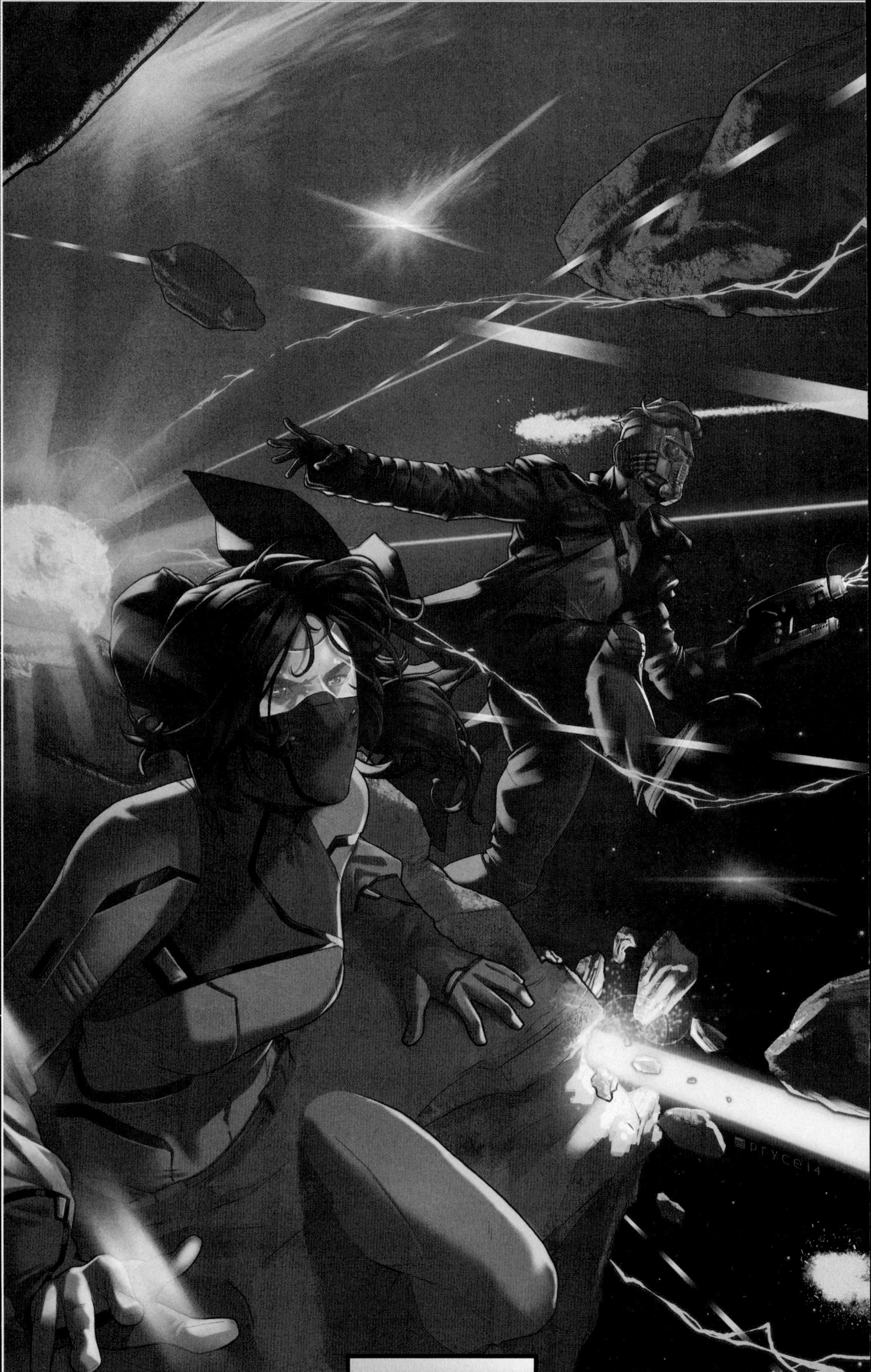

#6 VARIANT BY
JAMAL CAMPBELL

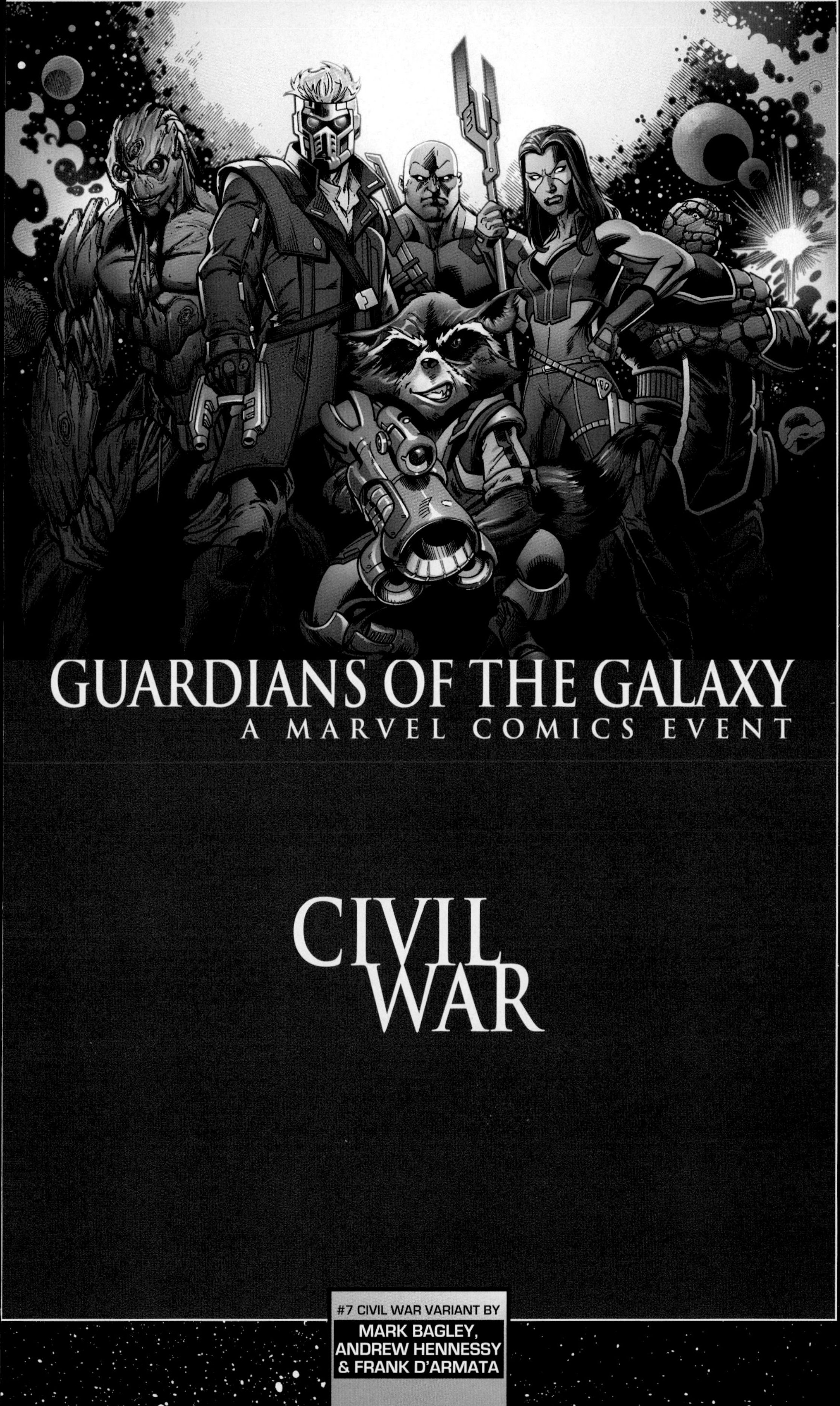
GUARDIANS OF THE GALAXY
A MARVEL COMICS EVENT
CIVIL WAR

#7 CIVIL WAR VARIANT BY
MARK BAGLEY,
ANDREW HENNESSY
& FRANK D'ARMATA

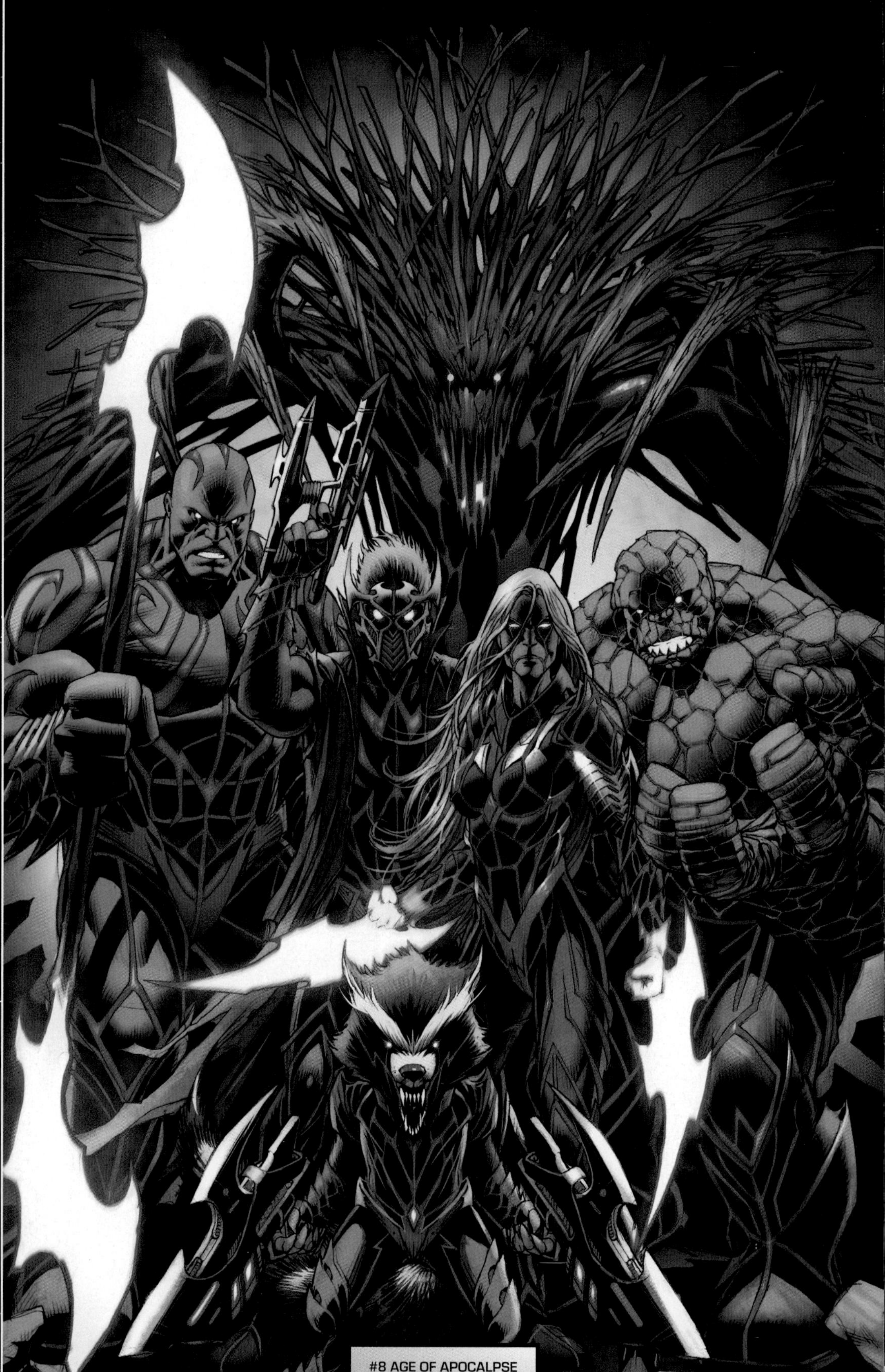

#8 AGE OF APOCALPSE
VARIANT BY
ARTHUR ADAMS
& JASON KEITH

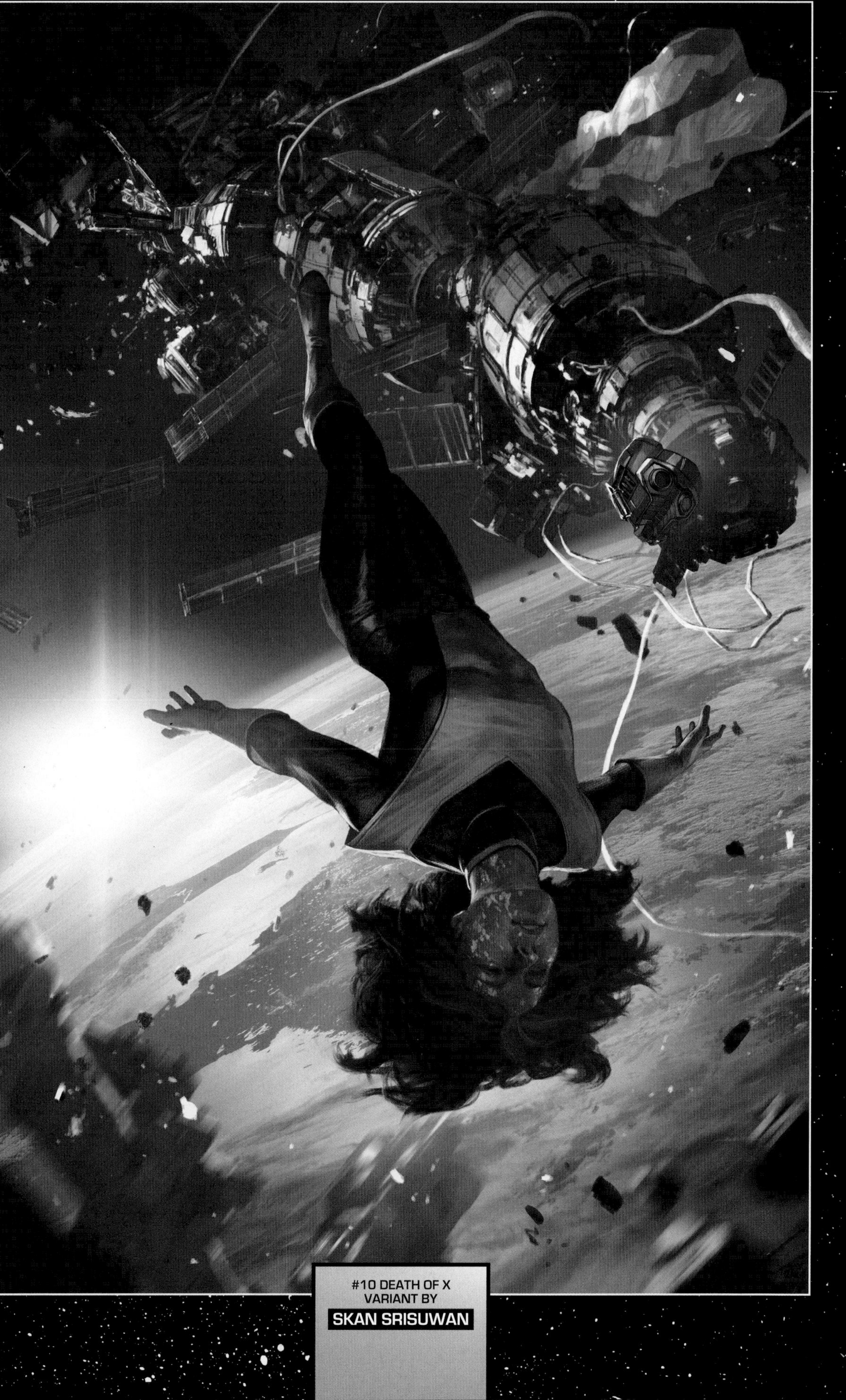

#10 DEATH OF X
VARIANT BY
SKAN SRISUWAN

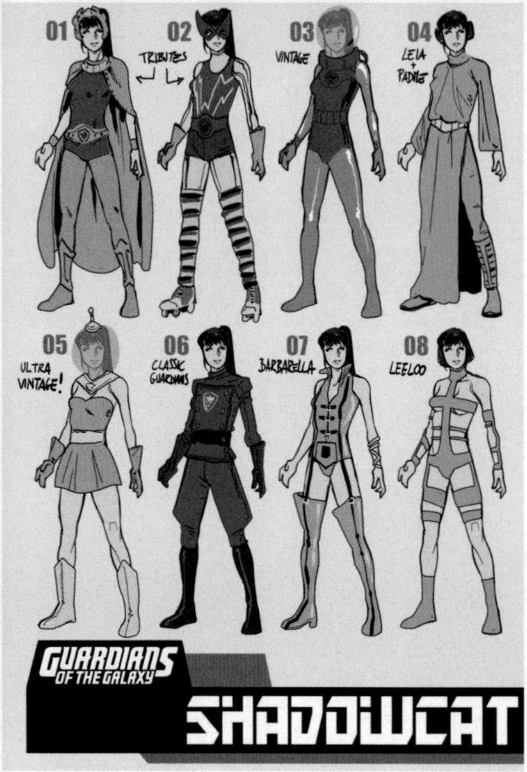
01
02
TRIBUTES
03
VINTAGE
04
LEIA + PADME
05
ULTRA VINTAGE!
06
CLASSIC GUARDIANS
07
BARBARELLA
08
LEELOO
GUARDIANS OF THE GALAXY
SHADOWCAT

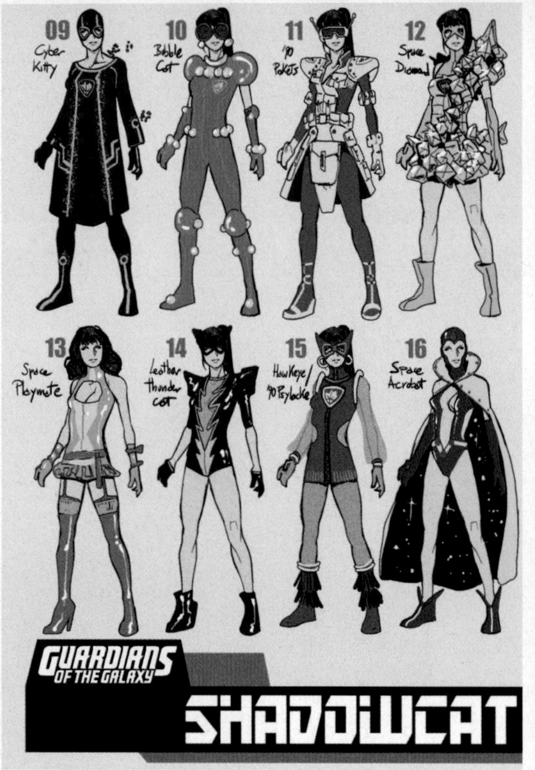
09
Cyber Kitty
10
Bubble Cat
11
'90 Pokets
12
Space Diamond
13
Space Playmate
14
Leather Thunder Cat
15
HawKeye/ '90 Psylocke
16
Space Acrobat
GUARDIANS OF THE GALAXY
SHADOWCAT

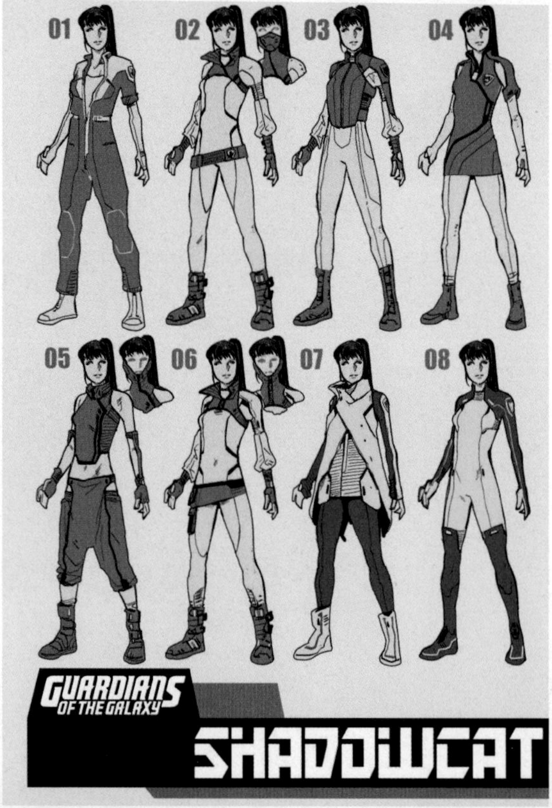
01
02
03
04
05
06
07
08
GUARDIANS OF THE GALAXY
SHADOWCAT

MOCK COSTUME DESIGNS BY
VALERIO SCHITI

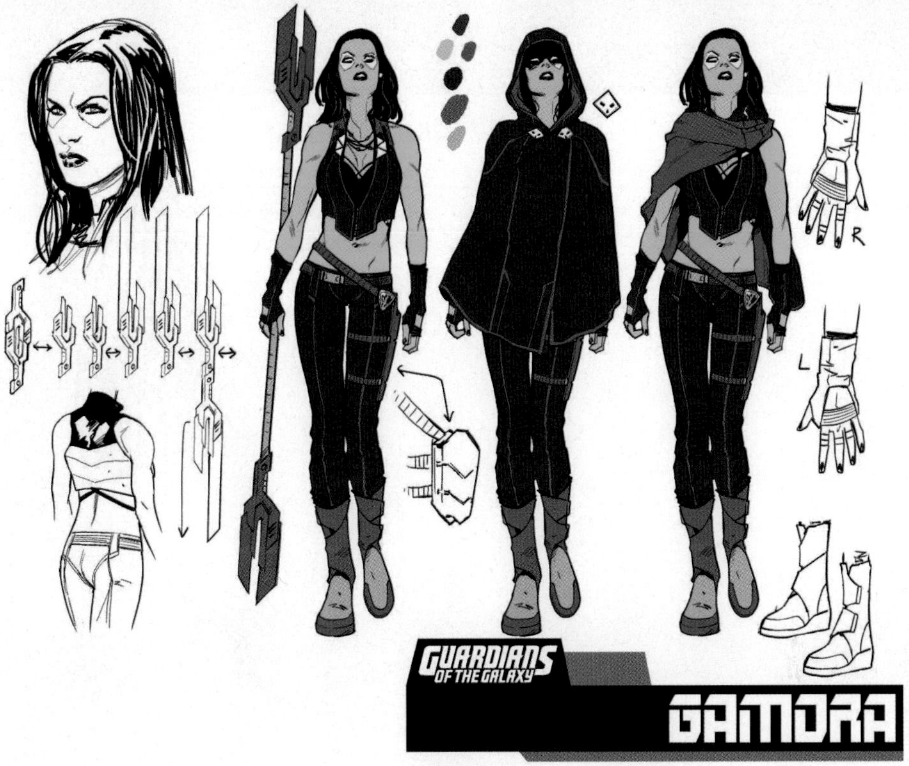
R
L
GUARDIANS OF THE GALAXY
GAMORA

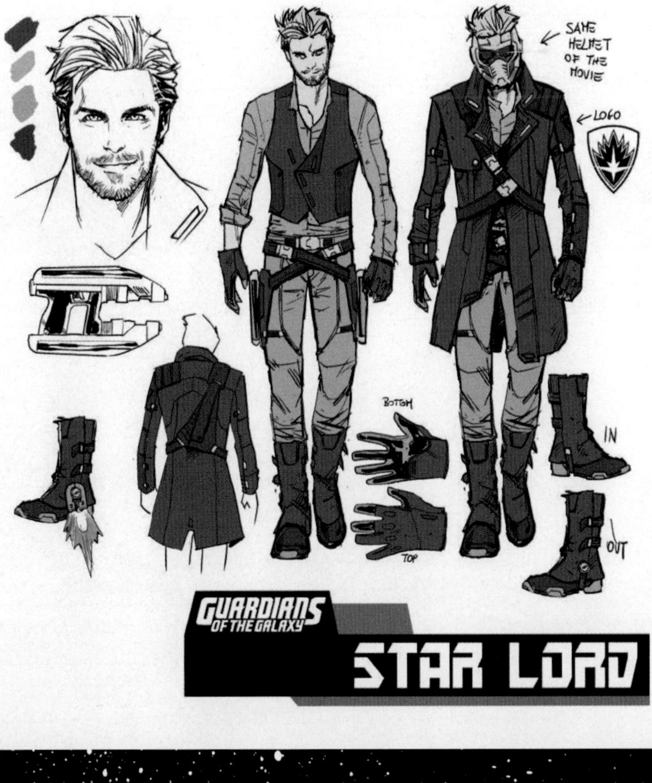
SAME HELMET OF THE MOVIE
LOGO
TOP
IN
OUT
GUARDIANS OF THE GALAXY
STAR LORD

CHARACTER DESIGNS BY
VALERIO SCHITI

FROM THE DESK OF
ARTHUR ADAMS

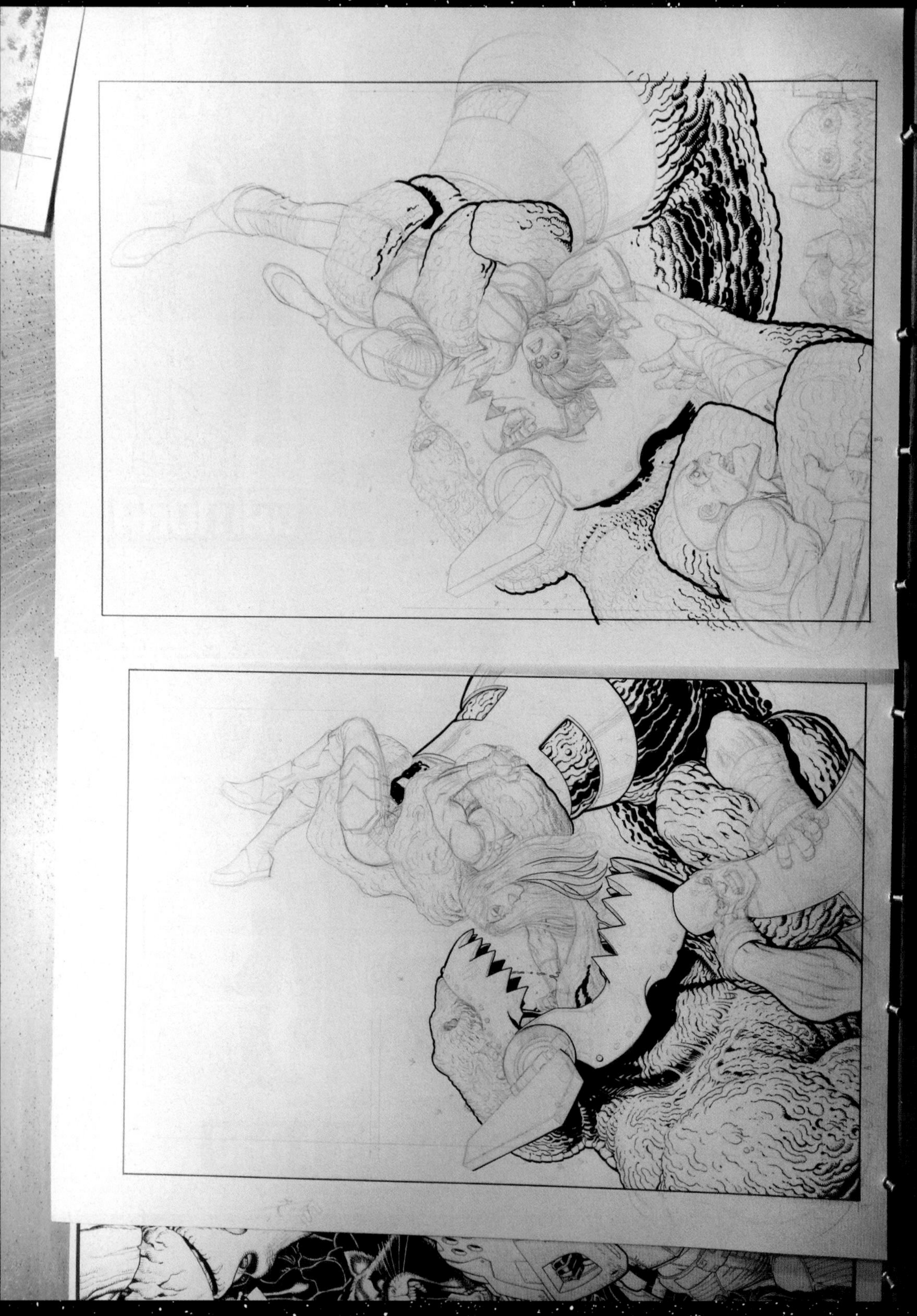

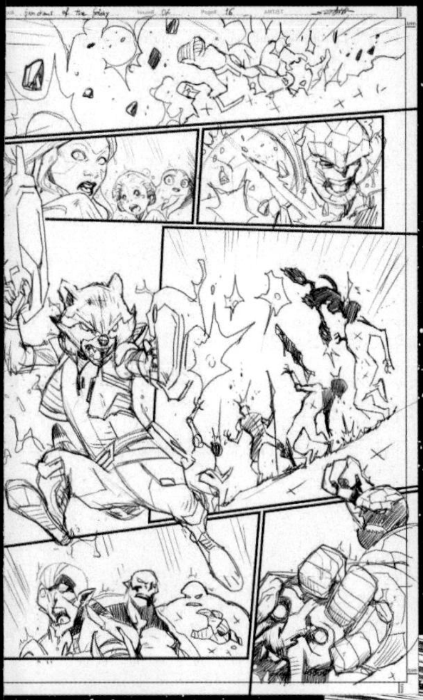

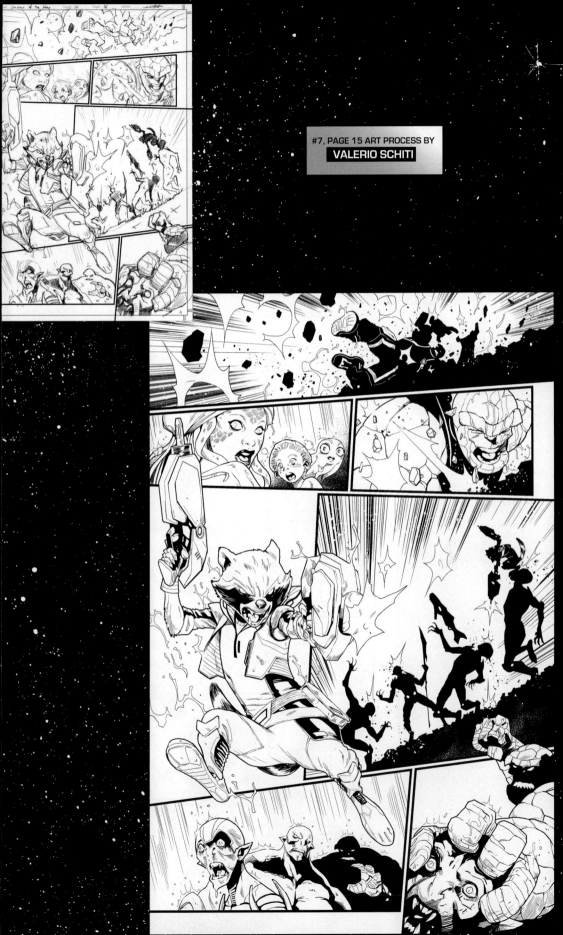

#7, PAGE 15 ART PROCESS BY
VALERIO SCHITI

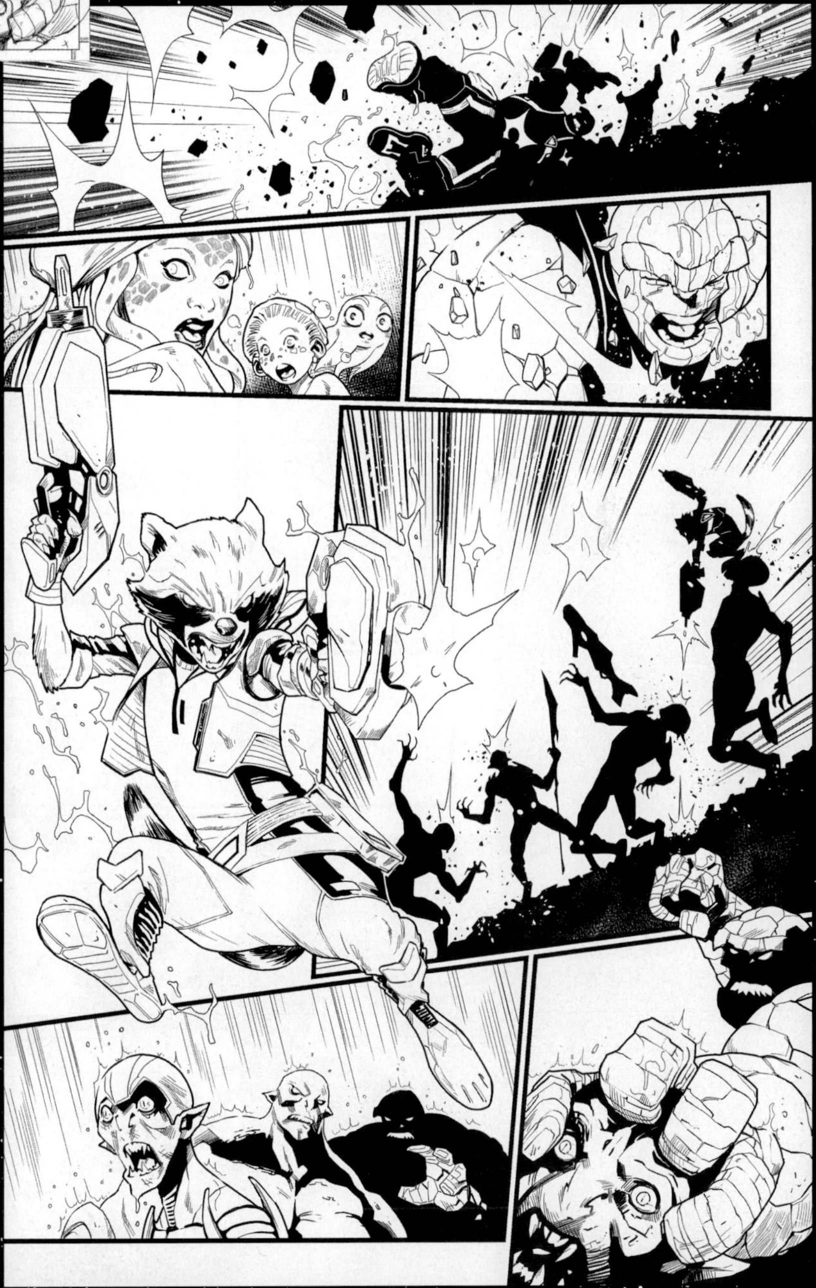

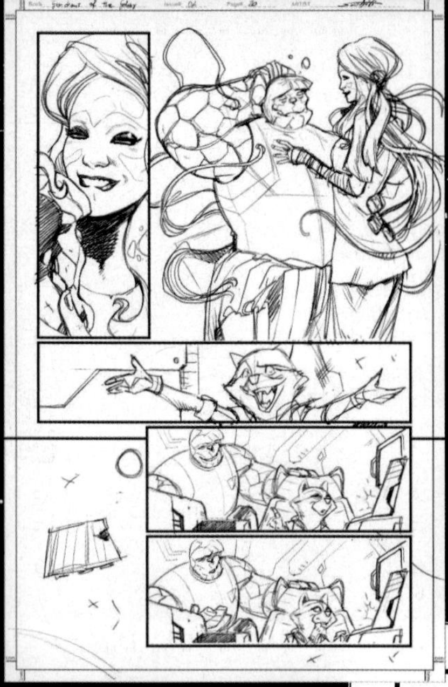

#7, PAGE 19 ART PROCESS BY

VALERIO SCHITI

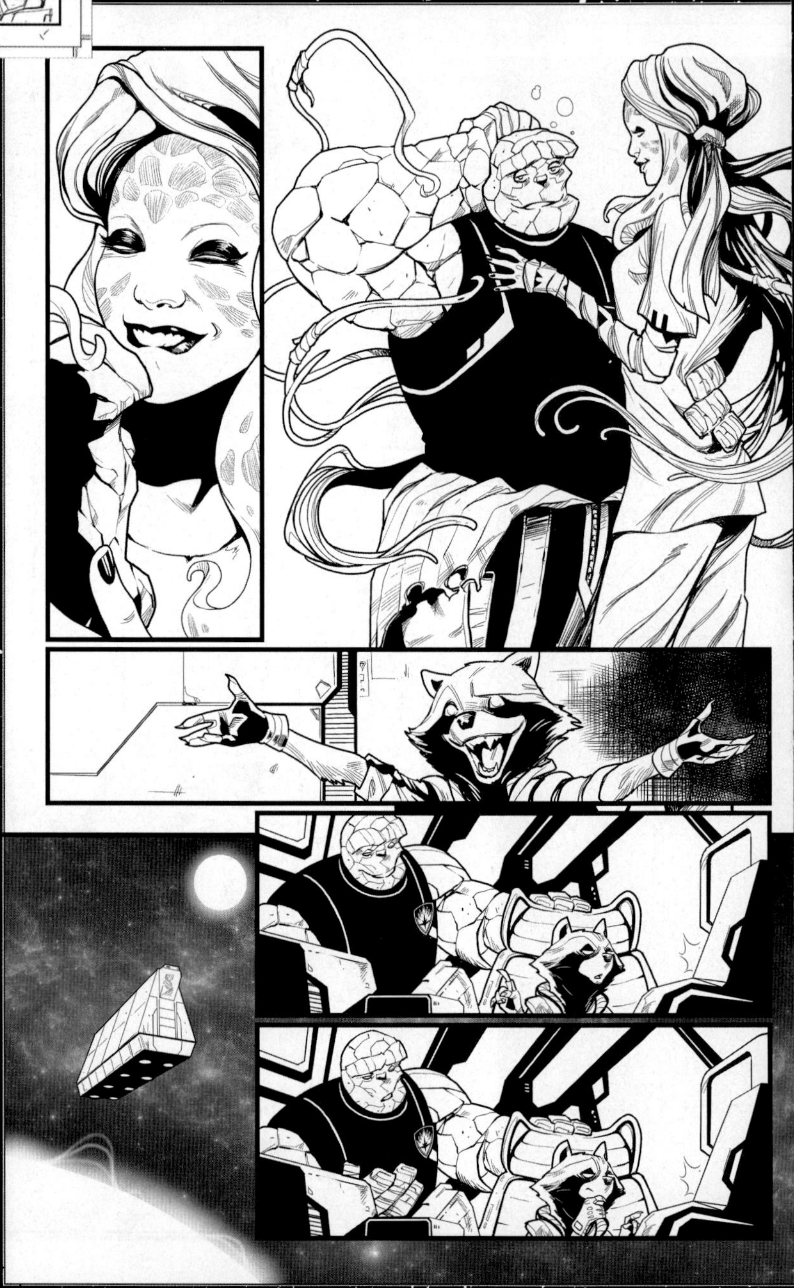

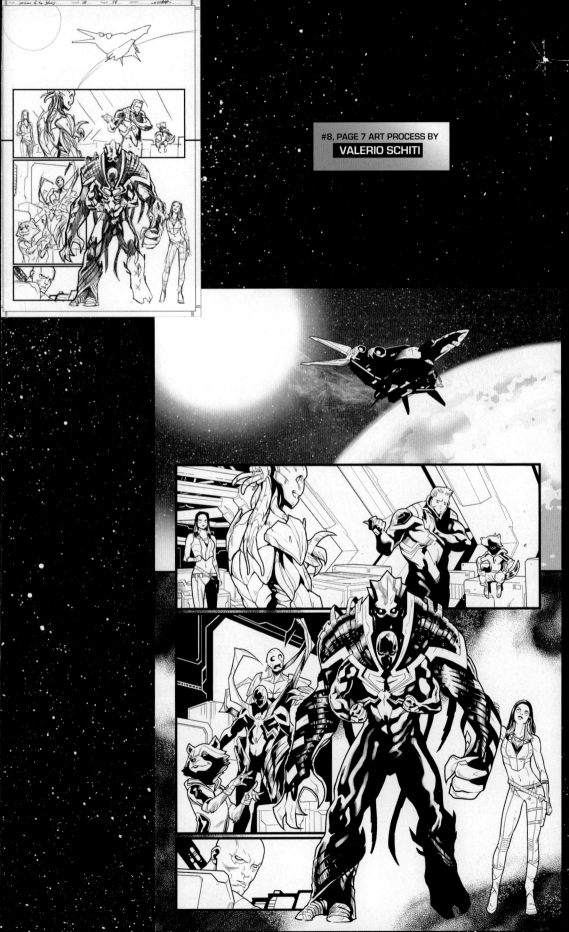

#8, PAGE 7 ART PROCESS BY
VALERIO SCHITI

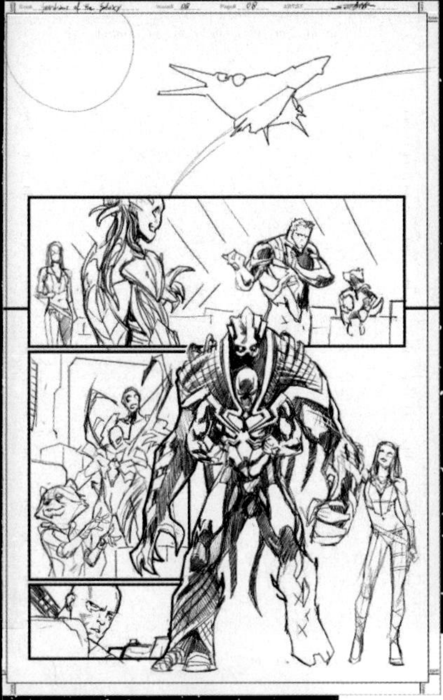

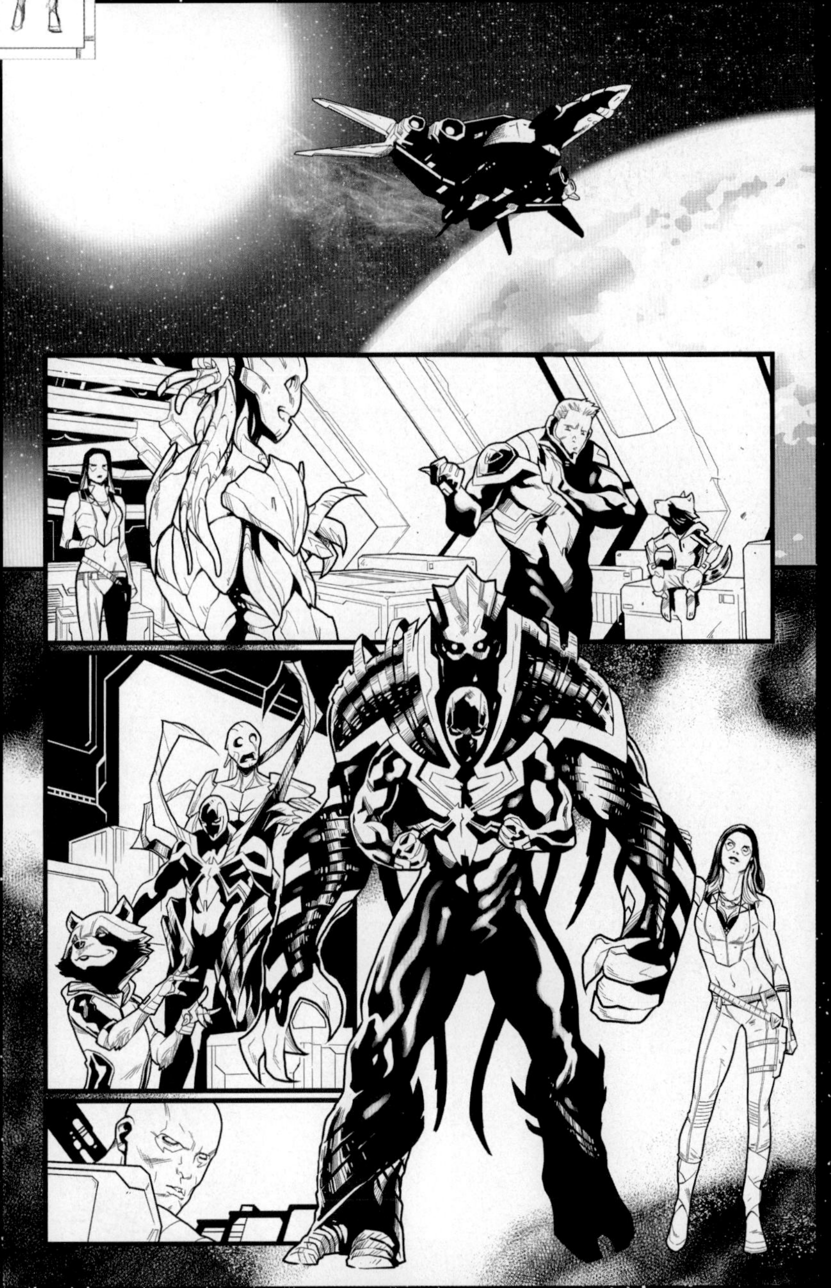

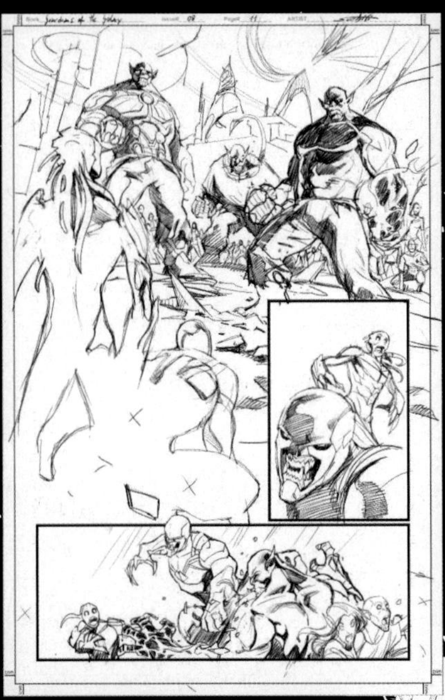

#8, PAGE 10 ART PROCESS BY
VALERIO SCHITI

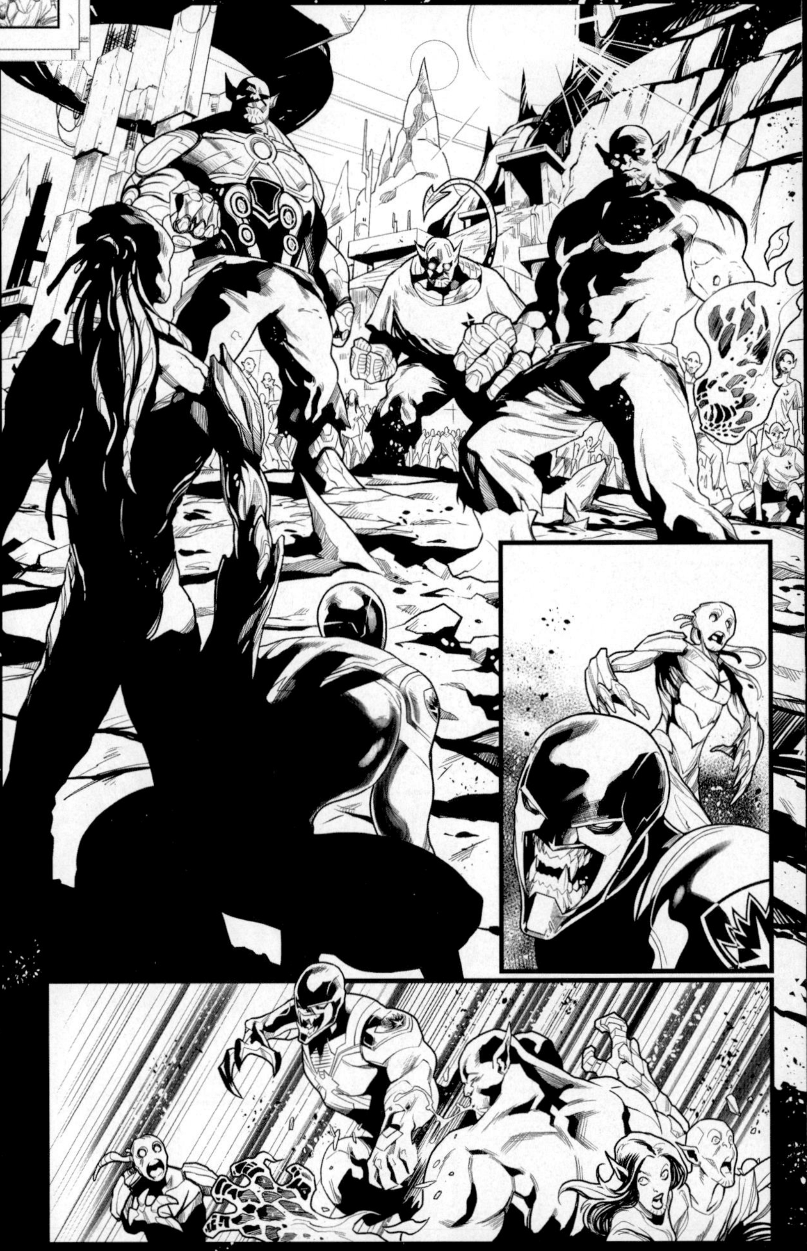

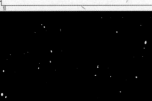

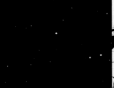

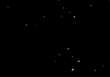

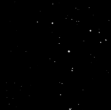

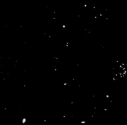

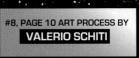

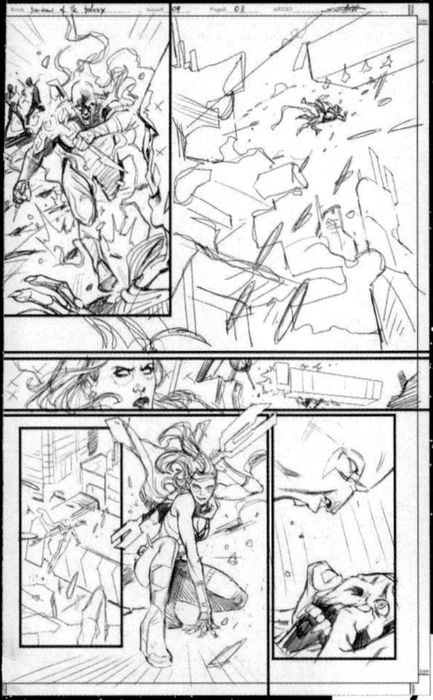

#9, PAGE 7 ART PROCESS BY

VALERIO SCHITI

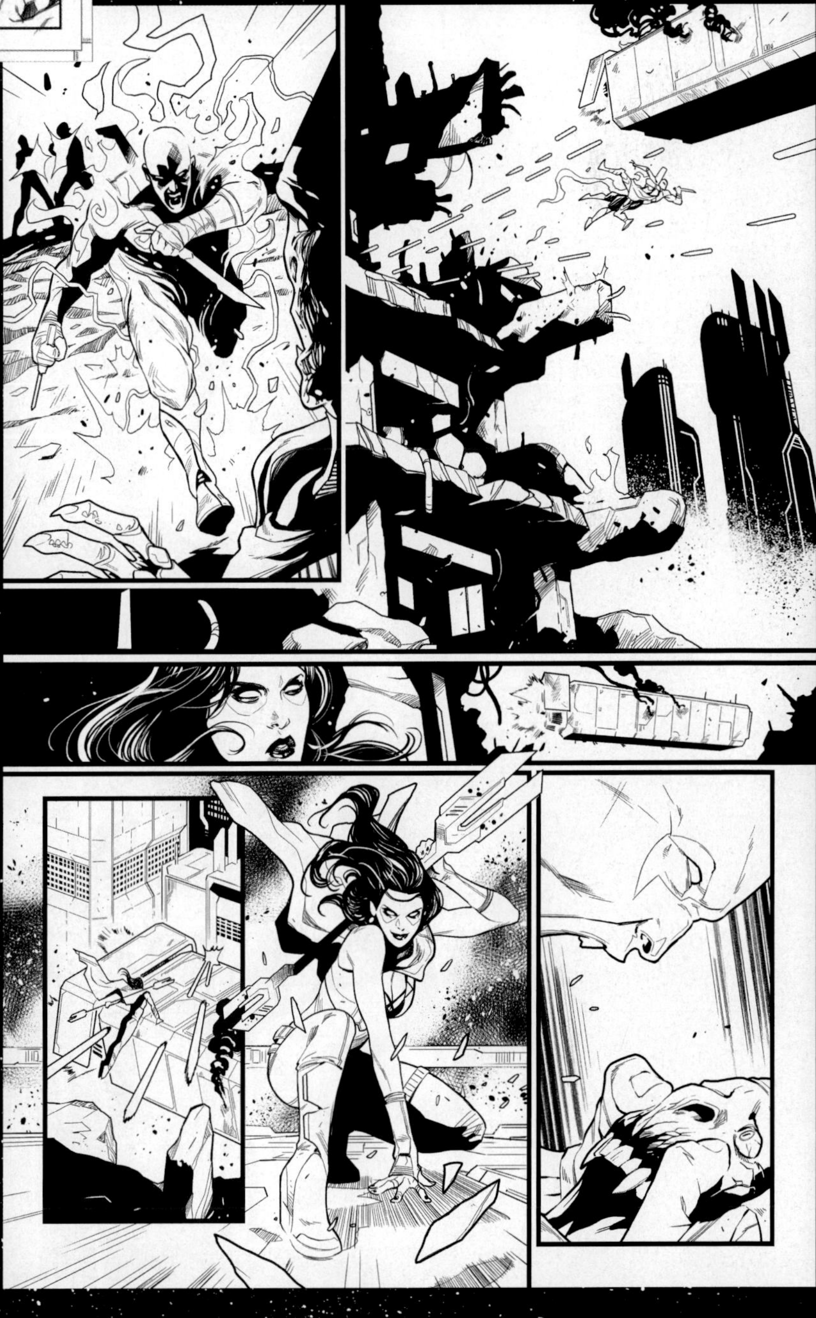

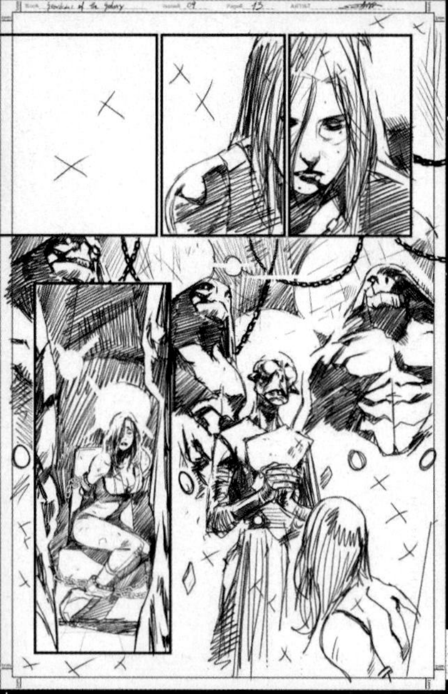

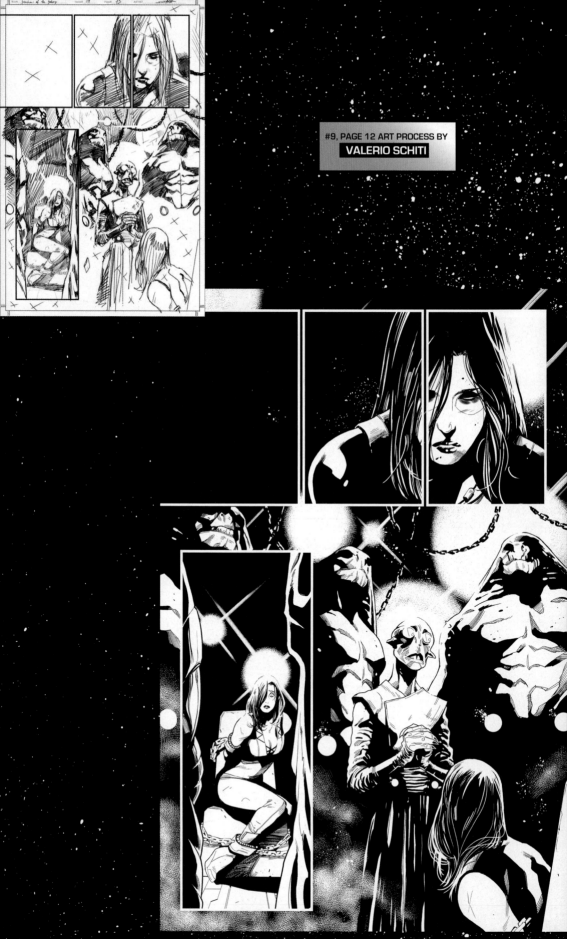

#9, PAGE 12 ART PROCESS BY

VALERIO SCHITI

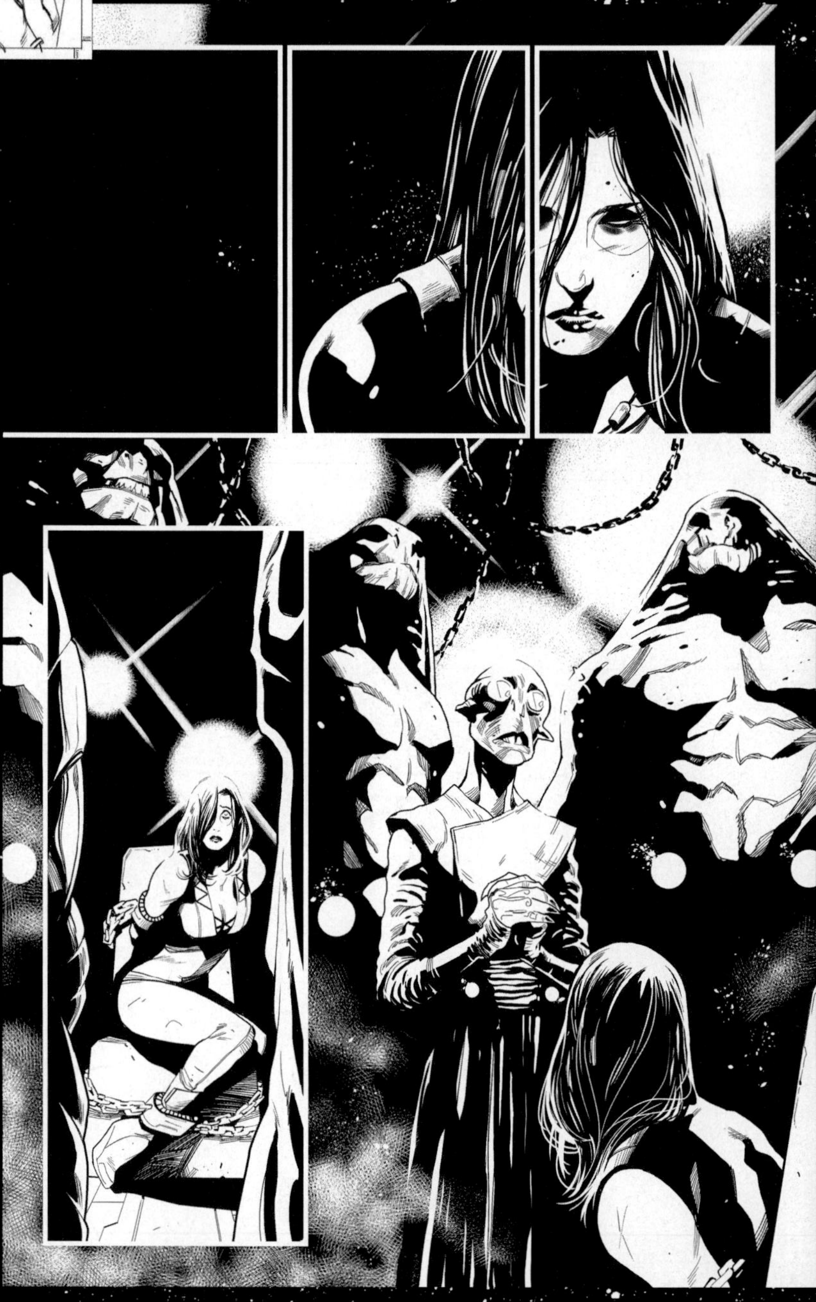

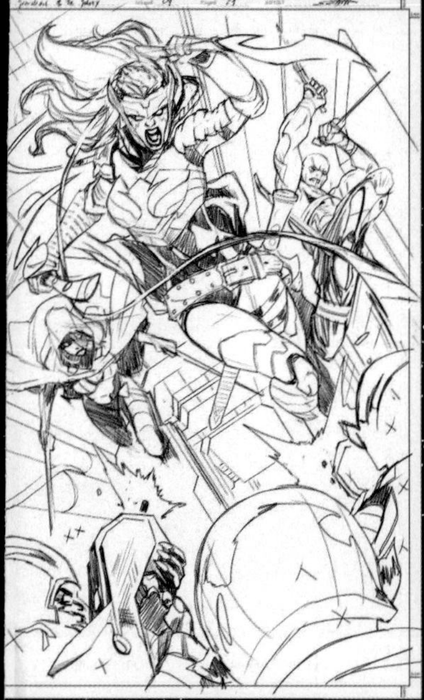

#9, PAGE 20 ART PROCESS BY
VALERIO SCHITI

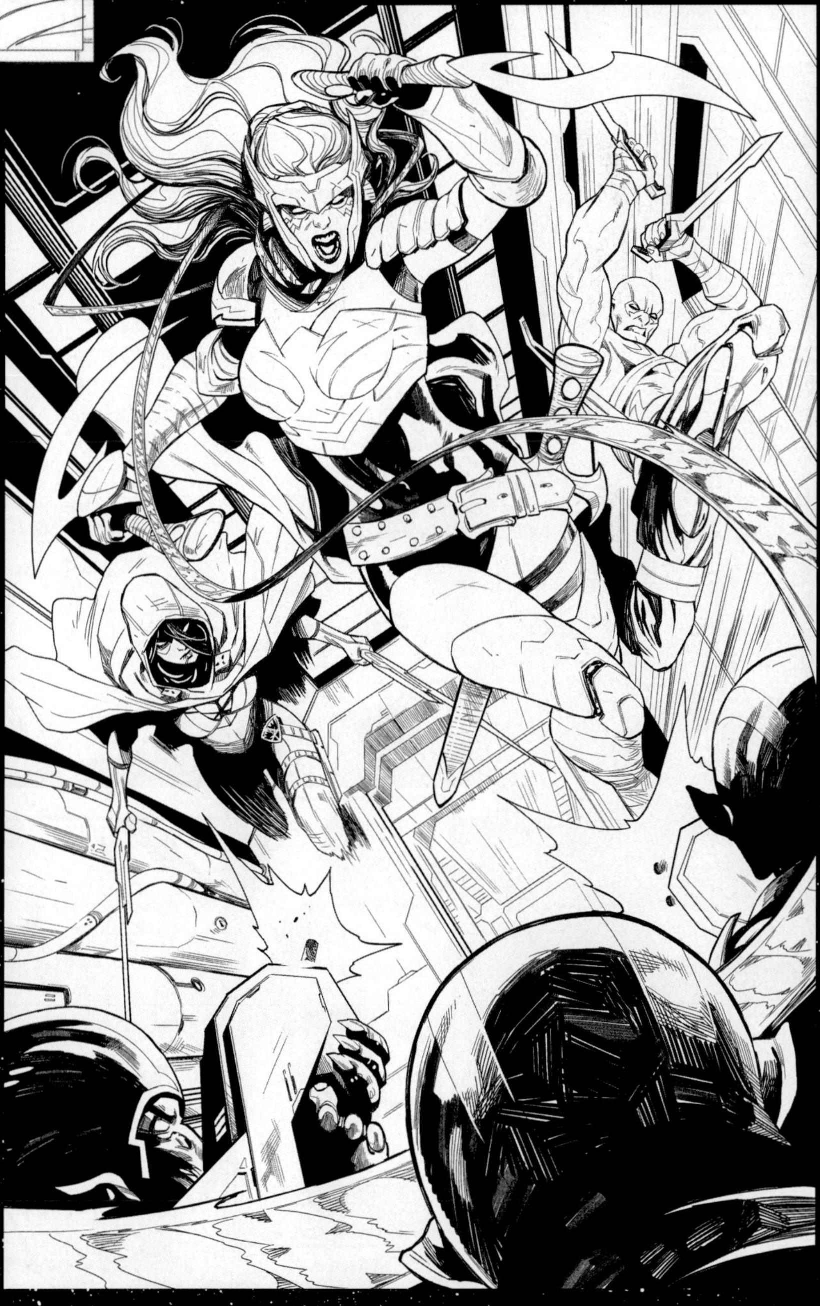

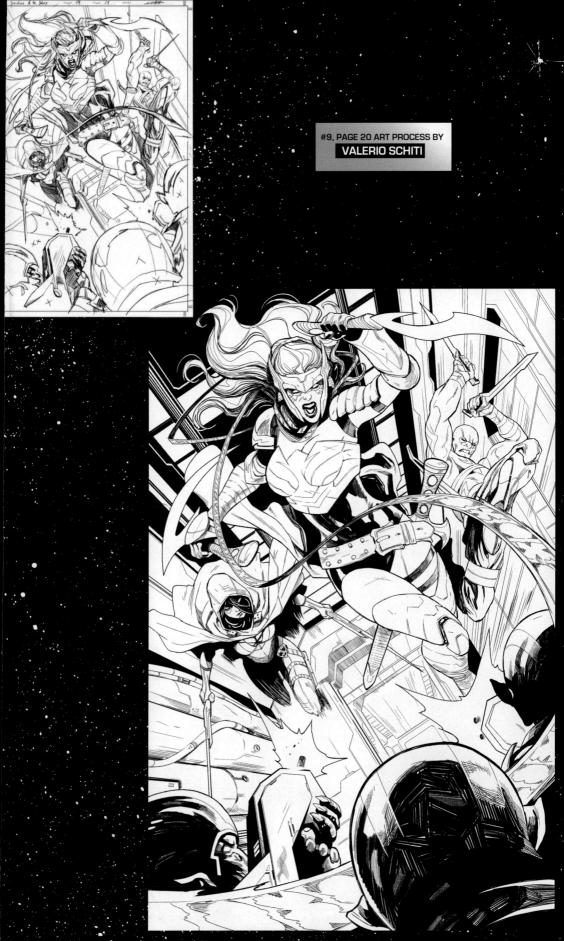

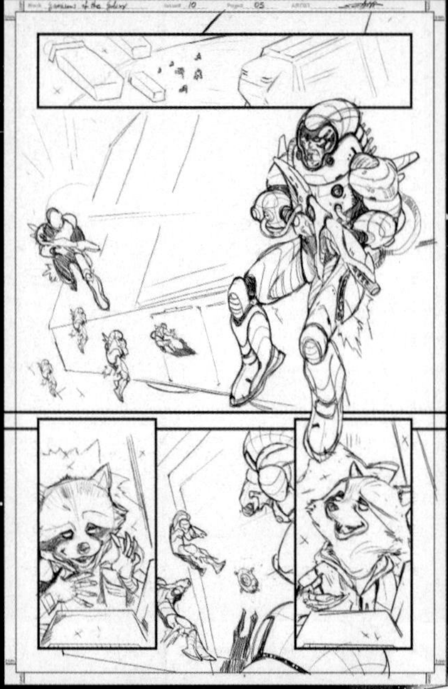

#10, PAGE 4 ART PROCESS BY
VALERIO SCHITI

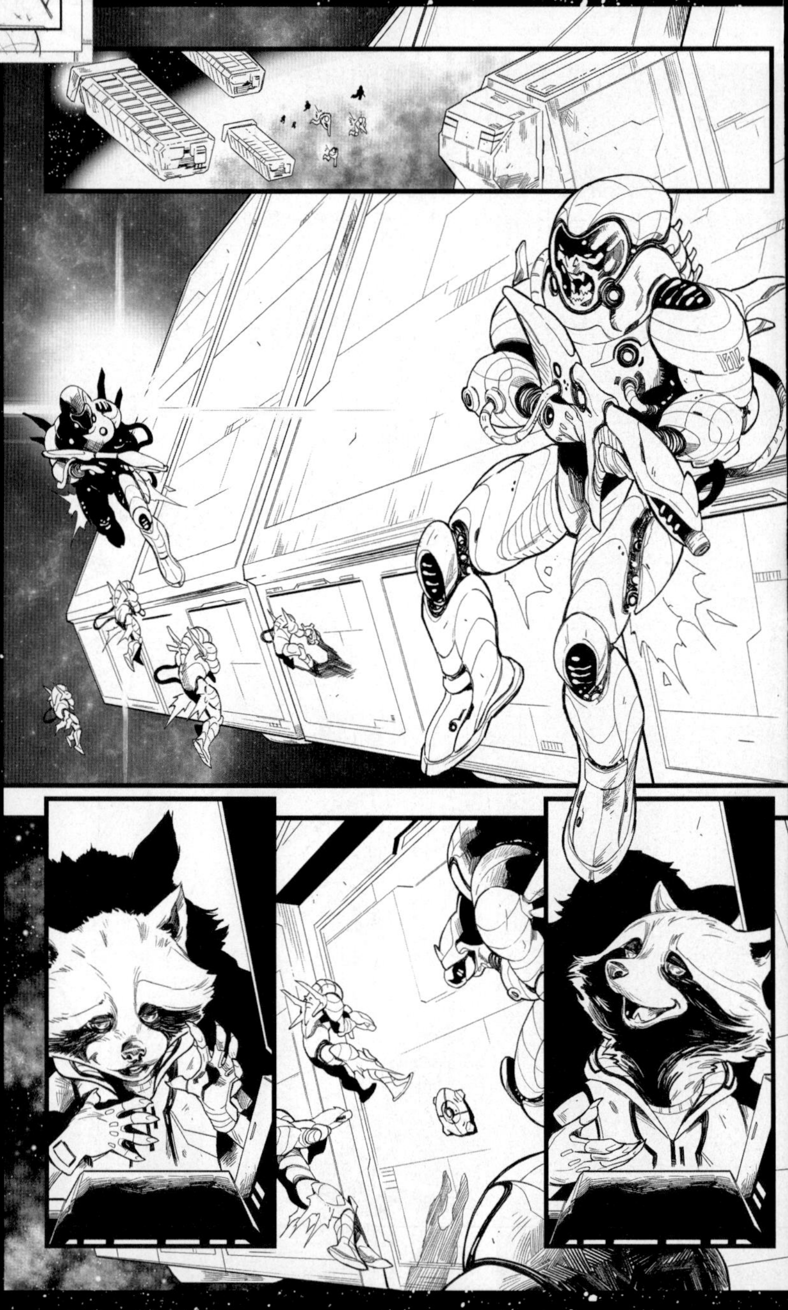

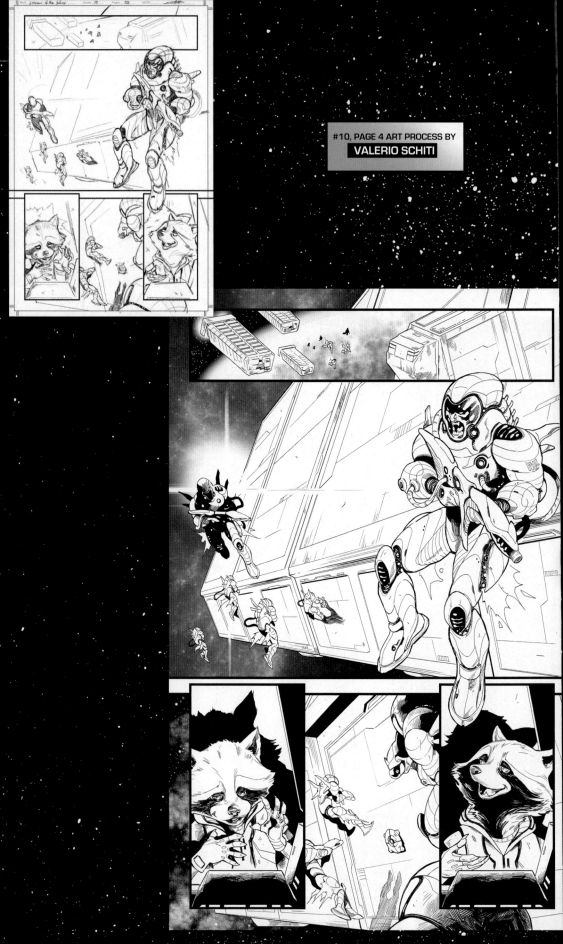

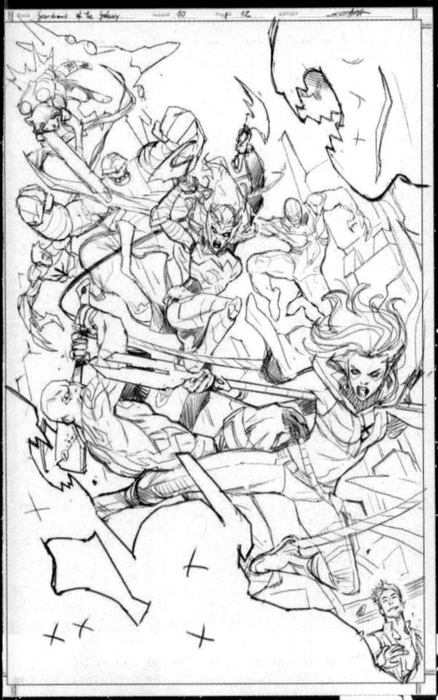

#10, PAGE 11 ART PROCESS BY

VALERIO SCHITI

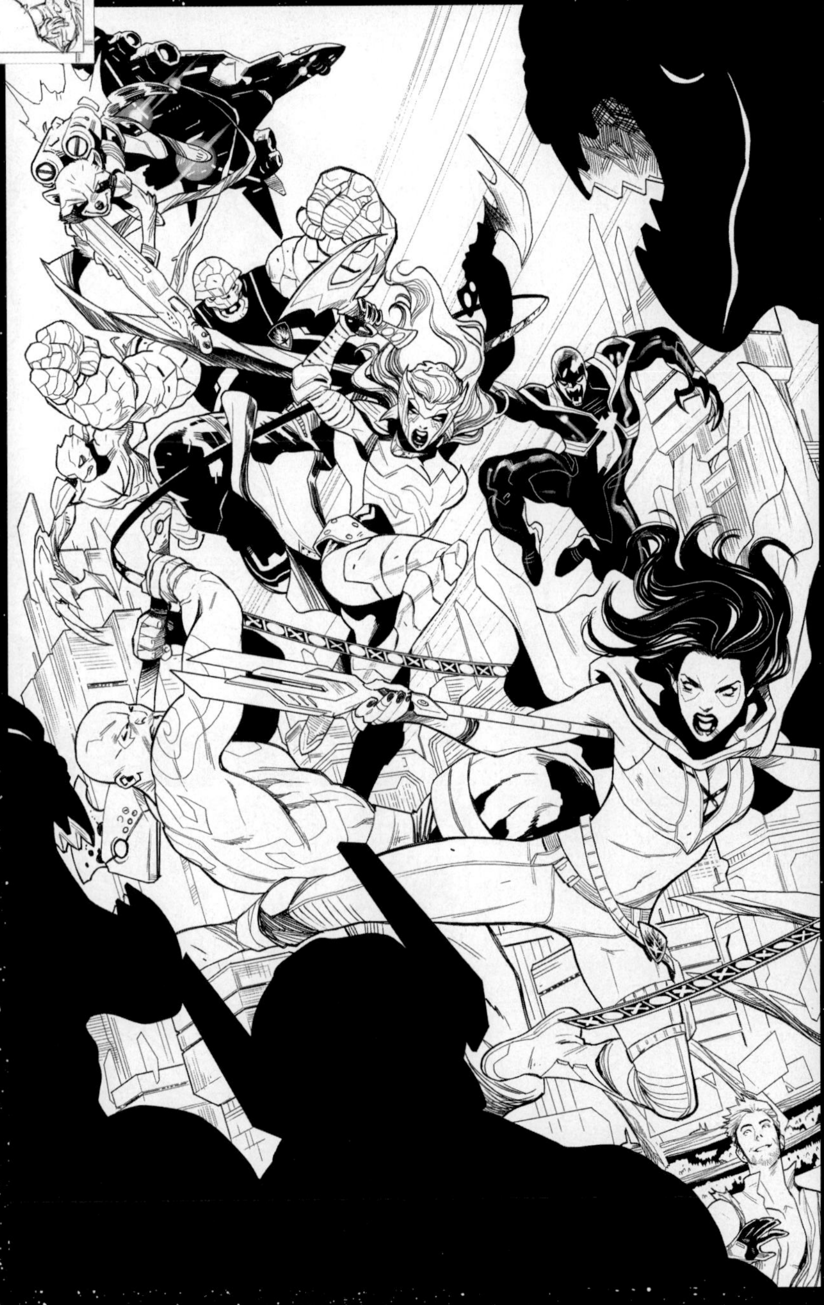

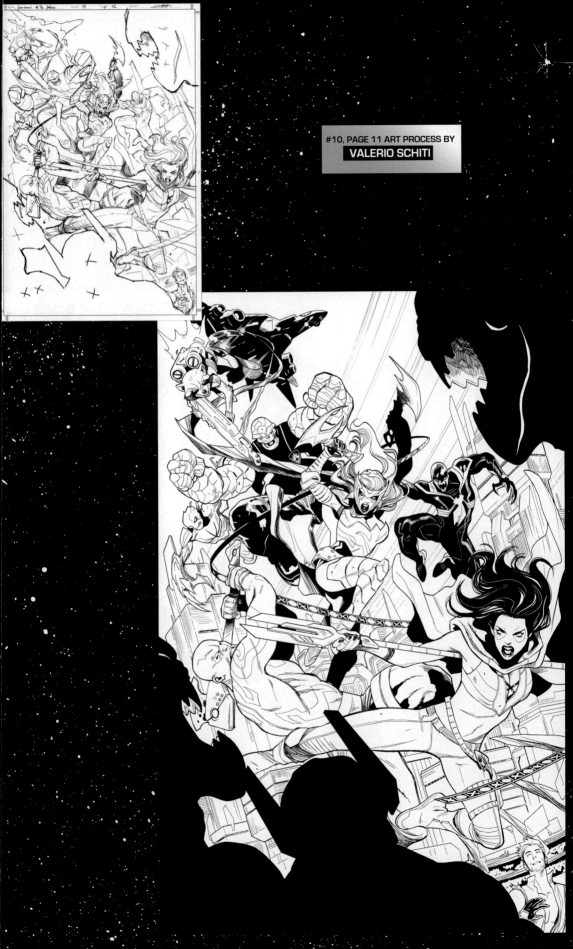

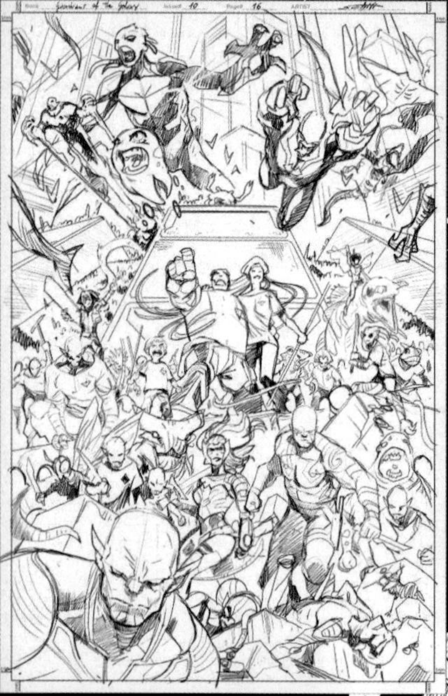

#10, PAGE 15 ART PROCESS BY
VALERIO SCHITI

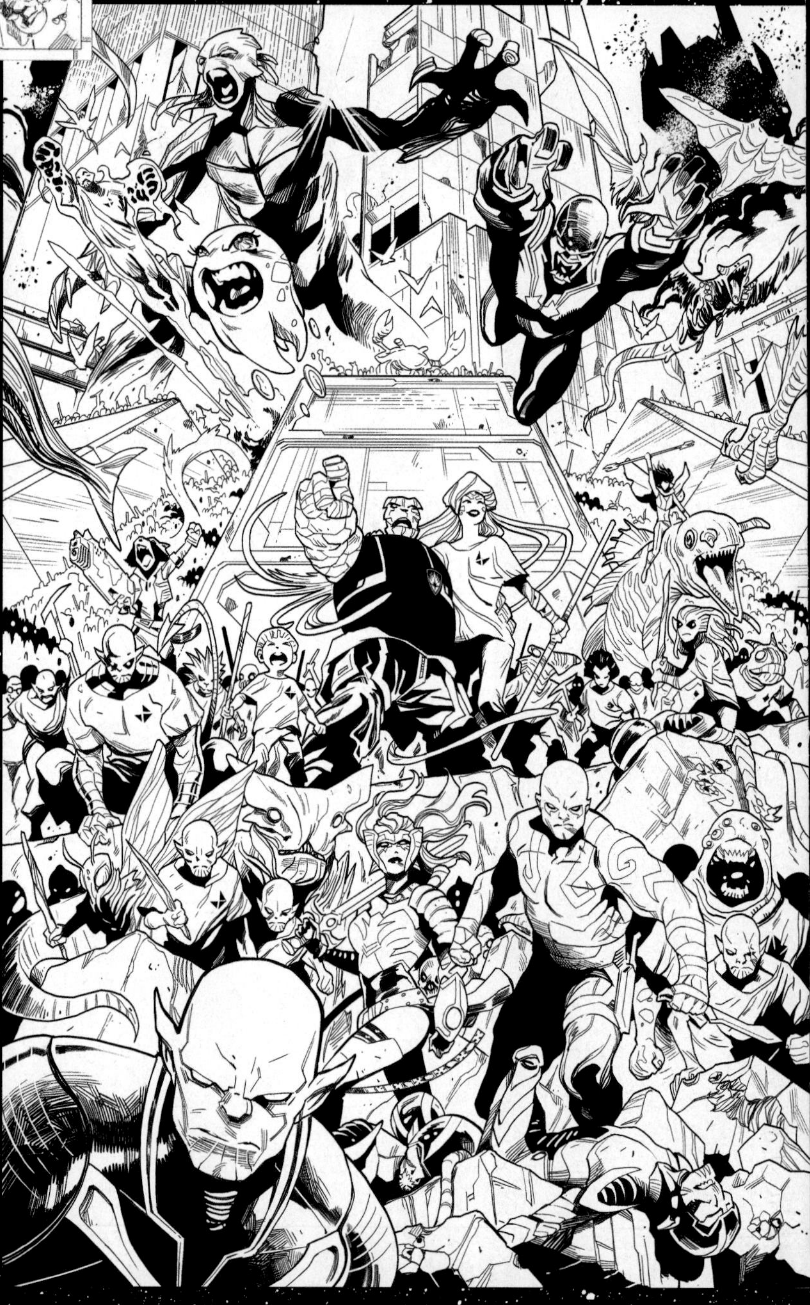

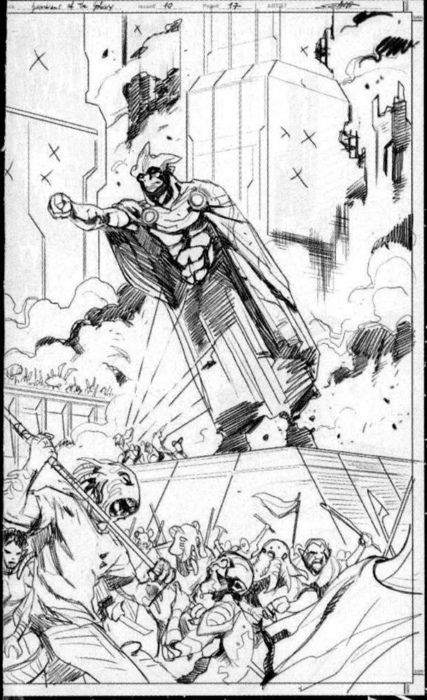

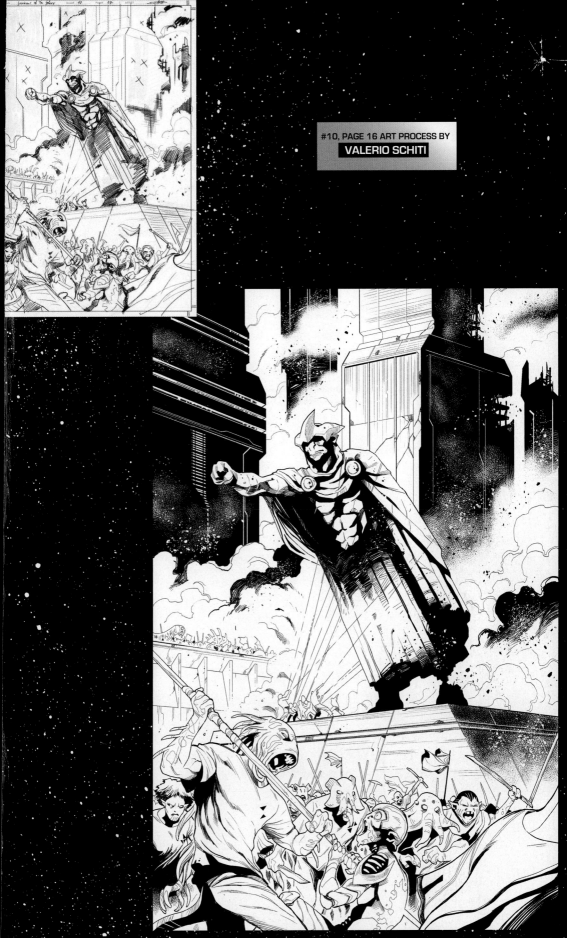

#10, PAGE 16 ART PROCESS BY
VALERIO SCHITI

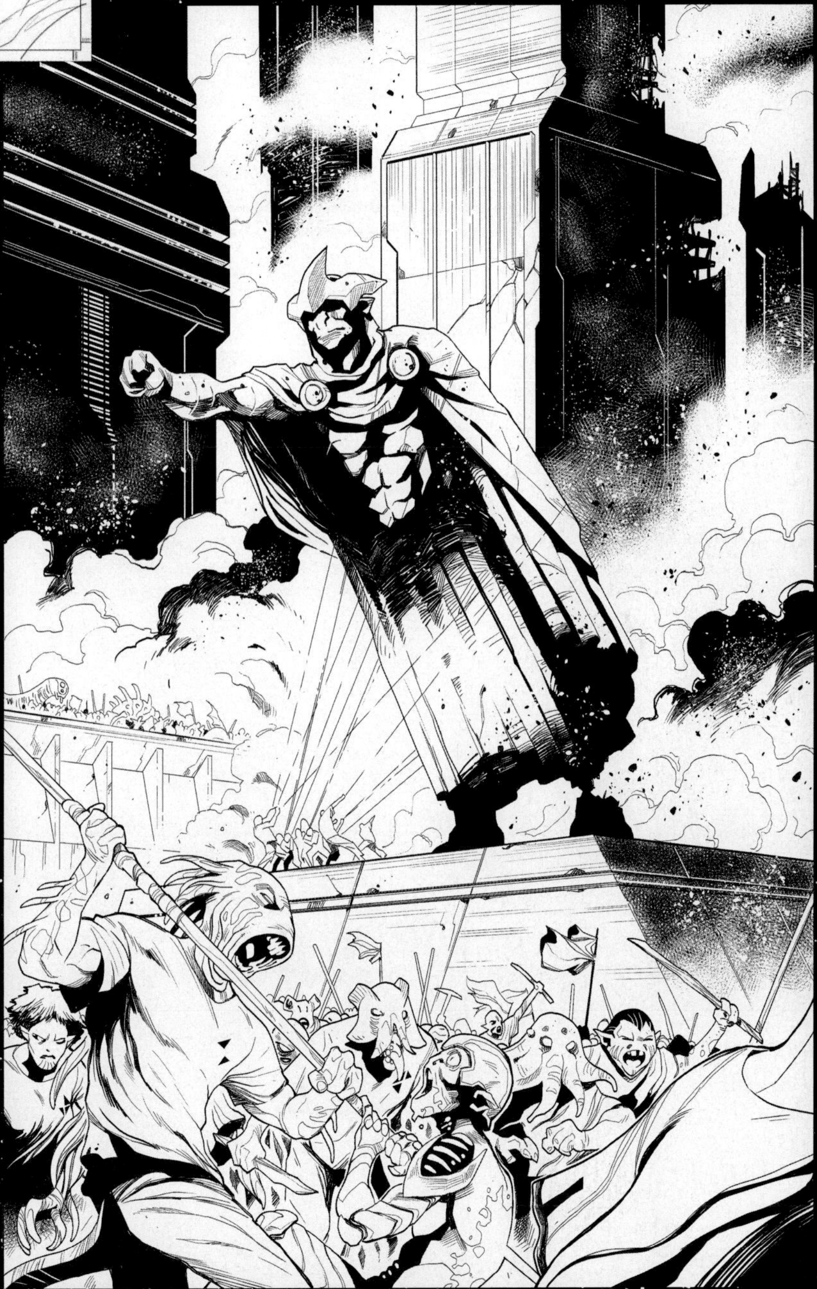

FREE
DIGITAL COPY

TO REDEEM YOUR CODE FOR A FREE DIGITAL COPY:

1. GO TO MARVEL.COM/REDEEM. OFFER EXPIRES ON 11/23/18.
2. FOLLOW THE ON-SCREEN INSTRUCTIONS TO REDEEM YOUR DIGITAL COPY.
3. LAUNCH THE MARVEL COMICS APP TO READ YOUR COMIC NOW.
4. YOUR DIGITAL COPY WILL BE FOUND UNDER THE 'MY COMICS' TAB.
5. READ AND ENJOY.

YOUR FREE DIGITAL COPY WILL BE AVAILABLE ON:
MARVEL COMICS APP FOR APPLE IOS® DEVICES
MARVEL COMICS APP FOR ANDROID™ DEVICES

TMAPS0MZMZY3

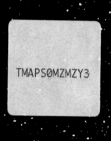